MENU

Today's Special

****

Soups	Appetizers
******	*********
******	*********
******	*********

MENU

Entrees

********** *********

********** *********

********** *********

Desserts

*******   *******

****

MENU PLANNING GUIDE FOR PROS

REMO MOFFA

MENU MASTER PRESS   2014

Original Text as;   *Moffa's Menus*
Library of Congress TXu 1-749-820

ISBN   978-0-9898494-0-1

Published by Menu Master Press
10465 Golden Avenue   Weeki Wachee, Florida 34613

First Edition

TABLE OF CONTENTS

7

INTRODUCTION

Do you often find yourself offering the same specials again and again? We all do. With all of the responsibilities we have in both the kitchen and the front of the house, there never seems to be enough time to search for new menu planning ideas. Unquestionably one of the most important functions of the kitchen is menu planning. It doesn't take much, just a reminder of combinations that go well together, or suggestions that you can improve on or customize for your particular operation. Whether you are just adding a few daily specials or building an entire new and exciting concept, innovative, forward thinking menus can set you apart from the place down the street. A great menu and daily specials can set the tone for the whole establishment. Being presented with dull menu choices speaks volumes about what lies ahead.

Menu Planning Guide for Pros is here to help. We have located, sifted through and categorized menu ideas found throughout the industry. We searched menus, trade magazines and restaurants for ideas that will help you transform your menus and special boards. We assemble them in a simple format to refresh your memory and your menus.
Make it easier on yourself; let *Menu Planning Guide for Pros* be:

"THE CHEF'S MOST VALUABLE TOOL"

FORWARD

I am not a writer, but a Chef. This guide did not start out as a book but as a list of menu ideas and specials that I had used over the years. I kept it around for those times when I needed an idea fast. I can't tell you how many times I had to produce a quick menu for a client or plan the daily specials at the last minute. I always enjoyed planning the menu, but many times this task was pushed until the end of a long day. After a full day of food and production, the last thing I wanted was to think "food" and brainstorm for specials. I would love this to be the most dog-eared book on your desk. This guide was never intended to be a book of recipes. It was intended to be used as a tool, just like your knives or sauté pans. It was meant to be a reminder, a source list of ingredients that work well together. This guide is meant to be used by experienced chefs, cooks and managers in the food service industry, as there are everyday terms indigenous to the professional kitchens, such as reduction, compote and coulis. There is a glossary at the end of this book to remind or update cooks on current terms and trends.

HOW TO USE THIS GUIDE

I have used only a limited amount of cross referencing as not to become too redundant. You might for example find a listing in the salad section for *Baby Spinach with Pecans, Caramelized Onion and a Maple Balsamic Vinaigrette*. You may additionally find the *Maple Balsamic Vinaigrette* listed in the Salad Dressing category. I do this in case you just need a quick idea for a salad dressing and not the entire dish.

In some instances, an item listed may just be a reminder of a basic preparation that you might not have considered for a while. *Mocha ice cream* is an example. We have all had it, but might not have used it in a while so it is off our radar. Now, I might also combine it with an additional ingredient for more flavor and texture, *Toffee Mocha*. Another step further and it becomes a compound preparation. *Toffee Mocha Ice Cream with Bananas Foster Syrup*. One suggestion might be too simple, another too complex, but there are applications for all three.

On occasion, I have chosen to include the complete description as the listing. Under the *Chicken Topping* category you might find *Grilled Breast of Chicken with Bacon and White Cheddar* or just the listing as *Bacon and White Cheddar*. I did this for readability of the text and to break up the repetition. I did not want you to be reading down a list like;

> *Breast of Chicken with Brie*
> *Breast of Chicken with Ham*
> *Breast of Chicken with Apples*

Every now and again, especially with the categories that have extensive listings, I felt the interjection of the category helps you to return to a reading rhythm.

Sometimes I do want to be specific about the combination. Here are two examples:

1) When there is a specific separation within the dish, as in

> *Caramelized Corn Waffle with Fried Green Tomatoes and Bacon Gravy*

I intended for the caramelized corn to be part of the waffle batter and the cooked waffle to be topped with the fried green tomatoes and bacon gravy, not a waffle topped with caramelized corn, fried green tomatoes and bacon gravy. Although it could work both ways, my intention here is to get you to think along the lines of flavoring the batter to add another dimension of flavor and texture to savory waffle dishes.

2) When I feel an ingredient is dish specific, like in

> *Fettuccine with Ribbons of Lamb, Wild Mushrooms and Mustard Cream*

The fettuccine noodles are long and will intertwine well with the ribbons of lamb, and they are wide enough to carry this heavier sauce. That does not mean that this is the only pasta that will work; it's just a recommendation and an indication that the pasta shape and size should be considered.

There are many instances where the ingredients in one dish are very adaptable to another. You will find great ideas for breakfast burritos or breakfast sandwiches in the omelet category. Some pancake batters make great waffles, and many cold sandwich combinations will make excellent melts or panini. If you still need more appetizer suggestions, you can use many of the entree seafood selections like shrimp, calamari, oysters and mussels for appetizers by just adjusting the portion size and presentation. There are Tex-Mex ideas available in the breakfast, appetizer and soup categories and many of the Tex-Mex entree category selections, in turn, will make suitable appetizers, pizza toppings or even risotto preparations. You will find many of these instances throughout the guide.

Furthermore, there are many inter-category changes that can be successful. Combinations that work for a New York Strip Steak will also work well for a Filet Mignon. You could also team beef combinations with veal chop or pork tenderloin. Halibut can be substituted for striped bass or a scallop preparation could be used with shrimp and so on. Sometimes, there are considerations as far as texture and flavor compatibility but don't be afraid to mix and match herbs, spices, sauces, and vegetable combinations.

Consider the use of local and regional ingredients on your menus. Not only is this a way to show support for the local suppliers in your area, but it is also an indicator of quality and freshness to your customers. There is a great variety of fresh vegetables, fruits, meats, cheeses, fish and shellfish being produced locally as well as second tier products like salsas, jams, syrups and condiments. Additionally, local hometown vineyards and craft breweries add local flair when offered as both beverage selections and in dish preparations.

And finally, I don't give names to most of these dishes. I always thought that unless you are preparing one of the classics, as in *Coquilles St. Jacques* or the like, it was always just a cumbersome bother to name dishes. There are a few exceptions. One is that if you have a signature dish, it is great to name it after your establishment so new patrons can be directed there. Sometimes the name of a dish is so descriptive you just have to include it. Flaming Ginger Shrimp, Firecracker Fries and Rum Painted Tuna are a few that come to mind. Just for fun I did apply names to some complete listings, and you can find examples of these at *Hot Dog and Sausage Combinations, Egg Rolls and Meeting Break* categories.

VARIETY AND SPECIALS

You may have a great basic menu, but many customers are looking for a little variety and innovation, even your regular customers that you see time and time again. The reason that they always order the same thing may not be because they like it so much, it may just be the only thing that they like on the menu. As your specials change, you may find some that are exceptionally popular. You can then add them to your regular menu.

DAILY SPECIALS

There are several ways to approach the need for variety and innovation. If you are concerned about having to overstock a lot of new inventory, try just starting with a few specials. This has advantages for a number of obvious reasons.

- ❖ <u>The ability to use fresh seasonal ingredients is the best reason.</u> You can purchase a small amount of a fresh ingredient and then "86" it when it has all been sold. As an example, let's look at fresh Soft Shell Crabs. For one thing, the daily availability from the watermen and, therefore the supply is limited. You might order six dozen "Jumbos" and receive four dozen "Hotels". This would necessitate a change in count per serving and possibly final menu cost. The next important factor is that you will receive them alive and dress them for service. They are best used that day, so when you are out you remove them from the special board and can start with fresh product the next day if they are available.

- ❖ <u>Highlight the particular skills of the kitchen.</u> If the chef has great skills with Thai Cuisine, highlight this with a few selections. Not only does it offer you customers a little variety, it keeps the Chef from being bored with the "same old same old".

- ❖ <u>Move the workload around the kitchen.</u> If you think that the sauté station might get an overload on a particular night, you can add a broiled special to shift the workload.

- ❖ <u>Effectively use inventory that you may have from a one-time banquet or special party menu.</u> Let's say that a group wanted hand cut Rib-Eye steaks. The party was for 20. One whole rib-eye would not be enough; two is more than you need. So you purchase two boneless rib-eye roasts. After you cut the steaks that you need for the party, the steaks that are leftover become your special for your a la carte menu. Let me clarify something right here: Contrary to what some people think, you never want to use your daily specials as a dumping ground for ingredients that are on the verge of going bad! This is a clear sign of lack of control of inventory. Professionals have control of the inventory, and never allow items to get to this point. This comes down to better menu planning, as well as superior inventory, purchasing and receiving procedures. Plain and simple.

❖ <u>A few notes on making purchases for specials.</u> When purchasing ingredients for specials that are only going to be used for a limited time, I find that it may be less expensive in the long run to purchase a small amount of an ingredient at a higher price and use it up rather than to purchase an entire case of something at a cheaper price that you may rarely use again. Sometimes a trip to a nearby gourmet grocery or even the local supermarket is a much better choice. It also may provide you with the opportunity to add some variety. Take a simple taco buffet table as an example. If you do not normally use taco shells, you might just order a whole case of one size or type of taco shell from your purveyor for a particular event. As a way of offering some choices to your guests, you go to the local store and you pick up regular, jumbo and mini hard taco shells. You also grab a few soft flour tortillas also in a variety of sizes and a few bags of tortilla chips. Look at the variety you are offering now using all of the same core ingredients at the buffet table. All of your basic ingredients like salsa, beef, cheeses and guacamole can be used with the different sizes of shells and chips. You can also think about what you might do with anything left over. Let's say you ran the taco table for a special party. The next day there are mini taco shells left. As a lunch special, I might offer a trio of mini tacos, one with shrimp, one with beef and one with chicken. Serve it with a guacamole salad or a cup of black bean soup, and you have a great use of you leftover ingredients. If you are still concerned about holding an increased inventory, but want more variety, try using the same core item and varying the accompanying sauce or garnish. I have used this format as the entrée selections for a single night dinner featuring a steak, a fresh fish, a shellfish combination and a veal sauté. This allowed me the variety of twelve items with only four main ingredients.

Seasoned Prime New York Strip
Prepared as you prefer

Caramelized Onion and Gorgonzola Crust
Wild Mushroom Hunter Sauce
Roasted Shallot and Horseradish Butter

Sautéed Veal Chop
Prepared as you prefer

Crisp Prosciutto and Aged Port Wine Reduction
Smoked Tomato Bordelaise
Fresh Mint and Capers

Grilled Fresh Alaskan Halibut
Prepared as you prefer

Red Onions and Toasted Pine Nuts with Kalamata Olive Butter
Pan Roasted Artichokes and an Orange Rosemary Sauce
Savory Cabbage, Bacon, Heirloom Beans and Fresh Basil

Shrimp, Scallop and Jumbo Lump Crabmeat Sauté
Prepared as you prefer

Caramelized Shallot, Lemon and Brandy Cream
Sweet Pepper Butter Sauce
Roasted Onion and Sherry Vinaigrette over Rice Noodles

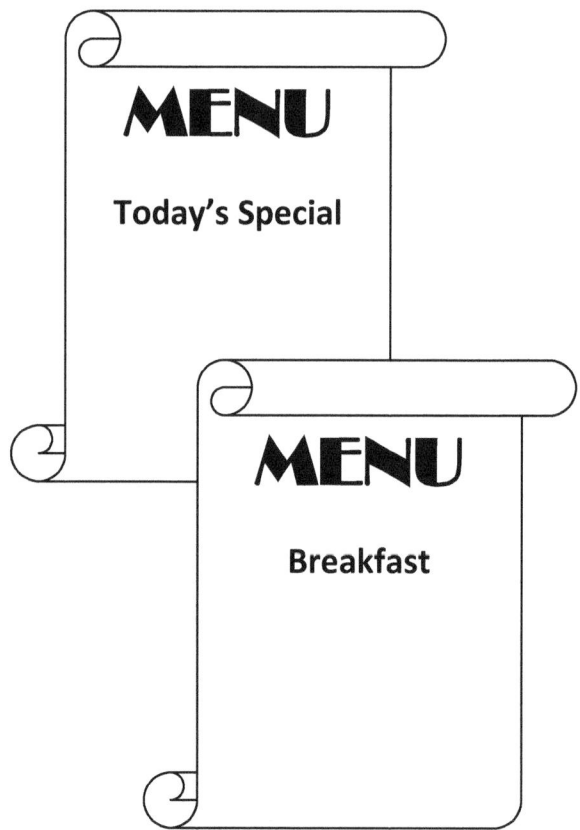

BREAKFAST

Breakfast Selections
Benedicts
French Toast
Omelets and Frittatas
Waffles and Pancakes
Breakfast Drinks

Chapter Notes, Ideas and Conversions

Main Ingredient	Element 1	Element 2	Element 3	Sauce	Texture

BREAKFAST

Morning Shepherd's Pie - Chive Scrambled Eggs, Crumbled Country Sausage and
Roasted Fall Vegetables with Cheddar Mashed Potatoes and Red Eye Gravy

Blueberry Lavender Blintzes with Lemon Zest Crème and Shaved White Chocolate
Fall Strata with Bacon, Pumpkin, Apples, Dates and Gruyere
Spiced Apple Couscous with Dried Fruit Compote and Cinnamon Cream
Spicy Grilled Shrimp served on Bacon Cheddar Grits with Fried Eggs
Scrambled Egg Sandwich on a Crisp Croissant with White Truffle Butter and Melted Brie

Grilled Rib Eye Steak with Fried Quail Eggs and a Cabernet Reduction
White Asparagus with Poached Eggs and a Whole Grain Mustard Vinaigrette
Skillet Scramble with Cracked Pepper Bacon, Gruyere and Charred Onions served with Texas Toast
Short Ribs with Sunny Side Eggs and Chipotle Onions served with Grilled Cornbread
Tex-Mex Skillet with Spicy Eggs, Fried Tortilla Strips, Chilies, Colby and Smoked Tomato Salsa
Gyros, Eggs and Feta Skillet with Roasted Potatoes and Grilled Onions
Apple Strudel and Egg Bake with Leeks and Manchego
New York Strip and Eggs served with Salsa Verde and Purple Potato and Poblano Hash

Pesto Scrambled Eggs on Ciabatta with Fried Salami, Grilled Tomatoes and Fresh Mozzarella
Egg and Chicken Enchiladas with Queso Fresco, Red Jalapeno Sour Cream, Roasted Tomato Salsa
Tasso Ham and Gruyere Quiche served on Arugula with a Caramelized Onion-Lemon Vinaigrette
Braised Short Rib served on Mushroom and Potato Cakes with Fried Egg and Béarnaise
Toasted Granola with Candied Ginger, Fresh Figs and Walnuts with Cranberry Goat Cheese Yogurt
Breakfast Pizza with Truffle Hash Browns, Charred Scallions, Diced Ham and Smoked Gouda
Charred Rib Eye Steak with Eggs, Black Pepper Tomato and Bordelaise
Pulled Pork Hash with Fried Eggs and Grilled Vegetables

Breakfast Pizza with Eggs, Italian Sausage, Mushrooms and Gorgonzola
Fried Green Tomatillos topped with Sunny Side Egg and Chorizo Gravy
Smokey Chicken with Roasted Peppers, Charred Scallions and Fried Eggs
Mojo Pulled Pork with Fried Eggs and Salsa Verde
Coffee Braised Short Ribs with Eggs and served with Green Chili Hash and Charred Texas Toast
Steel Cut Oatmeal with Roasted Peaches and Drambuie Cream
Open Face Sunrise BLT with Crisp Bacon, Red Leaf Lettuce, Smoked Tomato and Fried Egg
Dandelion Greens and a Sunny Side Egg over Crusty Croutons with Shaved Dry Aged Parmigianino

Scrambled Eggs with Wild Mushrooms on Chive Pancakes with Smoked Cheddar
Poached Eggs with Fresh Herbs served in Crisp Potato Nests
Spicy Grits with Eggs and Andouille Sausage
Toasted Brioche with Fresh Ricotta and Raspberry Marmalade
Country Ham, Grilled Asparagus and White Cheddar Panini on Peasant Rye Bread with a Fried Egg
Peppercorn Crusted Pork Tenderloin with Goat Cheese Grits and Molasses-Herb Reduction

BREAKFAST

Grilled Beef Medallions on Artichoke Ragout with Poached Eggs and Creole Mustard Hollandaise
Breakfast Empanadas with Crisp Bacon, Eggs, Smoked Salmon and Cotija Cheese
Soft Flour Tacos with Smoked Salmon, Scrambled Eggs, Grilled Scallions and Queso Blanco
Poached Eggs on Confit Potato with Grilled Andouille Sausage and Warm Salsa Verde
Ricotta-Mascarpone Blintzes with Warm Lemon Sauce and Fresh Blackberries
Chorizo, Jalapeño and Smoked Gouda Blintzes with Ancho Sour Cream

Harissa Marinated Skirt Steak and Eggs over Smoked Paprika Potatoes with Chimichurri Aioli
"Super Food" Oatmeal with Walnuts, Golden Flax Seed, Blueberries and Cinnamon Honey
Country Ham and Biscuits with a Pepper Jelly and Cream Cheese Spread
Roasted Fruit with Oatmeal Strudel Topping
Pan Seared Cheese Blintz with a Blackberry and Mint Compote
Egg Poached in Spicy Tomato Sauce served on a Sausage and White Corn Polenta Cake
Blue Claw Crab Fritter with a Tomato, Tarragon and Smoked Edam Fondue
Rösti Potato with Scrambled Eggs, Smoked Salmon, Crème Fraîche and Caviar

Grits with Fried Hot Peppers, Italian Sausage and Tomato Poached Eggs
Green Eggs and Ham - Pesto Scrambled Egg Whites and Honey Roasted Ham on Grilled Croissant
Granola with Candied Pecans, Toasted Coconut, Mango, Blueberries and Vanilla-Cinnamon Yogurt
Oatmeal with Brown Sugar, Roasted Bananas and Cream
Mascarpone Cheese Stuffed Crepes with Raspberry Jam
Sausage and Biscuits with Rosemary Gravy
Wild Mushroom Grits with Poached Egg, Charred Serrano Sauce and Cotija Cheese
Smoked Trout, Grilled Asparagus, Wild Mushroom and Feta Quiche

Eggs Benedict on Grilled Corn Cakes with Smoked Pork and Béarnaise Sauce
Crab and Red Potato Cake with Poached Eggs, Asparagus and Toasted Fennel Hollandaise
Flank Steak and Egg Empanadas with Chipotle Jam and Grilled Pears
Grilled Asparagus topped with Poached Egg and Brown Mustard Cream Sauce
Corned Beef Hash with Eggs, Gruyere and Grilled Onion Cream Sauce
Chorizo and Eggs with Sofrito, Roasted Potatoes and Queso Fresco
Roasted Hen of the Woods Mushrooms on Cheddar Grits with Grilled Onions and Bacon Gravy

Green Chili and Chorizo Breakfast Burrito with Fresh Avocado Slices and Ranchero Sauce
Toasted Bagel with Honey Walnut Cream Cheese and Grilled Pineapple
Breakfast Panini - Scramble Eggs, Crisp Pancetta, Sun Dried Tomatoes with
Sharp Provolone, Arugula and Caramelized Onions

Spicy Scrambled Eggs with Grilled Scallions, Jalapenos and Goat Cheese
Apricot and Dijon Glazed Ham and Eggs on Buttermilk Biscuits
Ranch Style Eggs Tostada with Grilled Poblano Chilies, Smoked Tomato Sauce and Monterey Jack
Fried Eggs, Crisp Pancetta and Gorgonzola on Wilted Frisée
Pan Fried Country Ham and Green Tomatoes with Coffee Gravy and Hash Browns

BREAKFAST

Johnny Cakes with Shaved Chocolate and Roasted Bananas
Pulled Pork Tostada with Fried Eggs, Monterey Jack and Poblano-Avocado Relish
Chilled Caramelized Grapefruit and Blackberry-Mint Salad
Poached Eggs on Sweet Corn Grits with Smoked Ham and a Chipotle-Cheddar Sauce
Soft Scrambled Eggs with Fontina, Chives and Crème Fraîche
Butter Poached Eggs with Arugula on Grilled Polenta
Caramelized Corn Grits with a White Cheddar and Jalapeno Sauce
Smoked Spicy Chicken on Sweet Potato Hash with Poached Eggs and Green Chili Hollandaise

Fried Eggs and Country Ham over Garlic and Rosemary Roasted Potatoes with Ranchero Sauce
Steak and Eggs with Black Peppercorn Crusted Tomato and Grilled Asparagus
Eggs on a Bed of Roasted Red Peppers, Grilled Onions, Tasso Ham, Jack Cheese and Jalapeños
Sage and Sausage Gravy on Cheddar and Scallion Biscuits
Lamb Sausage with Poached Eggs on Crispy Goat Cheese Polenta
Blackened Sirloin and Egg Tortilla with Grilled Red Onions, Roasted Peppers and Sliced Avocado
Potato, Grilled Onion and Spinach Hash with White Cheddar
Poached Eggs on Grilled Tomatoes with Sautéed Spinach, Wild Mushrooms and Pesto

Grilled Raisin Bread with Ricotta Cheese and Fruit
Tempura Shrimp with Sautéed Spinach, Sunny Side Up Eggs and Buttered Grits
Fried Eggs with Crisp Pancetta and Gorgonzola on Caramelized Onion Home Fries
Scrambled Eggs on Crisp Flour Tortilla with Roasted Tomatillo Salsa, Cotija and Sour Cream
Poached Eggs with a Lemon Chipotle Hollandaise and Spicy Sausage on a Grilled Croissant Crouton
Poached Eggs served over Spicy Braised Beef with Roasted Sweet Peppers and Red Potatoes
Shrimp and Scrambled Eggs in Potato Skins with Hollandaise
Blackened Pork Tenderloin with Eggs and Grilled Apples

Breakfast Empanadas with Bacon, Eggs, Smoked Tomatillo and Queso Asadero
Scrambled Eggs with Feta, Tomatoes and Basil
Golden Buck - Sautéed Veal, Sunny Side Egg with Grated Swiss on Rye Toast
Poached Eggs on Grilled Vegetables with Roasted Chili Hollandaise
Roasted Corn and Jalapeno Grits with Colby Jack Fondue
Smoked Salmon with Skillet Fried Potatoes, Sour Cream, Red Onion and Chives
Broiled Grapefruit with Honey and Almonds
Glazed Canadian Bacon

Bacon and Green Chili Deep Dish Quiche
Cinnamon Crepes with Apple and Pear Compote
Poached Eggs over Asparagus with Béarnaise
Sautéed Mushrooms on Toast Points with Bordelaise
Seafood Benedict --- English Muffin, Canadian Bacon, Shrimp and Scallops, Sauce Choron
Sautéed Chicken Livers with a Marsala Brown Sauce
Roasted Pepper and Egg Sandwich with Provolone

BREAKFAST

Wild Mushrooms and Brandy Cream in Puff Pastry
Pulled Pork Tostada with Fried Eggs, Jack Cheese and Poblano Compote
Beef Tenderloin with Asparagus, Poached Eggs and Sauce Béarnaise
Skillet Potatoes - Cheese, Onion, Mushrooms, Bacon and Roasted Peppers
Broiled Orange with Brown Sugar and Chopped Pecans
Scrambled Eggs with Chorizo, Cheddar, Scallions, Sour Cream and Salsa
Smoked Salmon on Scallion Scone with Poached Eggs, Crisp Potatoes and Dilled Hollandaise
Sausage, Pepper Jack and Green Onion Biscuit Bake

Grilled Pears and Scrambled Eggs with Chipotle and Red Onion Jam
Sautéed Granny Smith Apple and Ricotta Crepes
Grilled Corn Cakes with Smoked Salmon and Caviar Cream
Peppery Pastrami and Red Potato Hash
Fresh Cherries with Lemon Mascarpone
Grilled Sausage with Fresh Pear Relish
Poached Eggs on an English Muffin with Smoked Salmon and Fresh Dill Hollandaise
Baked Tomato, Egg and Smoked Mozzarella in Phyllo Cups

Grilled Vegetable, Cheddar and Sausage Bread Pudding
Potato Skins with Wild Mushrooms, Scrambled Eggs and Blue Veined Brie
Scrambled Eggs with Pesto and Scallions
Poached Eggs on Grilled Ripe Tomato Slices with Asparagus and Chardonnay Sauce
Rosemary and Caramelized Shallot Popovers
Eggs with Smoked Rainbow Trout and Four Onion Compote
Toasted Onion Bagel with Tomatoes, Thin Sliced Cucumbers and Wasabi Cream Cheese
Potato Pancakes with Scallions and Crisp Country Ham

Scrambled Eggs with Sautéed Crab on Shredded Grilled Potatoes and Horseradish Cream Sauce
Scrambled Eggs in Roasted Artichoke Bottoms with Light Cheese Sauce
Spinach and Swiss Quiche in a Sweet Potato Crust
Scrambled Eggs with Feta, Prosciutto and Cherry Tomatoes
Red and Gold Potato Frittata with Lemon and Herb Mayonnaise
Poached Eggs on Grilled Focaccia with Arugula, Sun Dried Tomatoes and Hollandaise
Poached Eggs in Puff Pastry with Mushroom Cream Sauce

Mushroom, Sausage and Cheese Bread Pudding
Scrambled Eggs with Smoked Salmon and Chives
Potato Crusted Jumbo Lump Crab Cake over Sautéed Spinach with Sun Dried Tomato Hollandaise
Blueberry Crepes with Mascarpone and Toasted Almonds
Shirred Eggs with Crab, Swiss Cheese and Cream
Goat Cheese Soufflé
Baked Apples with Ginger Cream
Poached Eggs in Grilled Artichoke Bottoms over Creamed Spinach with Béarnaise

BENEDICTS

All Benedicts use poached eggs unless otherwise suggested. You can change things up by using fried eggs or try using basted eggs. The advantage in using basted eggs is that they impart an additional flavor from the basting fat. One caution here be careful of the additional fat that basting will bring to the dish as it might overpower the preparation and if not blotted up it will seep onto the plate. Also if not noted a basic Hollandaise would be used in that particular preparation. It goes without saying that many sauces can be interchanged. In some instances I have suggested the bread base as something other than the traditional English muffin. There are all types and flavors of English muffins available as well as countless other substitutes. Grilled brioche, focaccia, biscuits even flavored cornbread can be used. Look for a bread base that will hold the liquid egg yolks and sauce. This is one of the reasons English muffins work so well. You may also want to use a potato cake, bean cake, rice or a potato hash variation. For non-starch bases grilled portabella caps really fit the bill and you can always substitute fresh baby salad greens or sautéed vegetables like zucchini or cooked spinach for the bread. End the dish with a flurry of chopped herbs, shredded cheese, truffles or toasted breadcrumbs to make a nice finish.

Lump Crab, Grilled Asparagus and Creole Hollandaise
Fresh Tomato Slices, Watercress and Sauce Choron on Sourdough Crouton
Sliced Beef Tenderloin, Wild Mushrooms and Double Yolk Hollandaise
Pulled Pork, Grilled Onions, Roasted Chilies and Adobo Hollandaise over Jalapeño Cornbread
Smoked Salmon, Fried Capers, Red Onions over Potato Pancakes with Chive Hollandaise
Butter Poached Lobster, Melted Leeks and Sautéed Spinach
Country Ham, Fried Green Tomatoes and Red Eye Hollandaise on Buttermilk Biscuits
Pancetta and Garlic Sautéed Radicchio on Grilled Portabellas

Cured Salmon on Rösti Potatoes with Sautéed Arugula and Béarnaise
Grilled Cajun Shrimp, Braised Mustard Greens and Spicy Rémoulade
Duck Confit and Charred Red Onions on Sweet Potato Hash with Béarnaise Sauce
Dungeness Crab with Avocado and Dill Hollandaise
Smoked Trout, Wilted Arugula, Oven Dried Tomatoes and Pesto Hollandaise
Crab Cakes, Roasted Red Peppers and Old Bay Hollandaise on Toasted Pretzel Bread
Black Peppercorn Bacon, Fried Artichoke Hearts and Sun Dried Tomato Béarnaise Sauce
Italian Sausage, Roasted Peppers, Sautéed Spinach and Fontina Cream Sauce on Crusty Focaccia
Sliced Turkey, Mushrooms and Dried Cranberry Hollandaise on Turkey Stuffing Griddlecakes

Grilled Shrimp, Sliced Avocado and Cilantro Hollandaise
Sliced Summer Tomatoes, Fresh Mozzarella and Basil Leaves with Lemon Olive Oil Hollandaise
Prosciutto, Grilled Asparagus and Pesto Hollandaise
Corned Beef Brisket, Caraway Onions and Herb Hollandaise on Rye Croutons
Serrano Ham, Fried Green Tomatoes, Wild Mushroom Hollandaise
Grilled Onion Slices, Crumbled Bacon and Roasted Tomato Hollandaise
Shredded Duck Confit on Wilted Radicchio with Chili Hollandaise
Butter Seared Crab with Béarnaise and a Truffle Oil Drizzle

BENEDICTS

Grilled Chorizo on Charred Corn Bread with Cilantro Hollandaise and Pico de Gallo
Sautéed Spinach, Grilled Lobster, Lemon-Dill Hollandaise
Short Ribs, Wild Mushrooms on Cheddar Biscuits with Hollandaise
Fried Green Tomatoes on Corned Beef Hash with Grilled Scallion Cream Sauce
Blue Crab and Asparagus with Fresh Fennel Hollandaise
Fried Eggplant Rounds and Crisp Pancetta on Ciabatta Toast with Alfredo Sauce
Butter Poached Salmon, Grilled Red Onions, Spinach and Caper Hollandaise
Lorraine Benedict - Crisp Bacon and Caramelized Onions on Hash Browns with Melted Gruyere
Country Ham, Sautéed Greens, and Whole Grain Mustard Hollandaise on Grilled Grits Cakes
Pork Belly, Caramelized Brussels Sprout Leaves and a Dried Cranberry Hollandaise
Surf & Turf Benedict- Grilled Beef Tenderloin, Rock Shrimp and Truffle Aioli
Lime Grilled Shrimp on Brioche Rounds, Sautéed Spinach and Crème Fraîche with Parmesan Crisp
Shaved Ham, Grilled Tomatoes and Mornay Sauce on Toasted Sourdough
Scotch Eggs Benedict - Panko Breaded Poached Eggs, Grilled Sausage and Creole Hollandaise
Smoked Shrimp on Stone Ground Grits with Marble Cheddar Sauce
Brandy Braised Morels on Venison and Potato Hash with Hunter Sauce Demi-glace

Crisp Prosciutto, Grilled Asparagus and Walnut Pesto Hollandaise
Grilled Mortadella, Roasted Mushrooms, Wilted Basil Leaves and Smoked Tomato Hollandaise
Grilled Lamb, Mint Hollandaise and Crumbled Feta
Sautéed Artichoke Hearts, Caramelized Shallots and Meyer Lemon Hollandaise
Duck Confit, Roasted Peppers and Ancho Hollandaise
Grilled Pastrami, Caramelized Onion and Melted Swiss on Butter Toasted Rye Rounds
Andouille, Blackened Chilies and Cajun Cream Sauce
Grilled Meyer Lemon Rounds and Poached Eggs on Lobster and Leek Hash

Crisp Potato Cake with Chorizo and a Roasted Chili Hollandaise
Grilled Country Pate and Roast Chicken on a Croissant Crouton with White Truffle Hollandaise
Smoked Salmon, Horseradish Hollandaise and Chopped Fresh Chives
Duck Sausage and Roasted Spinach on Polenta Cakes with a Honey Hollandaise
Grilled Avocado on Corncakes with a Smoked Ham Béchamel
Tasso Ham, Roasted Green Chiles and Tabasco Hollandaise
Fried Oyster, Bacon Collards and Old Bay Hollandaise

Andouille with Three Pepper Sausage Gravy
Grilled Summer Squash, Broccoli Florets, and Sweet Pimento Hollandaise
Prosciutto Di Parma Benedict on Focaccia with Truffle Hollandaise
White Asparagus on Grilled Brioche Crouton with Béarnaise
Grilled Chorizo with Green Chili Hollandaise
Warm Crab Cakes with Country Ham and Ruby Grapefruit Hollandaise
Smoked Trout served on Dill and Scallion Croutons with Lime Hollandaise

FRENCH TOAST

An easy way to add variety here is to change your bread type. Raisin bread, challah, cinnamon swirl, banana bread, thick cut Italian loaf and even croissants that have been sliced lengthwise in half make a great choice. For savory french toast, pumpernickel, oatmeal and sourdough make great choices.

Peanut Butter with Three Berry Compote
Strudel French Toast Topped with Whipped Maple Mascarpone
Brioche French Toast with Honey and Orange Blossom Syrup
Granola Encrusted with Bananas Foster Sauce and Hazelnuts
Mascarpone and Orange Stuffed with Grand Marnier Syrup
Peanut Butter and Marshmallow Fluff stuffed with Chocolate Drizzle
Raisin Nut with Roasted Fruit Syrup
Amber Malt French Toast with Blackberries and Maple Whipped Cream

French Toast stuffed with a Caramel-Apple and Mascarpone Filling
Pecan French Toast with Bananas and Nutella
Sticky-Bun French Toast with Cinnamon Syrup, Whipped Cream and Pecans
Cocoa dipped with Hazelnut filling and Espresso Crème Anglaise
Crispy French Toast with Strawberry Maple Marmalade
French Toast with Dark Rum Bananas and Butterscotch Chips
Vanilla Batter Dipped Challah with Almond Butter
Berry Filled Croissant French Toast with Raspberry Puree and Whipped Cream

Cinnamon Brioche French Toast with Peach and Cranberry Compote
Cornbread French Toast with Maple-Pecan Butter
Graham Cracker Crusted with Key Lime Custard Filling
French Toast stuffed with Honey Peaches and Mascarpone
Stuffed with Honey Flan and Topped with Maple tossed Pecans
Brioche French Toast with Apricot Compote and Cinnamon Whipped Cream
Cinnamon Swirl with a Rum-Date Compote, Whipped Cream and Crunchy Granola
English Muffin French Toast with Smoked Ham, Cranberry Jam and Honey Sour Cream

Streusel stuffed with Apple Cream Cheese and topped with Maple and Walnut Compote
Cap'n Crunch French Toast with Nutella Syrup and Chopped Peanuts
Croissant French Toast with Blueberry Compote and a Streusel Crumb Topping
Crème Brûleè French Toast with Burnt Orange Syrup
Peasant Bread with Oven Dried Strawberries and Black Pepper Maple Syrup
Stuffed with Cannoli Cream and topped with Powdered Sugar and an Espresso Dusting
Cornflake Crusted with Warm Carmel Sauce

Pecan with Streusel Topping and Maple Whipped Cream
Pumpkin Bread with Cranberry Marmalade, Whipped Cream and Shaved Nutmeg

FRENCH TOAST

French Toast with Roasted Apples, Dried Cherries and Pomegranate Syrup
Double Crunch French Toast with Crumbled Sausage and Poached Eggs
Raison Bread with Crystallized Walnuts
Brioche French Toast Served with Grilled Seasonal Fruits
Banana Stuffed with Streusel Topping
Pecan Crusted with Orange and Ginger Compote
Chocolate and Banana Stuffed with Espresso Whipped Cream
Pine Nut Crusted with Chicken Basil Sausage and Fried Eggs

Coco Crispy French Toast with Dark Chocolate Sauce and Whipped Cream
Raison Bread with Maple Fig Syrup
Ranch Cut Raison Bread with Merlot-Honey Syrup
Bread Pudding French Toast with Caramel Sauce and Crème Fraîche
Coconut Crusted with Roasted Bananas and Warm Honey
Sticky - Bun French Toast topped with Maple Pecan Compote
Whole Wheat with Grilled Figs, Maple Syrup and Granola Crunchies
Roasted Banana Stuffed with Vanilla Bean Gelato and Double Fudge Sauce

Almond Mascarpone Stuffed with Warm Orange Marmalade Syrup
Strawberry Stuffed with White Chocolate Sauce and Toasted Hazelnuts
Espresso French Toast with Fresh Raspberries and Dark Chocolate Shavings
Cranberry Walnut Layered with Warm Flan and topped with Dark Amber Maple Syrup
Orange Zest French Toast with Grand Mariner-Orange Compote and Whipped Mascarpone
Cornflake Crusted with Grilled Peaches and Cinnamon Syrup
Pumpernickel French Toast Stuffed with Crunchy Peanut Butter and Bananas
Brioche French Toast with Brandy - Cinnamon Crème Anglaise and Caramel Drizzle

French Toast with Glazed Peaches and Honey Cream
Brioche French Toast with Maple Whipped Cream and Caramelized Ginger
Hazelnut Crusted with Poached Pears and Stilton
Streusel Topped with Bananas Foster Syrup
Cinnamon Bread with Glazed Peach and Cream Cheese Filling
French Toast with Three Fruit Coulis and Seasonal Berries
Brioche with Applewood Smoked Bacon, Burnt Orange and Grand Marnier Syrup
Black Cherry Brioche with Toasted Hazelnut Syrup

Pecan Crusted with Warm Orange Marmalade and Cinnamon Whipped Cream
Stuffed with Bananas and Strawberries
Almond Crusted with Grilled Brie and Baked Apple Chutney
Stuffed with Pumpkin Mousse and topped with Maple Cardamom Cream
Ham and Cheese French Toast with Champagne Mustard and Honey-Plum Jam
Challah with Orange Vanilla Curd, Warm Orange Compote and Crunchy Granola Topping
Golden Raison and Mascarpone Stuffed with a Cinnamon and Maple Cream
Captain Crunch Crusted with Fresh Berries

OMELETS AND FRITTATAS

How do you decide on whether to make it a frittata, filled omelet or a folded omelet that has all of the ingredients mixed in with the egg? Frittatas work well when there are multiple or especially chunky ingredients. More seasoned or more savory ingredients also are more adaptable to the browning of the egg mixture normally associated with the frittata preparation. Whether to fill an omelet or mix the ingredients into the eggs for omelets is a personal choice. I think that by filling the omelet, as opposed to mixing in the ingredients, the egg is highlighted on its own and the separate filling adds another layer of flavor as well as texture. Sometimes you might want to use a combination of both techniques at the same time. An example might be to mix Fine Herbs into the egg mixture and fill the omelet with a light flavored cheese. Another preparation might mix crumbled chorizo and caramelized onion into the egg mixture and fill the omelet with a chili sour cream. The final considerations on filling as opposed to mixing would be time and cooking space. Working on a buffet line or with limited pan or grill space, you can use the same pan to heat the ingredients before adding the eggs and finishing the dish. Otherwise, you need two pans one to heat the filling and one to cook the omelet. The other option in these situations is to keep the fillings hot on the side, but this limits the number of filling options and creates the possibility for overcooking the fillings if they are not used quickly enough. One more note; many of these combinations will make great breakfast burritos when wrapped in a warm tortilla.

Grilled Shrimp, Bacon, Smoked Tomato and Asparagus
Potato and Roasted Garlic
Lobster Frittata with Asparagus, Red Peppers and Buffalo Mozzarella
Zucchini, Chive and Fontina Frittata
Caramelized Onion with a Smoked Tomato and Cheddar Cheese Sauce
Saffron Scented Omelet with Preserved Lemon, Harissa and Cumin Aioli
Fajita Steak, Roasted Peppers, Wild Mushrooms, and Asadero Cheese
Spicy Sausage, Caramelized Cauliflower, Ricotta and Fresh Parsley

Wilted Arugula with Oven Dried Tomato, Goat Cheese and Porcini Cream Sauce
Ricotta Cheese, Roasted Butternut Squash, Sun Dried Tomato and Baby Spinach
Pulled Chicken, Caramelized Shallot and Orzo
Caramelized Sweet Potato and Chorizo with Sun Dried Tomato Salsa
Smoked Salmon and Chive with Crème Fraîche
Mushroom and Goat Cheese with Melted Leeks
Prosciutto and Portabella with Truffle Oil
Goat Cheese, Sage and Red Onion Jam

Cheddar and Bacon with Honey-Chipotle Sour Cream
Spicy Chicken with Cilantro, Grilled Red Onion and Piquant Sauce
Grilled Potato and Chorizo with Sun Dried Tomato Salsa
Cobb Frittata with Chicken, Crisp Bacon, Avocado, Tomatoes and Gorgonzola over Wilted Arugula
Poached Salmon with Orange Hollandaise
Sautéed Thin Sliced Cucumbers and Smoked Salmon
Chorizo and Roasted Chilies
Smoked Sausage, Manchego Cheese, Roasted Chili and Caramelized Onion
Wild Mushroom and Black Forest Ham with Sharp White Cheddar

OMELETS AND FRITTATAS

Caramelized Apple and Gorgonzola
Chipped Beef with Grilled Onion
Saffron and Yukon Gold Potato
Smoked Bacon, White Cheddar and Crisp Potato
Sour Cream and Caviar with Frizzled Leeks
Andouille Sausage with Grilled Scallions and Smoked Tomatoes
Fresh Mint and Mascarpone

Smoked Salmon and Sautéed Cucumber with Tzatziki
Chorizo and Poblano with Cilantro
Artichoke, Crab and Brie
Saffron and Red Potato
Fruit Soufflé Omelet
Smoked Tuna and Three Pepper Frittata
Italian Sausage and Roasted Onion
Asparagus and Gruyere

Goat Cheese and Sun Dried Tomato
Applewood Smoked Bacon and White Cheddar
Shrimp and Fresh Mint
Spinach and Crispy Red Onion
Serrano Ham and Manchego Cheese
Spinach, Portabella and Gorgonzola Frittata
Avocado, Bacon, Tomato and Sour Cream
Broccoli and Stilton

Spanish Seafood
Grilled Pear and Blue Cheese
Smoked Eggplant Creole
Spiced Peach
Tomato, Bacon, Gruyere
Smoked Salmon and Sour Cream
Oven Dried Tomato and Wild Mushroom
Shiitake Mushroom, Ham and Gorgonzola

Asparagus and Ham
Camembert and Spring Herb
Red Potato Omelet with Lemon Garlic Aioli
Potato and Sorrel
Spinach, Lump Crab, Mushrooms and Fontina
Fresh Mozzarella, Tomato and Basil
Mint Omelet with Grilled Apples and Cider Crème Fraîche
Smoked Salmon with Herb Cream Cheese and Fresh Dill
Shiitake Mushroom, Seared Tofu, Grilled Japanese Eggplant
Grilled Peach and Caramelized Onion

WAFFLES AND PANCAKES

Many of these selections will work great for French Toast as well.
Try flavoring your waffle and pancake batter to add another layer to the dish.

Drunken Peach with Chopped Macadamias, Amaretto Butter and Whiskey Sauce
Lemon Soufflé with Raspberry Puree and Mint Cream
Toasted Coconut with Macadamias and Banana Syrup
Chocolate Chunk with Black Currant Syrup and Fresh Raspberries
Bananas Foster with Caramelized Bananas, Pecans and Brandy-Butter Syrup
Lavender Scented with Lemon Cream
Crisp Bacon Waffle topped with Poached Eggs and Hollandaise
Chocolate Chip with Orange Marmalade Syrup

Buttermilk with Crystallized Orange Syrup and Raspberries
Pumpkin with Maple Walnut Apples
Pecan with Lemon Curd and Maple Whipped Cream
Roasted Banana with Nutella Spread, Rum Butter and Hazelnuts
Oatmeal with Allspice Apple Butter
Chocolate with Fresh Raspberry Syrup
Spicy Ricotta Waffles
Banana Pancakes Drizzled with Warm Peanut Butter topped with Chocolate and Whipped Cream

Praline Waffles with Banana Syrup
Tangerine Ricotta with Toasted Pecan Butter and Candied Cranberries
Sweet Potato with Grilled Peaches, Toasted Pistachios and Brown Sugar Syrup
Whole Wheat and Honey Pancakes with Dried Cranberries and Maple Butter
Roasted Pumpkin with Apple Currant Chutney, Toasted Gingersnap Crumble and Molasses Butter
Blackberry with Vanilla Mascarpone Crème Anglaise with a Brown Sugar and Whole Oat Crust
Roasted Banana with Peanut Butter and Toasted Coconut
Chocolate Chunk Pancakes with Nutella Spread and Fresh Strawberries

Blueberry Thyme with Vanilla-Brandy Syrup
Upside Down Caramelized Pear Pancake with Cinnamon Honey Sour Cream
Blueberry with Caramelized Brown Sugar Lemon Rounds
Sweet Potato with Vanilla Mascarpone Crème and Candied Pecans
Walnut with Dark Rum Bananas and Toasted Coconut
Belgian Waffle with Roasted Fruits and Whipped Mascarpone
White Chocolate Macadamia with Coconut Syrup
Buckwheat with Wild Blueberries and Candied Walnut Butter

Blue Corn Buttermilk with Blackberry Bourbon Syrup and Sour Cream
Caramelized Apple Raisin
Macadamia Nut with Caramelized Pineapple Compote and Toasted Coconut Whipped Cream
Malted with Candied Walnuts and Loganberries
Chocolate Chip with Marshmallow Sauce

WAFFLES AND PANCAKES

Malted Milk with Captain Morgan Spiced Rum Bananas and Toasted Coconut
Grilled Peach with Hazelnuts and Nutella Sauce
Roasted Pumpkin Toasted Pine Nut
Blue Corn with Caramelized Oranges, Toasted Almonds and Honey Butter
Greek Yogurt with Lemon Curd, Candied Walnuts and Blood Orange Syrup
Wild Blueberry and Ricotta
Dark Chocolate Chunk
Sweet Potato with Mango Chutney
Orange Grand Mariner

Lemon Scented with Wild Blueberries
Roasted Banana with Toasted Walnuts and Malted Chunk Chocolate Gelato
Whole Wheat topped with Blackberry-Lemon Compote and Walnut Mascarpone Cream
Chocolate Chunk Pancakes with Chocolate Whipped Cream and a Bacon-Peanut Brittle Crumble
Pecan Pumpkin with Cranberry and Orange Chutney and Dark Amber Maple Syrup
Sweet Ricotta with a Dark Cherry Compote and Brandy Syrup
Roasted Apple Pancakes with a Pecan-Brown Sugar Streusel, Dark Rum Syrup and Nutmeg Cream
Orange Zest with Grand Mariner Butter and Mascarpone Crème

Blue Corn with Tangerine Honey Butter and Cinnamon Maple Syrup
Lemon Ricotta with Lemon Curd and Fresh Raspberries
Sweet Potato with Spiced Pecans, Peach Butter and Ginger Syrup
Pumpkin with Root Beer Syrup
Whole Wheat with Vanilla and Peach Compote
Toasted Coconut with Roasted Banana and Passion Fruit Syrup
Ricotta with Grilled Pears and Chopped Walnuts
Whole Wheat with Pistachios and Maple Syrup

Buckwheat with Honey Cranberry Butter
Roasted Corn with Cilantro
Lemon Yogurt with Poppy Seed
Crunchy Peanut Butter
Banana Chocolate Chip
Walnut Gingerbread
Pina Colada – Grilled Pineapple and Toasted Coconut

Maple Pear
Peanut Butter and Bacon
Whole Grain with Grilled Bananas
Glazed Pear with Molasses Crème Fraîche
Lemon Zest with Strawberry Butter
Cinnamon Oatmeal with Brandy Syrup
Buttermilk with Orange Orchid Butter
Bacon with Walnut Butter and Caramelized Onions

BREAKFAST DRINKS

A sprig of fresh mint and a citrus wheel or skewered fresh fruit make a great garnish. If using citrus wheels try aligning a thin orange, lemon and lime wheels together for a three-color effect.

Mint Raspberry Lemonade
Tangerine Iced Tea
Peach Sunrise-Peach Juice, Chardonnay and Pomegranate Juice Float
Gazpacho Tomato Cocktail
Rosemary Lemonade
Carrot Ginger Spritzer with Carrot Juice, Ginger Ale and Sparkling Water
Pineapple Cranberry Cooler
Mojito Iced Jasmine Tea with Mint, Key Lime Juice and Soda Water
Cinnamon-Apple Sparkler
Minted Grapefruit Cooler
Pino-mosa - Champagne with a Splash of Pinot Noir
Peach Nectar and Sparkling Water
Lime Ginger Iced Tea

Cappuccino Hot Chocolate
Sparkling Pear Blanc - Sauvignon Blanc, Pear Liqueur, Sparkling Water
Limeade with Pomegranate Syrup
Wasabi Spiked Bloody Mary
Apple Ginger Infusion with Apple Cider, Pickled Ginger and Club Soda
Pineapple Cilantro Iced Green Tea
Red Germain - Saint Germain with Blood Orange Juice and Fresh Raspberries
Cranberry-Lime Spritzer
Ginger Pumpkin Bloody Mary
Cucumber, Mint and Lime Spritzer
Cucumber Grigio - Pinot Grigio, Cucumber, Lime Juice and Orange Bitters
Blueberry Lemonade Mist
Pineapple Agave Nectar Crush

Mimosas

Pear	Apple
Guava	Lychee
Lavender	Key Lime
Raspberry	White Peach
Watermelon	Lemon Drop
Pomegranate	Blood Orange
Peach - Mango	White Cranberry
Strawberry-Kiwi	Dark Cherry

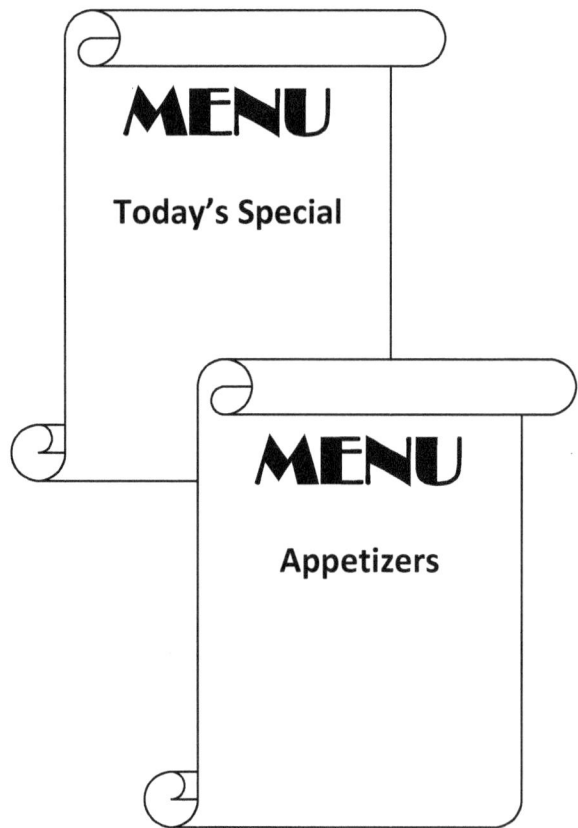

APPETIZERS

Appetizer Selections
Passed Hors D'Oeuvres
Bar, Tavern and Pub Fare
Savory Cheesecakes
Wing Sauces

Chapter Notes, Ideas and Conversions

Main Ingredient	Element 1	Element 2	Element 3	Sauce	Texture

APPETIZERS

In addition to items listed here, you will find many other items listed in the seafood, foie gras and other categories that will make excellent appetizer selections when served in the appropriate portion.

Lamb and Mushroom Skewers with Espresso Aioli
Mushroom Toast with Taleggio Cheese, Sun Dried Tomatoes and Roasted Garlic
Figs stuffed with Boursin Cheese and Wrapped in Prosciutto
Grilled Peasant Bread with Three Olive Tapenade and White Bean Puree
Crab Dip with Grilled Scallions and Smoked Bacon
Fried Green Tomatoes with Crab Rémoulade
Tomato, Herb and Chèvre Napoleon
Bacon Wrapped Dates stuffed with Montrachet Cheese and Apples

Chick Pea and Roasted Pepper Fritters with Spicy Tzatziki
Prosciutto Wrapped Asparagus with Lemon Aioli
Roasted Mushroom Napoleon with Scallion-Vermouth Cream
Grilled Andouille, Basil and Pineapple Kabobs
Duck Breast Skewers with Smoked Tomato and Ginger Jam
Fresh Sardines with Marinated Red Onions and Virgin Olive Oil
Sun Dried Tomato, Prosciutto and Fontina in Puff Pastry with Red Onion and Basil Marmalade
Duck Confit, Acorn Squash and Mushroom Ragu with Grilled Rustic Bread and White Truffle Oil

Melted Brie with Roasted Garlic, Sautéed Green Apples and Toasted Hazelnuts
Three Mushroom Napoleon with Layers of Red and
Yellow Tomatoes, Purple Basil and Fresh Mozzarella with Balsamic Drizzle

Deep Fried Pickles with Spicy Aioli
Crispy Duck Leg Confit with Rocket, Dried Cherries and Toasted Pistachios
Roasted Green Chili Hummus with Gaeta Olive Tapenade, Feta Crumbles and Warm Naan Bread
Jalapenos Stuffed with Manchego Cheese and Chorizo
Prosciutto with Fig Jam, Arugula and Fontina on Roasted Garlic Bread

Crisp Panko Fried Portabella with Grilled Peaches and Smoky Crème Fraîche
Slow Braised Beef Empanada drizzled with Jalapeno Honey served with Ancho Chili Dipping Sauce
Grilled Vegetable Napoleon with a Lemon Curry Sauce
Country Pâté with Green Tomato Relish, Lavender Mustard and Toasted Peasant Bread
Fire Cracker Shrimp - Crisp Spicy Shrimp, Coconut Curry Sauce, Pineapple Papaya Salsa
Grilled Portabella Mushrooms Stuffed with Blue Cheese and Caramelized Shallots
New Orleans BBQ Chicken Tenders Sautéed in Butter, Rosemary and Cayenne
Warm Pistachio Crusted Goat Cheese with Lemon Dressed Couscous and Southern Relish

Escargot in a Garlic Madeira Sauce
Baked Brie wrapped in Prosciutto and Puff Pastry served with a Reduced Merlot Demi-glace
Salmon and Scallop Pate with Roasted Pepper Puree

APPETIZERS

Baked Fresh Herb Ricotta
Asparagus wrapped with Sliced Rare Sirloin of Beef and Dijon Mustard
Crisp Smelts in a Sea Salt Batter with Scallion Aioli
Coconut Crusted Shrimp with an Orange Mustard Honey
Roasted Red Pepper Hummus with Cucumber and Kalamarta Relish and Herb Flatbread
Chicken Liver Pate with Pickled Green Tomatoes and Toasted Pine Nuts
Cured Scottish Salmon with Fresh Parsley Chimichurri
Homemade Soft Pretzels with Cheddar Stout Fondue and Purple Horseradish

Wood Oven-Roasted Bone Marrow with Honey Crisp Apple and Rum Raisin Bread Pudding
Scallops wrapped in Bacon with Smoked Paprika Aioli and Beet Hay
Wild Mushroom Risotto Fritters with Smoked Tomato Cream
Orange Glazed Chicken Lollipops with a Soy and Rice Wine Reduction
Balsamic Shrimp Bruschetta with a Sun Dried Tomatoes, Fresh Basil and Shaved Asiago
Roasted Red Pepper Hummus with Cucumber and Black Olive Relish and Charred Peasant Bread
Lump Crab Fritters with Sweet Cajun Rémoulade and Pickled Fennel
Duck Liver Toasts with Sour Cherries, Roasted Chestnuts and a Balsamic-Cabernet Reduction

Smoked Duck Dumplings with Chopped Fresh Chilies and Rice Vinegar Jam
Warm Burrata Cheese and Serrano Ham on Fresh Sage Biscuits
Artichoke Fritters with Maple-White Truffle Sauce
Wild Mushroom and Goat Cheese Flan on Wild Ramps with Truffle Oil
Ham and Smoked Swiss Fritters with Roasted Tomato Aioli
Phyllo Triangles Filled with Crab, Boursin and Fresh Tarragon
Poached Bone Marrow with Whole Grain Mustard and Pickled Vegetables on Crostini
Chopped Chicken Livers with Brandied Dried Fruit Compote

Fried Green Tomatoes drizzled with a Jalapeno Honey and Mango Ketchup
Roasted Bone Marrow with Red Onion Marmalade and Smoked Sea Salt
Black Bread Circles with Cilantro Guacamole and Smoked Shrimp
Smoked Pork Pot Stickers with Sweet and Sour Apricot Dipping Sauce
Crab Fritters with Cucumber and Cilantro Salsa and Ancho Chili Aioli
Pistachio Fried Goat Cheese with Green Tomato Salsa and Aged White Balsamic
Slow Roasted Pork Wontons with Guava Glaze and Chopped Mint
Roasted Red Pepper and Jalapeno Fondue over Grilled Artichokes and Toast Points

Serrano Ham Croquettes and Roasted Poblano Peppers with Smoked Gouda Fondue
Baked Brie with Gran Marnier-soaked Cherries and Toasted Hazelnuts
Cardamom Spiced Pumpkin Fritters with Sweet Pepper Jam
Lollypop Chicken Drumettes served with Blue Cheese Fondue and Spicy Hot Sauce
Smoked Duck Liver Pate with Pickled Watermelon, Sweet Pickle Chips and Pumpernickel Rounds
Cod Fritters with Pequin Pepper Aioli
Deep Fried Jalapeños Stuffed with a Chèvre Cheese and Peach Compote Filling
Black Lentil Hummus with Curried Eggplant and Fresh Oregano Olive Oil served with Warm Pita

APPETIZERS

Grilled Bruschetta with Manchego Cheese and a Serrano Chili and Cranberry Compote
Braised Oxtail and Smoked Cheddar Tart with Roasted Tomato Marmalade
Baked Fresh Mozzarella Crostini with Rosemary Prosciutto and Toasted Walnut Oil
Duck Confit Potato Skins with Goat Cheese and Scallion Crème Fraîche
Sun Dried Tomato Hummus on Grilled Bruschetta with Pomegranate Syrup Drizzle
Lobster, Roasted Pepper and Brie Fondue served with Rustic Basil Bread
Guinness Braised Short Rib Chili with Horseradish Cheddar
Fire Roasted Chèvre stuffed Medjool Dates wrapped in Parma Ham with Roasted Chestnut Puree
Short Rib Tacos with Pickled Cucumber, Spicy Kimchee and Korean BBQ Sauce
Napoleon of Smoked Salmon, Crispy Potatoes, Horseradish Cream and Grilled Green Apples

Bucket of Bones - Korean BBQ Beef Ribs, Tandoori Pork Ribs with
Lamb Chop Lollipops and Spicy Root Beer Chicken Wings

Oak Fired Black Mission Figs wrapped with Prosciutto served with Brie Fondue and Candied Pecans
Cracked Stone Crab Claws with a Toasted Coconut and Dark Rum Mustard Sauce
Brie Crème Brûleè with Sea Salt and Cracked Black Pepper Crostini
Roasted Fontina stuffed Dates wrapped in Veal Bacon with a Merlot Reduction Drizzle

Roasted Banana Won Tons with Mascarpone and Pear Chutney
Black Truffle and Wild Mushroom Risotto Croquets with Roasted Garlic Aioli
Flaky Crust - Crab and Gruyere Pop Tarts with Orange Caper Hollandaise
Sundried Tomato Brie with Toasted Pecans, Granny Smith Apple Relish and Dark Rum Butter
Sun Dried Tomato Flan with Burrata Cheese, Fresh Basil and White Balsamic Drizzle
Grilled Shrimp Kabob Marinated in Green Thai Curry and Coconut Milk with Roasted Peanut Sauce
Conch Fritters with Brown Butter and a Key Lime and Charred Pineapple Salsa
Roasted Poblano and Smoked Gouda Fondue over Grilled Artichokes and Toast Points

Carmel Glazed Lamb Chops with Red Jalapeño and Mint Salsa
Crostini with Eggplant Caponata, Sliced Figs, Burrata Cheese and Spicy Tomato Coulis
Smoked Salmon and Green Apple Salad with Shaved Fresh Horseradish
Butter Poached Alaskan King Crab with Roasted Peppers and Whole Grain Mustard on Crostini
Shrimp and Maui Onion Stuffed Mushrooms with Béarnaise Sauce

Phyllo with a Ground Lamb, Dried Cherry and Toasted Pine Nut Filling served
with Tzatziki Dipping Sauce

Roasted Duck Liver Mousse with Dried Plums
Grape Leaves Stuffed with Goat Cheese and Roasted Eggplant with Balsamic Syrup
Caramelized Stilton, Melted Leeks and Baby Watercress on Grilled Peasant Bread Croutons
Warm Parmesan and Roasted Asparagus Flan with Lemon Brown Butter
Cured Salmon Bruschetta with Pickled Red Onions, Capers and Chive Mascarpone
White Anchovy Tart with Roasted Mushroom and Smoked Tomato Confit

APPETIZERS

Crab and Lobster Crêpe with Whipped Mascarpone and White Truffle Oil
Crispy Pork Belly with Soy Pickled Ginger
Crab and Risotto Fritters in a Tomato Basil Broth
Sautéed Spinach and Goat Cheese in a Warm Potato Basket with Summer Tomato-Coriander
Vinaigrette Gorgonzola in Puff Pastry served over a Warm Apricot-Walnut Relish
Slow Roasted Tomato Tart with Balsamic Onion Confit and Fresh Burrata Cheese
Beets with Goat Cheese, Wilted Arugula and Meyer Lemon Dressing
Crispy Asian Chicken tossed with Thai Spicy Chili Sauce and
served over Sweet and Sour Sesame-Cucumber Slices

Grilled Artichokes with Hummus, Feta, Olives and Rosemary Olive Oil on a Fire Toasted Crouton
Lamb and Caramelized Onion Meatballs with Mint Pesto
Roasted Eggplant and Smoked Tomato Terrine on Frisée with Anchovy Vinaigrette
Cilantro, Radish and Red Curry Salmon Rolls with Lime Aioli
Toasted Flat Bread with Brie and Smoked Tomato Marmalade
Mini Reuben on Pretzel Bread with Whiskey, Green Apple and Caraway Sauerkraut
Stilton and Granny Smith Apple Tart with 75 Year Balsamic
Baked Brie in Puff Pastry with a Guava and Pomegranate Reduction

Smoked Salmon and Crisp Potato Galette with Parsley Shallot Cream
Warm Brie En Croute with Sun Dried Tomato Pesto
Steamed Artichoke with a Roasted Garlic and Lemon Aioli
Spicy Steamers - Littleneck Clams with Five Spice and Chili-Garlic Butter served with Crusty Bread
Fried Green Tomatoes with Crisp Bacon and Ranch Aioli
Dungeness Crab Stuffed Artichokes with Red Chili Hollandaise
Roasted Asparagus Crostini with Fontina Fondue
Pan Seared Jumbo Prawns on Baby Bok Choy with a Vanilla Lime Emulsion

Dates Wrapped In Serrano Ham Stuffed with Asiago Cheese with a Roasted Pepper Coulis
Spicy Tuna with Jicama and Thai Basil Salsa and Mint Crème Fraîche
Eggplant and Fig Caponata with Sweet Butter Crostini
Crispy Stuffed Squash Blossoms with Boursin and Toasted Hazelnuts
Wild Mushroom and Goat Cheese Strudel with Charred Tomato Demi-glace
Smoked Trout and Horseradish Dill Parfait
Artichoke Bottoms Stuffed with Tomatoes, Wild Mushroom and Melted Brie
Marinated Sardines with Heirloom Tomatoes and Pickled Onions on Crisp Rye Croutons

Grilled Pears with Parma Ham, Fresh Ricotta and Balsamic Glaze
Spinach Pancakes with Feta and Sun Dried Tomato Compote
Yellow Tomato Carpaccio with Fresh Basil and White Truffle Oil
Layered Roasted Vegetable Terrine with Sweet Red Peppers and Grilled Shitakes
Crisp Queso Fresco Wonton with Raspberry and Mint
Smoked Trout Mousse in Phyllo with Black Truffle Cream Sauce
Roasted Pepper, Basil and Fontina Popovers
Leek And Gruyere Tart served with Arugula Salad and Caper Vinaigrette

APPETIZERS

Fontina, Pistachio and Grilled Pear Soufflé with Pomegranate Syrup
Escargots with Wild Mushrooms in a Burgundy sauce over Toasted Peasant Bread
Alaskan King Crab Parfait
Stuffed Mushrooms Casino
Cured Salmon on Grilled Polenta with Caviar and Crème Fraîche
Toasted Goat Cheese Crouton with Champagne Mustard Dipping Sauce
Gorgonzola Stuffed Dates with Honey and Balsamic Aioli
Phyllo Wrapped Shrimp over Feta Couscous with Chunky Tomato, Olive and Caper Chutney

Escargots in puff pastry with Spinach, Mushrooms, Chives and Garlic Butter
Clam and Conch Fritters with Scotch Bonnet Tartar Sauce
Crab and Leek Tarts
Grilled Flatbread with Warm Brie and Dried Fruits
Mango Pomegranate Glazed Chicken Satay with Jicama Relish
Smoked Trout with Horseradish and Caper Sauce on Black Bread Rounds
Escargots with Spinach, Toasted Pine Nuts and Roasted Garlic in a Pastry Shell
Shrimp and Pecan Dumplings with Wilted Greens and Habanero Vinaigrette

Oyster Mushroom Tartlets Glazed with Fontina and served with Madeira Wine Sauce
Tureen of Duck with Black Pepper Cumberland Sauce
Tenderloin Tidbits of Lamb with Lime Hollandaise for Dipping
Country Pate' with Creole Mustard Sauce
Shiitake Mushroom and Brie Toast
Salmon and Crawfish Cakes with Avocado and a Sweet Red Onion Pickle
Kobe Steak Sashimi with Pickled Cucumbers and Spicy Radishes
Black Sesame Crusted Seared Ahi with Orange Cilantro Vinegar

Baked Artichoke, Parmesan and Roasted Green Chili Dip with Crostini
Deep Fried Panko Crusted Asparagus with a Pineapple and Shallot Relish
Thai Spiced Chicken Lollipops with Green Papaya Relish
Grilled Pears wrapped in Prosciutto with a Balsamic Reduction
Brie and Sweet Red Pepper Pie
Wild Mushroom and Goat Cheese Strudel with Demi-glace
Pork and Veal Pate with Sun Dried Cranberries
Warm Gorgonzola Baguettes with Lightly Browned Lemon Wheels

Rolled Tortillas Filled with Chorizo and Green Chili Potatoes
Smoked Ham and Roquefort Tart
Spicy Gingered Beef Pot Stickers with Thai Chili-Pineapple Sauce
Roasted Eggplant and Yellow Pepper Dip with Grilled Pumpernickel Rounds
Seared Scallops with Riesling and Fresh Sage
Roasted Garlic with Mascarpone Cheese on Grilled Sour Dough
Spinach, Crab, Ricotta and Onions baked in Puff Pastry served with Red Pepper Beurre Blanc
Beef Capriccio with Lime and Fresh Thyme

PASSED HORS D'OEUVRES

You know the rules, small enough to pick up with one hand and eat in two bites.
No sauces or toppings that might drip.

Chorizo and Manchego Cheese Stuffed Dates Wrapped in Bacon
Prosciutto and Crab Meat Cigars
Spicy Scallop Mousse in Mushroom Caps
Seared Foie Gras with Dried Currants on Melba
Rare Lamb Tidbits on Béarnaise Toast
Fried Port-Salut and Smoked Ham Squares
Herb Cheese in Belgium Endive
Cubes of Camembert Wrapped in Prosciutto and Deep Fried
Brie in Phyllo Purses with Pistachio Nut Butter
Tandoori Chicken and Curry Pineapple Skewers

Baby Romaine Leaves filled with Roasted Eggplant and Sesame Mascarpone
Coconut Breaded Scallops
Cucumber Coins filled with Saffron Scented Lobster
Pepperoncini Peppers Stuffed With Feta
Rare Beef Tenderloin and Caramelized Pearl Onion on Rosemary Picks
Peanut Butter and Crisp Bacon Canapés
Shrimp Grilled with Jerk Seasonings and Orange Honey
Crab, Prosciutto and Fontina in Puff Pastry
Thai Spiced Shrimp Toast
Chicken Basil Pot Stickers

Bacon Wrapped Mission Figs with Goat Cheese
Duck and Citrus Mousse in Phyllo Cups
Veal and Prosciutto Meatballs
Asparagus Wrapped with Fontina and Cappicola
Smoked Chicken Tenders with Hoisin Glaze
Ham, Green Onion and Blue Cheese in Puff Pastry Triangles
Shrimp and Caviar Baguette with Fresh Chives
Roasted Pepper and Red Onion Hushpuppies
Grape Leaves stuffed with Fresh Ginger Rice and Cremini Mushrooms

Quail Eggs wrapped in Smoked Salmon and Tarragon
Grilled Chorizo and Baby Portobello Skewers
Kalamata Olive and Red Onion Bruschetta
Dried Beef on Pumpernickel Rounds with Spinach and Horseradish Butter
Jalapeno Meatballs
Pastrami, Dill Pickle and Sweet Red Pepper Wraps
Smoked Trout with Lemon Mayonnaise on Melba Rounds
Scallop Puffs with Fresh Dill and Gruyere
Fresh Tuna and Wasabi Won Tons
Smoked Duck and Avocado on Pumpernickel Crusts

BAR, TAVERN AND PUB FOOD

Guinness and Cheddar Fondue with Crisp Potato Wedges and Toasted Irish Soda Bread for Dipping
New Orleans BBQ Shrimp - Shell on Shrimp sautéed in Butter, Rosemary and Cayenne
Flaming Ginger Prawns
Littleneck Clams Steamed in Dark Beer and Herbs
Brie and Mango Quesadillas with Minced Jalapenos
Raw Vegetables with Spicy Dipping Salt - Cumin, Coriander, Cayenne, Kosher Salt
Grilled Smoked Sausage Rounds with Mustard Glaze
Quesadilla with Goat Cheese and Spiced Walnuts
Key West Conch Fritters with a Whole Grain Honey Mustard and Caribbean Cocktail Sauce
Aged Gouda and Dark Ale Bread Pudding with Horseradish Cream and Grilled Scallions
Smoked Chicken Spring Rolls
Fried Cheddar and Bacon Squares
Shrimp Au Poivre with Jack Daniel's Dipping Sauce
Orange and Honey Glazed Back Ribs
Fresh Tuna and Pineapple Kabobs with Rum Pepper Glaze
Dark Ale, Cheddar, Hot Mustard and Horseradish Fondue
Red Pepper Meatballs
Baked Artichoke and Dill Havarti Spread with Cheddar Toasted Pita Chips
Chilled Vegetables with Sweet Pepper Vinegar and Crème Fraîche
Toasted Walnut and Caramelized Shallot Dip

Cajun Shrimp Fritters with Salsa Verde
Jalapeno Crab Balls
Deep Fried Mushrooms stuffed with Sausage and White Cheddar
Grilled Shark Bites with Habanero Mayonnaise
Shrimp Glazed with Maple Syrup and Crushed Red Pepper Flakes
Sun Dried Tomato, Chipotle and Sharp Cheddar Dip
Fresh Cod Brochettes with Calypso Sauce
Five Spice Chicken with Peanut Dipping Sauce
Grilled Shrimp with Chipotle Strips wrapped in Bacon
Crisp Jalapeno Wontons
Spicy Puff Pastry Cheese Straws
Deep Fried Crab Fingers served with Red Crab Vinegar
Cajun Meat Pies
Grilled Scallops with Spicy Chili Dipping Sauce
Three Cheese Chimichanga with Chorizo
Thai Chicken and Red Pepper Satay
Grilled Pork Kabobs with Lime Ginger Glaze
Mussels with Vermouth and Green Onions
Smoked Chicken Tenders
Scallops wrapped in Bacon served with Three Peppercorn Cream
Crab Fingers Served with Eastern Shore Red Vinegar Sauce
Chipotle Crab Balls

SAVORY CHEESECAKES

These selections make a quick lunch or brunch item when garnished with a small side salad or a cup of soup. Use an unsweetened cream cheese and egg cheesecake base. Add savory ingredients and flavor with additional cheeses or other components as desired. Crusts can include any corresponding spices, fresh or dried herbs or seasonings and can be prepared with a variety of crushed crackers, corn flakes or a traditional pie crust. Add a puree, salsa or accompanying reduction as a base for the plate, taking into consideration texture and color. Flavored unsweetened whipped cream can be piped on top or on the side to add additional level of flavor. Savory Cheesecakes are also a great way to utilize less used components from butchering. An example might be the legs and thigh meat left from a whole duck. You have many offerings for the breast meat but don't have a use for the remainder of the meat. By slow braising it you can now make it lead component of the cheesecake.

Butter Poached Lobster, Sun Dried Tomato and Mascarpone
Scallop and Tarragon with Lemon Aioli
Santa Fe Roasted Chicken and Monterey Cheese with Cilantro Pesto
Smoked Salmon and Horseradish Cheddar
Crab and Wild Mushroom with a Green Onion Coulis
Gulf Shrimp and Smoked Gouda with Creole Mustard Sauce
Chèvre Cheese and Rosemary with Shaved Prosciutto and Armagnac-Macerated Figs
Scallop and Asparagus on a Port Wine-Vanilla Reduction

Dried Chipped Beef with Caramelized Onions and Horseradish Cheddar
Savory Mini-Blue Cheese Cakes with Port Reduction
Warm Creole Cheesecake with Crawfish, Roasted Peppers and Goat Cheese
Prosciutto and Fontina with Sun-Dried Tomatoes and Pesto
Smoked Salmon and Brie with a Lemon and Dill Coulis
Goat Cheese Cake with Sweet and Sour Cherries on Arugula
Serrano Ham and Manchego Cheese with Smoked Tomato and Cilantro

Chipotle Marinated Shrimp and Grilled Scallion with a Sweet Mango Puree
Roasted Medjool Dates with Prosciutto and Gorgonzola
Caramelized Granny Smith Apple, Country Ham and Double Crème Brie
Smoked Chicken with Broccoli, Artichokes and Havarti
Gorgonzola Cheese with Candied Walnuts and Pear Vinaigrette
Parma Ham with Roasted Chestnuts and Port Salute
Fresh Basil, Summer Tomato and Ricotta
Smoked Oyster and Bacon with Poblano

Blackened Scallop with Thyme Roasted Vegetable Confit on a Yellow Pepper Coulis
Old Bay Crab and Colby Jack served on a Black Bean and Roasted Corn Salsa
Savory Duck, Caramelized Onion, Charred Tomato with Port-Salut
Shrimp and Lemongrass on a Braised Fennel Confit
Mixed Shellfish and Boursin Cheese with a Roasted Garlic Scampi Sauce
Smoked Mussels with Roasted Peppers and Chopped Scallions
Braised Short Rib, Wild Mushroom and Goat Cheese

WING SAUCES

There once was a day when even the staff would not eat chicken wings. The only thing we used wings for was to make stock. How times have changed. What a lesson in the practice of supply and demand. Wings are now so popular that they far out-price any of the other cuts of the chicken. Certainly whole chickens, all of the dark meat cuts and even the once most prized breast are less expensive to purchase than the wings. The original Buffalo style will always be the most popular seller, just as vanilla is by far the most popular flavor of ice cream. But any number of interesting preparations, marinades, glazes and coating sauces as well as dipping sauces can make wings more appealing. You can add additional layers of flavor and textures by incorporating end of preparation coatings such as chopped peanuts or other nuts, chopped fresh herbs, dried or fresh chilies or a spice shake just before serving. For more ideas for wings, look in the "BBQ Sauces" list on page 177 in this book. Many of those selections will work as a glaze or as a dipping sauce. And don't forget your house aioli as an accompaniment. You may have several that you use in your existing menu items that can also be used for wings. A *Honey Wasabi Aioli* that is served with your seared tuna might be an example. It's already a prep item so there is no addition work needed to offer it. For speed of preparation the deep fryer works great for wings. Blanching and allowing the wings to cool not only decreases you final cooking time but adds to the crispness of the final product. If you are working with a coal or wood fired oven you can get a fantastic charred flavor into your preparation. Of course wings take well to char broiling and some preparations can even be done in a hot oven.

Golden Asian Chili Glaze
Mango Chipotle
Root Beer and Vodka Syrup
Spicy Hoisin BBQ
Mango, Fresh Chilies and Mint
Apple Cider and Red Jalapeño Jam
Spicy Thai Peanut
Teriyaki
Citrus Glaze and Fresh Thyme
Garlic, Ginger and Orange
Citrus Chipotle Glaze

Spicy Plum and Dark Rum
Sticky Sesame Caramel
Chipotle BBQ
Far Diablo Marinara
Lemon Pepper
Ginger Wasabi
Orange Habanero
Chili Lime
Double Dijon and Honey
Habanero Ranch
Szechwan Chili

Cracked Black Pepper Crusted with Jack Daniel's Sauce
Irish Whiskey Glaze with Guinness Ranch Dip
Chicken Wing Lollipops with Honey Buffalo Sauce
Caribbean Jerk Seasoned with Caramelized Pineapple Glaze
Bourbon, Brown Sugar and Hot Sauce
Peanut Crusted with Sriracha Honey and Chopped Cilantro
Cherry Coke Glaze and Red Pepper Flakes
Crispy Wings tossed with Diced Papaya, Sweet Chili Sauce and Chopped Fresh Pasilla Peppers
Dark Rum Glaze with Kaffir Lime Dipping Sauce
Thai Chili Sauce with Cucumber-Wasabi Cream
Chinese Five Spice with Sweet and Sour Glaze
Wood Fire Roasted with Caramelized Onion, Garlic and a Squeeze of Fresh Lemon
Cajun Blackened with Honey, Lime and Tequila
Jerk Chicken Wings with Spicy Lemon Dipping Sauce
Pilsner-Brined Wings with a Pickled Carrot and Stilton Salad

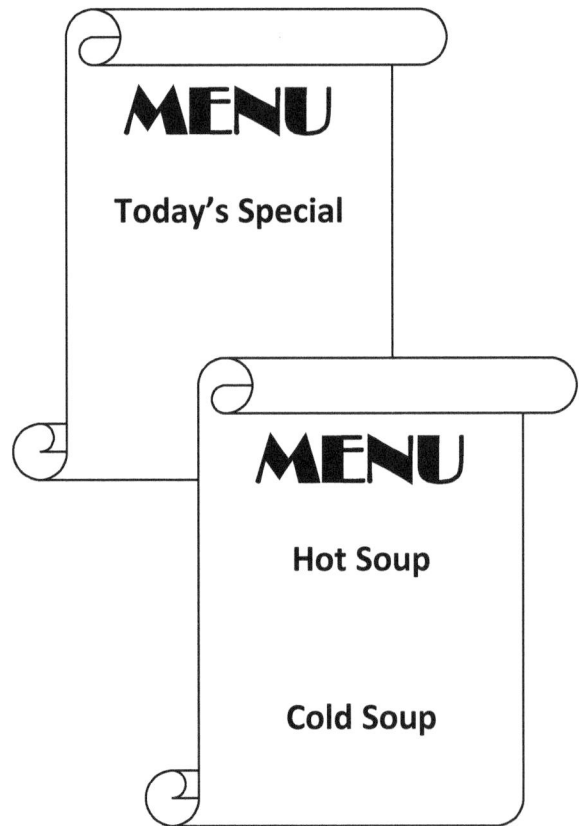

SOUPS

Hot Soups
Cold Soups

Chapter Notes, Ideas and Conversions

Main Ingredient	Element 1	Element 2	Element 3	Sauce	Texture

SOUP

Roasted Golden Chestnut Bisque with Bacon and Spiced Maple Butter
Cuban Black Bean with Cubanelle Pepper Relish
Wild Ramp Soup with Braised Smoked Pork Shoulder and Roasted Carrots
Thai Hot and Sour Asparagus with Seared Scallops
Spicy Lobster with Truffle Butter
Meatball and Grilled Fall Vegetable
Caramelized Corn Chowder with Bacon and Sweet Butter Crostini
Dried Lima Soup with Smokey Bacon and Vidalia Onion Fritter
Roasted Sweet Potato Bisque with Maple Cream
Sweet Corn and Leek Soup with Black Truffle Oil

All White Lobster Bisque
New England Clam Chowder with Black Pepper and Chive Biscuits
Apple and Turnip Soup with Whole Wheat Spaetzle
Seafood Chowder with Boston Brown Bread Croutons
Roasted Parsnips Soup with Amber Maple Syrup
Smoked Haddock and Mushroom Chowder
Spicy Miso with Grilled Shrimp, Oyster Mushrooms, Chiles and Chives
Tuscan Three Bean Soup with Shaved Logatelli and Olive Oil Swirl
Roasted Chicken and Poblano with Aged Jack and Tortilla Strips
Green Apple and Celery Root Soup with Chive Oil

New York Steak Hot and Sour
Country Tomato with Blue Cheese Puff Pastry Crust
Butternut Squash and Roasted Apple with Duck Confit
Charred Golden Tomato and Grilled Fennel Chowder
Spicy Vegetable with White Cheddar Croutons
Sun Dried Tomato Stew with Burrata Cheese over Grilled Country Bread
Three Onion Soup with a Fried Cod Cake and a Lemon and Green Onion Garnish
Celery Root and Apple with Fried Sage
Sunchoke and Lobster Bisque
Curried Squash and Roasted Onion Puree with Coconut Milk

Roasted Butternut Squash and Sage Bisque with Cranberry Crème Fraîche
Fresh Rockfish Chowder
Red and Yellow Pepper Soup with Shrimp Dumplings
Dungeness Crab and Grilled Scallop Chowder with Ginger Crème Fraîche
Curried Cauliflower with Toasted Almonds
Country Minestrone with Prosciutto
Acorn Squash Bisque with Gorgonzola Croutons
Parsnip Celery Root and Duck Confit Chowder with Fried Sage
Cauliflower and Blue Cheese

SOUP

Grilled Lobster Chowder with Lemon Verbena and Black Pepper Beignets
Spicy Shrimp and Crayfish Bisque
Hot and Sour Soup with Chili Seared Scallops
Poblano and Caramelized Corn Chowder
Roasted Tomato Bisque with Gorgonzola Croutons
Sausage and Lentil
Vidalia Onion Soup with Blistered White Cheddar Croutons
Coconut Curry
Chicken Tortilla with Tomatoes, Chipotle, Roasted Corn and Cilantro Crème Fraîche
Oyster Stew with Potatoes and Crisp Bacon

Onion Soup with Truffles, Foie Gras and Gruyère Puff Pastry Triangles
Cream of Roasted Garlic
Dried Lima Bean with Smoked Pork, Cilantro and Lime
Butternut Squash and Grilled Apple with Cider Crème Fraîche
Cream of Watercress Soup, Lemon Oil, Yogurt
Parsnip Soup with Diced Apple and Hazelnut Oil
Caramelized Corn Chowder
Smoked Shellfish Broth
Lemon Egg Drop with Crab
Caramelized Cauliflower and Wild Mushroom Broth with Sage Crostini

Spinach and Oyster Bisque
Roasted Chestnut Soup with Smoked Bacon
Cream of Tomato with Tarragon Oil
Cauliflower with Black Truffle
Cream of Artichoke with Wild Mushrooms
Creamy Lobster Bisque with and Oven Dried Tomato and Lobster Confit
Garlic Potato Puree
Sunchoke Soup with Wild Mushrooms and Smoked Bacon
Chicken Soup with Caramelized Corn Dumplings
Pasta and Three Bean

Fire Roasted Tomato and Cracked Pepper Chowder
Butternut Squash Puree with Tarragon Crème Fraîche
Tomato Basil with Tortellini
Porcini Mushroom and Smoked Lobster Bisque with Black Truffle Oil
Root Vegetable Soup with Ricotta Croutons
Black Bean and Rosemary
Lobster and Cascabel Chili Chowder
Curried Potato and Crawfish
Roasted Carrot Soup with Lime Butter

SOUP

Lobster, Green Chili and Caramelized Corn Chowder
Shellfish Broth with Cilantro
Charred Lobster Bisque with Shaved White Truffles
Roasted Pumpkin with Smoked Chili and Pomegranate Crème Fraîche
Corn Soup with Crispy Okra Strips
Cream of Crab and Artichoke
Fennel, Leeks and Spinach in a Savory Broth
Grilled Chicken Soup with Corn, Green Chilies, Caramelized Onions and Crisp Tortilla Strips

Carrot Soup with Cardamom Crème Fraîche and Cilantro Oil
Spring Vegetable with Ginger
Southern Crab and Sweet Corn Chowder
Cream of Fennel with Scallops and Shrimp
Lemony Mushroom Basil
Herbed Haddock Chowder
Chicken Bonnet Pepper
Spicy Red Shrimp Chowder
Butternut Squash with Shitake Mushrooms and Orange Zest
Truffle Scented Broth with Wild Mushroom Ravioli

Roasted Beet Soup with Yogurt, Cilantro and Garam Masala
Lobster Champagne Bisque
Hot and Sour Soup with Shiitake Mushrooms
Cream of Squash with Herb Poached Oysters
Smoked Turkey with Fennel Ravioli
Pumpkin Apple Cider
Asparagus Cream with Lump Crab
Curried Mussel and Potato Chowder
Harvest Vegetable with Pasta, Beans and Pesto

Cream of Pumpkin with Prosciutto
Steak and Potato
Dried Lima Bean with Country Sausage
Cheddar Vegetable with Puff Pastry Crust
Roasted Apple and Cheddar with Crisp Croutons
Beef, Mushroom and Tomato
Smoked Lobster and Black Bean Soup with Sun Dried Tomato Jam
Sesame Chicken and Rice
Sausage and Bean with Pasta
New England Cioppino with Roasted Garlic-Cheese Crostini
Cajun Potato and Crawfish
Lentil with Lamb and Rice

SOUP

Smoked Chicken Broth with Artichoke Ravioli
Cream of Leek with Mussels and Pesto
Salmon Chowder with Potatoes, Bacon and Corn
Celery Root and Oyster Chowder
Cream of Four Onion
Florentine Bean - Cannelloni Beans with Pancetta, Spinach and a Splash of Vermouth
Cream of Broccoli with Blue Cheese
Pasta and Artichoke
Southwestern White Bean

Curried Butternut Bisque
Pumpkin Tortellini in Chicken Broth
Winter Squash and Sage
Oven Dried Tomato and Wild Mushroom
Cauliflower and Colby
Creamy Roasted Garlic with Brie
Oyster Mushroom Chablis
Jersey Lobster and Corn Chowder
Chicken Curry

Avocado Veloute with Citrus and Crab
Shrimp and Orzo
Beef and Fresh Spinach with Tortellini
Lobster and Asparagus
Peanut Sweet Potato Bisque
Pumpkin Soup with Herbed Croutons
Turkey and Wild Rice Chowder
Leek, Mushroom and Clam Volute

Squash and Sage
Roasted Asparagus with Fresh Thyme
Cream of Avocado with Cracked Black Pepper
Little Neck Clam with Andouille
Chicken Chipotle with Bell Peppers and Lime
Mushrooms and Artichokes with Tomato Pesto
Grilled Chicken and Roasted Red Potato
Pumpkin with Fresh Ginger and Chives
Grilled Tomato and Caramelized Eggplant with Parmesan Croutons
Smoked Salmon and Rosemary Chowder
Caramelized Corn and Red Pepper Bisque
Five Mushroom Consommé
Roasted Garlic Velouté with Prosciutto Croutons

COLD SOUPS

Watermelon Gazpacho with Cucumber, Thai Basil and Fresh Mint
Chilled Cantaloupe with Citrus Crème Fraîche and Lemon Verbena Oil
Smoked Tomato and Red Onion with Basil Oil and Lime Crème Fraîche
Chilled Zucchini Soup with Blistered Cherry Tomatoes, Nicoise Olives and Basil
Roasted Red Pepper and Poblano Puree with Goat Cheese Mousse
Ancho Gazpacho Verde with Lobster and Crème Fraîche
Cool Fresh Pea Velouté
Watermelon, Cherry Tomato and Jicama
Strawberry and Mango with Lemongrass

Cucumber and Buttermilk with Sorrel
Blackberry Lime
Summer Tomato Soup with Diced Cucumbers and Smoked Shrimp
Cold Honeydew Melon, Cilantro and Scallop
Cantaloupe and Blueberry Gazpacho with Honey Crème Fraîche
Cucumber with Smoked Lobster and Citrus Oil
Peach Soup with Fine Herbs
Honeydew and Cucumber Gazpacho with Agave Nectar and Fresh Mint
Pumpkin and Ginger
Golden Tomato with Chive Sour Cream
Scallop and Cucumber Cream with Ancho Oil

Strawberry Gazpacho
Peach and Champagne with Mint Crème Fraîche
Cool Crab Asparagus
Cucumber and Yogurt with Fresh Cilantro
Roasted Tomato and Fresh Herbs with Olive Oil and Crumbled Feta
Chilled Cauliflower and Potato
Cucumber Gazpacho with Feta, Toasted Almonds and Greek Yogurt
Summer Tomato with Basil Crème Fraîche
Strawberry and Honey with Balsamic Vinegar
Avocado, Tomatillo and Cilantro with Lime

Creamy Orange with Honey and Mint
Vichyssoise with Fresh Fennel
Creamy Cucumber and Crab
Tomato and Roasted Pepper
Cantaloupe Mint
Avocado and Fresh Cilantro
Vegetable Gazpacho with Crab
Cool Champagne and Raspberry
Old Bay Crab, Summer Tomato and Sweet Yellow Peppers
Salmon and Cucumber Soup
Kiln Dried Cherry and Sour Cream
Three Melon Soup with Coconut Milk

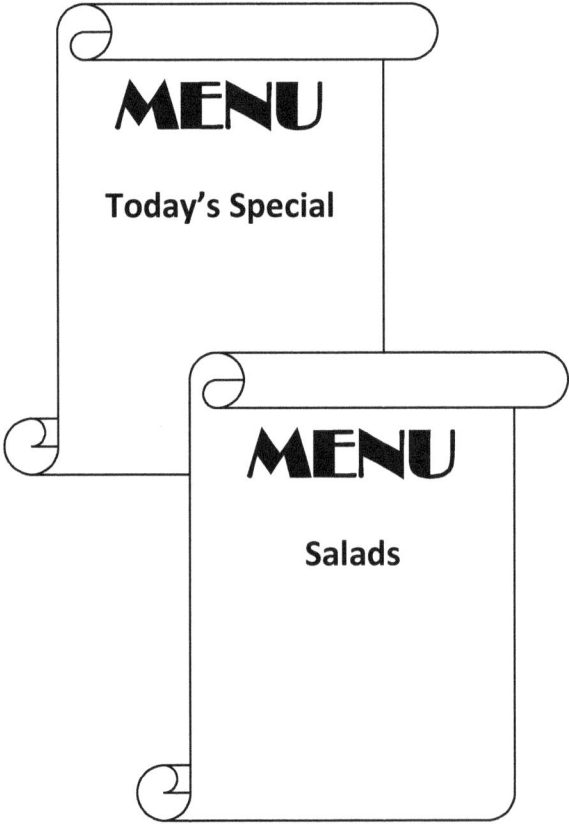

SALADS

Assorted Salads
Salad Dressings, Vinaigrettes

Chapter Notes, Ideas and Conversions

Main Ingredient	Element 1	Element 2	Element 3	Sauce	Texture

SALAD

Many selections can be served over baby greens as a lunch, dinner or appetizer salad.

Country Ham, Black Mission Figs and Spiced Pecan with a Dijon Molasses Dressing
Grilled Baby Romaine with Crisp Chorizo and Cotija Cheese Croutons with Roasted Garlic Dressing
Smoked Salmon over Baby Greens with Boursin, Dill Vinaigrette and Toasted Onion Crostini
Fresh Green and Yellow Beans with Fingerling Potatoes, Green Olive Puree and Feta

Thai Crunch Salad - Shredded Napa Cabbage, Julianne Cucumbers, Crispy Wontons with
Toasted Peanuts, Wilted Red Cabbage and Fresh Scallions with a Lime, Mint and Cilantro Dressing

BBQ Chicken, Black Beans, Grilled Corn, Scallions, Smoked Tomatoes, Cilantro Ranch Dressing
Belgium Endive, Radicchio, Spiced Walnuts, Roasted Pears and Roquefort with Vanilla Vinaigrette
Grilled Romaine with Crisp Pancetta, Gorgonzola and Sweet Fig Vinegar
Roasted Red and Golden Beets, Baby Spinach, Shaved Red Onion and a Chardonnay Vinaigrette
Tangerines, Plums, Toasted Almonds, Golden Raisins, Bel Paese and a Sherry Honey Dressing
Arugula, Apples, Grapes, Pine Nuts, Smoked Chèvre, Basil and Crisp Pancetta Vinaigrette
Seared Salmon Salad with Shaved Red Onion, Avocado and Green Goddess Dressing
Roasted Pumpkin on Arugula with Toasted Pumpkin Seeds and Warm Bacon Dressing

Grilled Peaches and Dandelions with Fresh Ricotta and Chopped Hazelnuts
Spinach, Candied Kumquats, Boursin, Crisp Bacon and Ginger Vinaigrette
Warm Wild Mushrooms with a Gorgonzola Flan and a Port Wine Vinaigrette
Grilled Pears and Apples with Candied Walnuts, Blue Cheese and Orange-Fennel Vinaigrette
Spinach Salad with Blueberries, Red Onion and Almond Grilled Brie, Mission Fig Vinaigrette
Baby Arugula with Candied Walnuts, Manchego Cheese and Mango Vinaigrette
Roasted Chicken over chilled Vermicelli Salad with Mint, Roasted Peanuts, Lime Chili Dressing

Penne Pasta Salad with Spring Vegetables and Goat Cheese Pesto
Breast of Duck with Avocado and Papaya Ginger Vinaigrette
Lobster Medallions, Grilled Shrimp and Crisp Calamari over Red Leaf with Citrus Ginger Dressing
Sliced Sweet Sopressata, Balsamic Onions, White Beans, Roasted Hot Peppers
Marinated Squid and Wilted Cucumbers with Coriander and Three Onions
Sweet Red Peppers and Snap Peas with Fresh Savory and Toasted Almonds
Avocado and Fresh Beets with a Dijon Vinaigrette

Grilled Eggplant Caprese with Fresh Mozzarella, Tomatoes, Basil Leaves and 75 Year Balsamic
Warm Goat Cheese Salad with Prosciutto, Summer Fruits and Toasted Pistachios
Yellow Beets, Fresh Fennel, Watercress and Ricotta with Orange Hazelnut Vinaigrette
Oven Roasted Shrimp with Field Greens, Avocado, and Champagne Vinaigrette
Arugula with Goat Cheese, Pears, Candied Walnuts and Three Citrus Dressing
Crispy Fried Artichoke Hearts with Spicy Lemon Aioli and Field Greens
House Cured Salmon on a Potato Galette with Mixed Greens and Parsley-Shallot Cream
Caramelized Fig, Fresh Ricotta, Basil Leaves, Toasted Almonds and Yellow Heirloom Tomatoes

SALAD

Boston Bibb with Toasted Walnuts, Stilton and a Blueberry Port Dressing
Southern Style Caesar with Crisp Fried Oysters
Cucumber and Beefsteak Tomato, Boursin, Green Onions and Dark Balsamic Drizzle
Cornmeal Crusted Goat Cheese, Pine Nuts, Sun Dried Tomatoes and Ancho Chili Vinaigrette
Crispy Calamari with Garlic Green Beans, Cilantro and a Harissa and White Balsamic Dressing
Asian Spiced Chicken, Jicama, Crisp Wontons, Peanuts and Sweet Chili Vinaigrette

Grilled Chicken, Roasted Anaheim Chilies, Asadero Cheese and Avocado with
Blue Corn Tortilla Strips and a Creamy Cilantro Ranch

Southern Fried Chicken, Cheddar, Caramelized Corn, Grilled Onions and Spicy Buttermilk Dressing
Spinach, Boursin, Candied Walnuts, Grape Tomatoes, Raspberries and Shallot Sherry Vinaigrette
Smoked Mussels and Chèvre Cheese with Lime Ginger Vinaigrette
BLT Salad with Monterey Jack
Blackened Steak, Red Onion, Mushrooms, Tomatoes and Blue Cheese
Lightly sautéed Green Beans with Sweet Butter, Parmigianino and Fresh Cracked Pepper
Red and Yellow Potatoes with Smoked Salmon, Pear Tomatoes and a Warm Vinaigrette
Marinated Fresh Mozzarella with Crispy Fried Peppers

Grilled Shitakes, Spiced Pistachios, Pickled Red Onions and Chèvre with
a Crystallized Ginger Vinaigrette

Breast of Duck Au Poivre with Shaved Fennel
Chilled Black Bass with Lime Vinaigrette in Avocado Shell
Mushrooms, Fresh Fennel and Shaved Parmesan with Port Wine Vinaigrette
Grilled Scallops and Cashews with Lemon Herb Dressing
Mediterranean Shrimp with Meyer Lemon and Olive Oil
Lobster, Watercress, Asparagus, Kiwi and Cherry Tomatoes with a Ginger Apple Dressing
Marinated Asian Vegetables with Grilled Shrimp

Jumbo Lump Crab, Foie Gras and Papaya on Baby Greens
Pacific Rim Caesar Salad with Tempura Shrimp and a Cilantro Wasabi Dressing
Spinach Salad with Bleu Cheese, Grapefruit and Maple-Balsamic Vinaigrette
Honey-Dijon Smoked Chicken, Wonton Crisps, Spicy Peanuts and a Sesame-Garlic Dressing
Roma and Yellow Tomatoes, Avocado, Belgian Endive, Gorgonzola and Basil Oil
Crisp Chicken Tenders with Grilled Pineapple, Bacon, Colby and Honey Mustard Dressing
Gingered Beef, Granny Smith Apples, Roasted Corn, Jicama and Cilantro-Lime Vinaigrette
Caesar Salad Garnished with Oven Dried Tomatoes and Parmesan Eggplant Croutons

Black Pepper Fried Chicken, Pears, Bacon, Pecans and a Buttermilk Cucumber Dressing
Tossed Greens with Warm Mussels, Bacon and Anchovy Dressing
Red Oak and Baby Romaine with Crepe Sautéed Brie
Warm Scallops and Cumin over Baby Greens
Grilled Portobello and Oyster Mushrooms with Italian Parsley
Smoked Breast of Duck with shavings of Parmigianino and Truffle Olive Oil

SALAD

Smoked Mozzarella finished with a Reduced Red Wine Vinaigrette
Fresh Fennel, Sliced Pears and Toasted Hazelnuts in Radicchio Cups
Asian Spiced Beef and Watercress with Caramelized Ginger Vinaigrette
Greek Salad with Grilled Lamb, Feta, Kalamata, Cucumbers and a Mint Yogurt Dressing
Pesto Chicken with Red Potatoes and Tri-color Peppers
Spinach Salad with Tomatoes, Warm Bacon Maple Dressing and Blue Cheese Crostini
Smoked Salmon and Wild Mushrooms and a Creamy Scallion Dressing
Grilled Onions and Red Pepper Marinated Mozzarella over Greens

White Beans, Grilled Breast of Duck and Smoked Gouda with Olive Oil and Thyme
Hearts of Romaine with Blue Cheese, Spiced Pecans and Shaved Red Onion
Broccoli, Black Olives and Roasted Eggplant Hummus
Spinach, Smoked Bacon, Grilled Red Onions, Gruyere Cheese, Fresh Herb Dressing
Wilted Spinach with Pancetta and Pine Nuts
Wilted Greens with Oven Roasted Tomatoes, Grilled Portabellas and Fresh Mozzarella
Seared Duck with Grilled Zucchini, Mushrooms, Tomatoes, Wild
Rice and Spiced Shrimp over Greens with Orange Cumin Vinaigrette

Chilled Lobster, Papaya and Seared Foie Gras over Tossed Greens
Calamari, Mushrooms and Sweet Red Peppers with Warm Vermouth Dressing
Bibb Lettuce, Wild Mushrooms, Hazelnut Vinaigrette
Scallops and Mussels in Mustard Vinaigrette over Fresh Asparagus
Belgian Endive with Macadamias and Goat Cheese
Sliced Beef Tenderloin and Fresh Horseradish over Watercress with Cracked Pepper Dijon

Wild Greens, Roasted Tomatoes, Grilled Porcini and Smoked Mozzarella with
a Warm Bacon Dressing

Shrimp, Crab Meat and Avocado with a Golden Pineapple Salsa Dressing
Green Beans, Red Pepper Strips and Roasted Garlic
Napa Cabbage, Smoked Chicken, Water Chestnuts and Sno-Peas with a Ginger Dressing
Arugula, Sliced Fennel, Rounds of Orange and Balsamic Vinaigrette
Shrimp and Avocado Vinaigrette
Chicken Salad with Grapes, Walnuts and Blue Cheese Chunks
Smoked Turkey with Avocado and a Fresh Tomato and Cilantro Dressing
Fresh Spinach, Bacon, Toasted Sesame Seeds and Yellow Grape Tomatoes
Greek Salad with Feta and Crab Meat

Grilled Shrimp and Spiced Cashews with Lemon Herb Dressing
Oriental Chicken with Crispy Won Tons and Chili Sesame Vinaigrette
Boston Lettuce with Asparagus, Oranges and Red Onion
Lobster Salad with Ginger and Lemongrass
Baby Greens with Fresh Sage Leaves, White Beans and Grilled Duck with an Orange Vinaigrette
Hazelnut Crusted Goat Cheese, Fresh Spinach, Pears and Grapes
Lobster Salad with Poppy Seed Dressing

SALAD

Sautéed Foie Gras over Salad of Apples and Endive with Walnuts and Pomegranate Vinaigrette
Baked Plum Tomatoes on Baby Greens with a Melted Brie Dressing
Hummus, Cured Olives, Roasted Vegetables and Fresh Basil Oil with Grilled Yogurt Bread
Smoked Duck, Peppers and Blue Cheese with Raspberry Vinaigrette
Cold Sesame Noodles with Asparagus, Ginger, Scallions and Orange Zest
Szechuan Marinated Beef with Toasted Sesame Dressing
Crisp Fried Chicken Breast with Ham, Red Peppers, Colby, Bacon and Blue Cheese
Poached Seafood, Green Beans, Tomatoes, Tender Potatoes, Olives, Herb Dressing
Seared Salmon on Beefsteak Tomatoes served with Caramelized Shallot Mayonnaise

Crab Meat and Grapefruit on Endive
Warm Goat Cheese rolled in Pecans, Bacon and Horseradish over Mache
Smoked Duck Breast sliced paper thin with Shavings of Parmigianino, Greens and Truffle Oil
Panache of Greens with toasted Gorgonzola Garlic Croutons
Warm Goat Cheese in Phyllo over Greens with Curry Vinaigrette
Spinach and Persimmon Salad with Ginger Vinaigrette
Roasted Golden Potatoes with Whole Cloves of Roasted Garlic over
Arugula with Creamy Smoked Paprika Dressing

Grilled Fruits over Dandelion Greens with Ginger Dressing
Sliced Tomatoes with Fresh Mozzarella marinated in Pepper Flakes and Basil Olive Oil
Seared Salmon and Cool Cucumber Slices with Chunky Gazpacho Salsa
Spinach with Strawberries and Candied Almonds served with a Balsamic Vinaigrette
Roasted Green Tomatoes with Goat Cheese over Baby Greens
Jumbo Lump Crab with Sweet Red Pepper Strips, Hearts of Palm and Caper Mayonnaise
Pomegranate and Endive Salad with Spiced Pecans
Spinach and Goat Cheese with Fresh Mint

Grilled Pineapple and Fresh Asian Vegetables with Crisp Noodles over Baby Greens
Tex-Mex Tomatoes with Fresh Poblano
Cucumbers with Spiced Cashews and Scallions
Grilled Vegetables and Smoked Mozzarella
Warm Brie and Roasted Peppers with Crispy Fried Leeks
Wilted Spinach with Pancetta and Pine Nuts and Smoked Tomato Vinaigrette
Grilled Onions and Chèvre Cheese
Asparagus, Oranges and Red Onion

Wild Mushroom and Grilled Peach Salad with White Truffle Vinaigrette
Heirloom Tomatoes with Fresh Ricotta and Brandy-Saffron Drizzle
Cajun Salad with Three Olive Tapenade, Tasso Ham and Shredded Colby-Jack
Shaved Watermelon Salad with Port Salut and Aged Balsamic Drizzle
Apple and Pear Salad with Burrata Cheese and Cider Balsamic
Radishes, Spiced Pecans, Pickled Ramps, Herbed Boursin and Shallot Vinaigrette
Roasted Baby Beets with Goat Cheese, Arugula, Walnuts and a Black Plum Vinaigrette

SALAD DRESSINGS, VINAIGRETTES AND COMBINATIONS

You can use many of the vinaigrette combinations as a creamy or heavier base dressings and vice versa. Many of the vinaigrettes may also be heated and served as a warm dressing. A fantastic, carefully chosen house dressing is a great way to set you apart from everyone else. Many times a customer will order the house dressing, whatever it is, just to have something new and different. Often the salad is the first course that your guest will have and it is an opportunity to get the meal off to a great start.

Mission Fig Vinaigrette
Creamy Smoked Paprika
Grilled Mango Vinaigrette
Roasted Poblano Buttermilk
Creamy Orange Hazelnut
Roasted Shallot-Red Wine Vinaigrette
Lemon, Tequila and Chipotle
Toasted Sesame and Miso

Ancho Chili Vinaigrette
Tarragon-Merlot Vinaigrette
Balsamic-Black Peppercorn Vinaigrette
Asian Pear-Vanilla Seed Vinaigrette
Champagne Vinaigrette
Basil-Lemon Vinaigrette
Ancho Caesar
Green Onion, Avocado and Sour Cream

Red Chili and Toasted Peanut
Vanilla Bean Vinaigrette
Orange-Fennel
Chardonnay Vinaigrette
Lime Ginger
Maple-Balsamic Vinaigrette
Caramelized Ginger Vinaigrette
Meyer Lemon and Tarragon Vinaigrette

Dijon Molasses
Roasted Garlic Dressing
Lime, Mint and Cilantro
Sherry Honey
Meyer Lemon and Chili Dressing
Blueberry Port Dressing
Mango Ginger Vinaigrette
White Balsamic Dressing
Creamy Cilantro Ranch
Horseradish Tomato

SALAD DRESSINGS

Cilantro Wasabi Dressing
Warm Creamy Melted Brie
Thai Sweet Chili Vinaigrette
Mint Yogurt Dressing
Golden Pineapple Salsa Dressing
Warm Vermouth Dressing
Smoky Green Chili Ranch
Lemon Ginger Vinaigrette

Pernod Buttermilk
Blueberry Balsamic
Red Wine Dijon Vinaigrette
Toasted Coriander Seed and Citrus
Coconut Sweet Chili Vinaigrette
Ginger-Miso
White Balsamic Vinaigrette
Lemon Pecorino

Dijon Buttermilk
Creamy Lemon Fennel
Cranberry Citrus
Warm Pecan
Fig-Balsamic Vinaigrette
Sherry Honey Dressing
Basil and Bacon Vinaigrette
Crystallized Ginger-Champagne Vinaigrette

Shallot Sherry Vinaigrette
Spicy Roasted Garlic
Tomato Ginger
Tamarind Mint
Cucumber Sesame
Bitter Orange Vinaigrette
Strawberry Balsamic
Spicy Roasted Corn and Molasses

Thai Chili and Cilantro
Lemon Pesto
Spicy Miso
Mango Ginger
Creamy Orange Shallot
Whole Grain Mustard Vinaigrette
Shaved Horseradish and Whole Grain Mustard
Tangy Maple
Spicy Buttermilk Dressing

SALAD DRESSINGS

Honey and Brown Butter Vinaigrette
Scallion, Dill and Buttermilk
Grilled Onion and Blue Cheese
Meyer Lemon Caesar
Bacon Cider
Blackberry Walnut
Roasted Sweet Pepper
Yogurt, Cumin and Mint

Papaya Ginger Vinaigrette
Bacon Lime Ginger
Red Onion, Sherry and Orange
Kalamata Olive and Cilantro
Curry Grapefruit
Feta and Roasted Garlic
Creamy Cilantro
Caramelized Red Onion and Saffron

Toasted Hazelnut and Bacon
Citrus Chili Vinaigrette
Rosemary and Cracked Black Pepper
Orange and Cumin Dressing
Buttermilk and Toasted Walnut
Lemon and Roasted Garlic
Tangerine and Fresh Rosemary Vinaigrette
Cumin and Cracked Pink Peppercorn

Creamy Smoked Tomato
Spicy Peanut and Rice Wine Vinaigrette
Parmesan, Basil and Pine Nut
Lime and Red Onion Vinaigrette
Green Olive and Dijon
Thai Palm Sugar and Mint
Chipotle and Scallion Ranch
Orange Saffron

Lemon, Thyme and Olive Oil
Creamy Smoked Bacon
Walnut Dijon
Roasted Shallot and Citrus
Orange Cumin
Toasted Hazel Nut Vinaigrette
Creamy Lemon Mascarpone

SALAD DRESSINGS

Chili Sesame Vinaigrette
Smoked Almond
Pomegranate Vinaigrette
Lemon Caper
Cool Cucumber Mint
Walnut Mustard
Curry Champagne
Roasted Tomato and Cumin

Spring Onion and Bacon
Georgia Peanut
Caramelized Shallot and Citrus Vinaigrette
Warm Red Onion, Sherry and Lemon
Oven Roasted Tomato with Gorgonzola
Raspberry Vinaigrette
Orange-Cilantro Ranch
Creamy Fennel-Black Pepper

Tangerine and Goat Cheese Vinaigrette
Red Miso Ranch
French Mustard with Herbs
Blackberry Mojito Dressing
Honey Lavender Vinaigrette
Pinot Grigio Vinaigrette
Caramelized Walnut and Orange Vinaigrette
Cherry Port Vinaigrette

Warm Bacon Raspberry Vinaigrette
Lemon Grass and Ancho
Brown Butter
Spicy Orange
Sweet and Sour
Grilled Pear and Gorgonzola
Apple Cider and Caramelized Onion
Green Onion Ranch

Guinness Ale Buttermilk
Smoked Almond
Scallion and Toasted Coconut
Creole Sour Cream Dressing
Ginger Apple Dressing
Creamy Poppy Seed

SANDWICHES

Assorted Sandwiches
Burger and Chicken Combinations
Grilled Cheeses
Hot Dog and Sausage Combinations
Mustard and Ketchup Varieties
Melts and Panini
Sandwich Wraps

Chapter Notes, Ideas and Conversions

Main Ingredient	Element 1	Element 2	Element 3	Sauce	Texture

SANDWICHES

Summer Lobster Roll with Papaya, Thai Basil and Vanilla Chili Sauce
Rare Roasted Beef, Baby Spinach, Red Onion Marmalade, Pickled Cucumber and Chili Aioli
Soft Shell Crab Po-Boy with Grilled Onions and Lime Chipotle Sour Cream
Cider Braised Kielbasa with Charred Onions and Caramelized Apple Jam on Pretzel Roll
Cuban Sliders - Slow Roasted Pork, Smoked Ham, Salami and Colby Cheese
Griddled Pastrami with Pale Ale Braised Onions and Melted Gruyere
Lobster Club with Arugula, Roasted Tomato, Crisp Pancetta and Lemon Verbena Aioli
Ancho BBQ Pulled Pork with Apple Slaw, Crispy Shallots and Blackberry Whole Grain Mustard

Slow Roasted Turkey Club with Brie and Roasted Peppers
Mexican Meatball Sub with Pork and Chorizo Meatballs, Pepper Jack, Lettuce and
Tomatoes, Red Onion, Salsa Verde and Cilantro Mayonnaise

Roasted Leg of Lamb with Kalamata, Arugula, Preserved Lemon, Hummus and
Sun Dried Tomato Aioli

B.G.L.T. - Smoked Bacon, Goat Cheese, Red Leaf Lettuce, Heirloom Tomato on Sourdough Toast
Ancho Marinated Skirt Steak with Grilled Onions and Smoked Tomato Ranch
Turkey with Brie, Tomato, Fresh Spinach and Rosemary Aioli on Ciabatta
Roast Pork with Tomato, Onion and a Poblano Goat Cheese Spread

Pressed Pork Sandwich with Red Onion Marmalade, Arugula and Ancho Mayonnaise
Jerk Chicken and Roasted Banana with Spicy Peanut Sauce on Wood Grilled Peasant Bread
Tomatoes, Grilled Figs, Taleggio Cheese and Baby Greens on Roasted Garlic Focaccia
Meatloaf with Oven Dried Tomato, Watercress and Fontina on a Soft Cuban Roll
Smoked Turkey and Crisp Prosciutto with Cranberry Mascarpone Spread on Toasted Focaccia
Baked Apple and Brie with Watercress and Balsamic Aioli on Rustic Walnut Bread
Pastrami, Bacon, Green Tomato, Butter Lettuce and Sun Dried Tomato Mayonnaise on Marble Rye
Smoked Salmon B.L.T with Artichoke, Tarragon and Boursin Spread

Country Ham, Pickled Red Onion, Heirloom Tomato and Lemon Aioli on Grilled Sourdough
Meatloaf Patty Melt with Caramelized Onions, Thousand Island Dressing and Fontina Cheese
Shrimp Po' Boy with Pickled Red Onion, Arugula and Cajun Rémoulade
Roasted Pork Belly, Caramelized Apples, Grilled Onions, Baby Greens and Sage Aioli on Focaccia
Shrimp Salad Sandwich with Watercress and Crisp Cucumbers
Panko Crusted Soft Shell Crab with Bacon, Tomato and Lemon Mayonnaise
Smoked Oyster Po Boys

Pulled Pork Sliders with Sharp Cheddar and Apple Cider Slaw
Spicy Grilled Ham with Roasted Garlic Spread, Pickled Red Onions and Grilled Green Tomatoes
Chicken Satay - with Chicken, Peanut Butter, Mango Chutney and Dried Apricots in Flatbread
Cobb Sandwich - Chicken, Tomatoes, Bacon and Blue Cheese with a Avocado and Pepper Relish
Marinated Charbroiled Lamb in Pita with Tomato, Baby Spinach with
Cucumber-Cilantro Salsa and Buttermilk Dressing

SANDWICHES

Truffle Croque Monsieur with Ham, Gruyere, and Black Truffles on Toasted Brioche
Cajun Chicken in a Chipotle Chili Wrap with Crispy Fried Onions, Lettuce and Tomato
Grilled Lobster and Bacon with Lemon Rémoulade
Braised Pork with White Cheddar and a Golden Raison Compote on Sourdough
Lemon Pepper Chicken with Marinated Mozzarella, Red Pepper Salad and Roasted Olive Tapenade
Crab "Louis" - Crab, Tomato Confit, Avocado, Hard Boiled Egg, Sweet Chili Sauce Aioli
French Dip with Caramelized Shallots, Gruyere, and Thyme Au Jus
Chili Dusted Chicken with Asadero Cheese and Green Tomatillo Sauce in Rustic Bread

Wasabi Lobster Salad with Avocado Relish
Peppercorn Crusted Smoked Salmon with Salmon Caviar, Red Onions and Chive Sour Cream
Leg of Lamb with Kalamata Tapenade, Arugula and Sun Dried Tomato Aioli on Charred Ciabatta
Grilled Portobello with Spicy Cress, White Bean Hummus and Lemon Olive Oil
Charred Beef Brisket with a Roasted Garlic and Wild Mushroom Tapenade and Pickled Carrots
Lemongrass Pulled Pork with Thai Chilies, Grilled Eggplant and Mint Crema on Toasted Baguette
Smoked Beef Brisket with Caramelized Onion Slaw and Horseradish Cheddar
BBQ Pork with Gouda, Roasted Tomatoes and Grilled Red Onions on Charred Texas Toast

Portabella with Goat Cheese, Fresh Basil Leaves and White Truffle Oil on Brioche
Yellow Fin Tuna Melt with Roasted Tomato and Gruyere
Meatloaf with Bacon, Blue Cheese and Red Onion Marmalade
Warm Pita with Eggplant Hummus, Ricotta Salata, Fresh Basil Leaves and Grilled Artichokes
Goat Cheese on Charred Sourdough with Yellow Beets, Arugula and Walnut Pesto
Olive Oil Poached Salmon with Gaeta Olives on Black Russian Bread with a White Truffle Aioli
Grilled Tandoori Chicken with Avocado, Scallions and a Mandarin-Mint Tzatziki on Naan
Charred Chicken Salad with Lettuce and Tomato and a Honey-Lime Sour Cream

Garlic Roasted Pork with Fried Long Hot Peppers, Sharp Provolone and Apple Slaw
Pan Roasted Sausage with Sun Dried Tomatoes, Arugula and Sharp Provolone on a Herb Baguette
Spicy Grilled Catfish with Bacon and Tomatoes on Toasted Sourdough with a Cajun Rémoulade
Seared Tuna with Seaweed Salad and a Ginger Aioli on Egg Bread
Grilled Shrimp with Butter Lettuce and a Spicy Tomato Relish on a Pretzel Roll
Garlic Roasted Chicken with Baby Romaine, Ricotta Salata and a Apple Sherry Aioli
Meatloaf with Horseradish Cheddar, Crispy Fried Onions and Smoked Tomato Ketchup
Grilled Tex-Mex Spiced Flank Steak, Charred Scallions, Pepper Jack and Chimichurri Aioli

Chili Crusted Chicken, Jack Cheese, Grilled Onion and Cilantro-Lime Mayo
Roasted Eggplant, Charred Red Onion, Sun Dried Tomato Pesto and Sharp Provolone
Fried Oyster "Po Boy" with Crisp Country Ham and Spicy Rémoulade
Chipotle BBQ Beef with Ranch Slaw and Crispy Onions
Dry Rubbed Chicken with Jack Cheese, Guacamole and Jalapeño Tapenade
Mint Pesto Chicken Salad with Goat Cheese, Arugula and Baby Spinach
Oven Roasted Turkey Breast with Agave Cream Cheese and Bibb Lettuce

SANDWICHES

Fried Lobster Roll with Celery Root and Three Apple Slaw
Slow Roasted Five Spice Pork with Spicy Carrot Pickle and Cumin Aioli on Crisp Cuban Roll
Grilled Portobello with Roasted Peppers, Fontina and Mint Pesto
Smoked Turkey BLT on Toasted Cranberry-Walnut Bread with a Maple-Chipotle Mayonnaise
Dry Rubbed Chicken with Jack Cheese, Jalapeño Salsa and Black Bean BBQ on Texas Toast
Grilled Eggplant, Caramelized Onions, Goat Cheese and Caper Tapenade
Brisket and Pickled Onions on Horseradish Rye
Pepper Jack Crab Cake with Smoked Bacon

Pulled Pork Shoulder with Granny Smith Apples and Red Cabbage Slaw on a Pretzel Roll
Grilled Portobello with Goat Cheese, Ripe Tomatoes and Kalamata Tapenade
Duck Breast with Sun Dried Tomato and Onion Confit and Spinach on a Charred Baguette
Smoked Turkey, Grilled Pears, Fontina and a Dried Cherry Jam
Honey Roasted Bacon with Red Onion Jam, Three Pepper Slaw and Crispy Onion Straws
Turkey with Tomato Confit and Fresh Tarragon Aioli

Char Grilled Chicken with a Cherry Tomato and Golden Raisin Relish
Butter Lettuce and Balsamic Syrup

Grilled Hanger Steak with Charred Leeks and Smoked Tomato Aioli
Fried Green Tomato BLT with Cilantro Aioli
Crispy Portobello with Fontina and Horseradish
Burrata Cheese, Roasted Eggplant, Oven Dried Tomato and Fresh Basil
Slow Roasted Pork with Manchego and Romesco
Fresh Ricotta, Portobello, Sun Dried Tomato, Shaved Parmesan and Toasted Almond Pesto
Honey Glazed Flank Steak, Shitake Mushrooms and Grilled Red Onions

Mesquite Smoked Yellow Squash, Zucchini and Portobello with
a Tomato-Roasted Pepper Relish and Cotija Cheese

Grilled Sandwich of Fontina and Seared Black Trumpet Mushrooms
Meatloaf with Smoked Gouda and Spicy Tomato Relish
Seared Salmon, Roasted Tomato, Green Olive Pesto, Shaved Red Onions
Grilled Chicken, Cherry Pepper-Pineapple Salsa and Fresh Tomato
Warm Lobster Club with Citrus Aioli
Crisp Pancetta, Boston Lettuce and Roasted Tomatillo with Fresh Basil Dressing
Cheddar, Smoked Ham, Grilled Pears and Champagne Mustard on Cranberry-Pecan Bread

Grilled Portobello, Smoked Mozzarella, Oven Dried Tomato and Rosemary Aioli
Roasted Mushrooms, Hummus, Baby Spinach and Goat Cheese
Slow Cooked Pork BLT with Crisp Bacon, Lettuce, Tomato and Smoky Mayonnaise
Prosciutto, Goat Cheese and Fig on Grilled Ciabatta
Bresaola and Fresh Spinach with Pecorino and White Balsamic Aioli
Marinated Flank Steak, Arugula, Pickled Onions and Horseradish Cream
Thai Chicken with Shredded Napa Cabbage, Mango, Peanut and Cilantro Pesto and Fresh Chilies

SANDWICHES

The "Breadless" Chicken Club - Boneless Grilled Chicken Breast Layered with
Baby Romaine, Pancetta, Munster and Smoked Paprika Aioli

Wild Boar Sloppy Joe with Crispy Sage, Pickled Onions and Marbled Cheddar
Grilled Salmon, Lemon Pickles, Butter Lettuce and Mint Aioli
Grilled Eggplant, Roasted Tomatoes, Shaved Parmesan and Fresh Basil Leaves on Ciabatta
Sliced Grilled Sirloin Steak with Baby Romaine and Tomato Pesto
Summer Tomatoes, Pickled Onions and Fresh Coriander on Whole Wheat Flatbread
Prosciutto, Fresh Mozzarella, Plum Tomatoes and Kalamata Olives served on Parmesan Focaccia
Grilled Shrimp on Flat Bread with Spicy Coleslaw, Tomato Chutney and Honey Dijon
Cheese Salad Sandwich - Shredded Cheese mixed with Pickle Relish and Hard Boiled Eggs

Spicy Sliced Chicken with Watercress and Fresh Chive Butter on
Curried Chicken Croissant with Cashews and Grapes
Chopped Chickpeas with Roasted Peppers, Kalamata, Flat Leaf Parsley on Country Bread
Seared Tuna, Grilled Fennel, Black Olives and Preserved Lemon Relish on Grilled Pumpernickel
Meatloaf with White Cheddar, Bacon and Smoked Tomato
Slow Roasted Pork, Braised Red Cabbage and Dijon Pepper Relish on Marbled Rye
Tomato Bruschetta with Sun Dried Tomatoes, Pesto, Artichokes, Black Olives and Fresh Mozzarella
Bacon, Roasted Banana and Peanut Butter on Toasted Raison Bread

Crisp Prosciutto, Cantaloupe and Red Leaf Lettuce with a Honey Aioli on Toasted Brioche
Flatbread with Cucumbers, Alfalfa Sprouts, Garbanzos, Roasted Garlic and Lemon Mayonnaise
Smoked Turkey Club with Cranberry Sauce and Cinnamon Aioli
Peanut Butter, Granny Smith Apple and Alfalfa Sprouts
Avocado, Red Onion and Gruyere on Sun Dried Tomato Bread
Rare Roast Beef with a Cream Cheese-Sour Cream Horseradish Spread served with Onion on Rye
Prosciutto, Brie, and Watercress with a Rosemary Fig Confit on Focaccia
Grilled Shrimp, Prosciutto, Smoked Tomato with Fresh Basil

Cajun Crusted Grouper with Roasted Corn and Red Pepper Salsa, Cilantro and Lime
Country Ham, Grilled Pears, Red Leaf Lettuce and Honey Sour Cream on Toasted Sourdough
Mexican Hero - with Smoked Ham, Chorizo, Pepper Jack, Grilled Onions, Peppers and Tomato
Fried Oyster Poor Boy with Chipotle BBQ Sauce and Crunchy Blue Cheese Slaw
Grilled Striped Bass with Caramelized Onions and an Old Bay Tomato Chutney
Goat Cheese, Avocado, Crisp Celery and Watercress with Walnut Pesto in a Multigrain Pita
Roast Bcef, Grilled Red Onions, Three Pepper Slaw and Black Pepper Aioli
Chicken Salad with Toasted Walnuts, Roasted Tomatoes, Pickled Red Onion on Marbled Rye

Spicy Grouper on Grilled Peasant Bread with Baby Spinach, Mango and Spicy Rémoulade
Thai Marinated Chicken Breast, Avocado, Sesame Mayonnaise
Roasted Vegetables and Feta on Crunchy Country Bread
Shrimp Louis - Shrimp and Hard Boiled Eggs with Sweet Chili Sauce and Horseradish Mayonnaise

Grilled Zucchini, Tomatoes, Olives, Yellow Peppers and Red Onion with
Cucumber, Feta and Toasted Almonds served in Grilled Flatbread

SANDWICHES

Cowboy Reuben-Smoked Prime Rib, Dry Jack Cheese, 3-Pepper Slaw and
Ancho Mayo on Texas Toast

Pork Confit with Honey, Goat Cheese, Dark Cherries and Watercress
Jerk Coffee Spiced Chicken with Grilled Pineapple, Avocado and Cilantro Butter
Braised Pork Shoulder, Black Bean Paste, Charred Red Onion and Chipotle Sour Cream
Smoked Pastrami with Horseradish Cheddar and Guinness Mustard on Grilled Pretzel Roll
Wild Mushroom and Goat Cheese on Rosemary Focaccia with Wilted Arugula and Roasted Shallots
Shaved Venison with Cipollini Onion Jam, Smoked Hatch Chilies and Dry Asadero
Fig Glazed Oven Roasted Pork Meatballs with Wilted Escarole and Gorgonzola

Grilled Ahi, Crispy Tabasco Shallots, Sunflower Sprouts, Pickled Ginger and Wasabi Sour Cream
Smoked Turkey, Oven Roasted Tomato and Bleu Cheese Slaw with Toasted Pumpkin Seeds
Slow Cooked Lamb, Thin Sliced Cucumbers, Honey Yogurt and Pickled Onions on Irish Soda Bread
Pulled Beef Short Rib Sliders, Roasted Peppers, Charred Onions, Horseradish Bleu Cheese
Adobo Roasted Pork with Grilled Scallions, Oaxaca Cheese and Chipotle Caramelized Red Onions
Roasted Mushroom Grinder with Asiago, Fried Hots and Oven Dried Tomatoes
Orange Poached Chicken Salad with Caramelized Fennel and Baby Mache on a Grilled Croissant
Chicken and Pear with Port-Salut, Arugula and a Cranberry-Pecan Aioli on Rustic Pumpernickel

Short Rib Cheese Steak with Cherry Pepper Relish, Grilled Balsamic Shallots and Sharp Provolone
Blackened Shrimp "Po Boy" with Smoked Tomato Rémoulade and Three Pepper Slaw
Garlic Roasted Leg of Lamb, Charred Escarole, Caramelized Wild Mushrooms and Gouda
Open Faced Pork Cheese Steak with Smoked Portabellas, Fontina and Fried Eggs on Bruschetta
Korean BBQ Pulled Pork with Napa Slaw and Green Apple Chutney on Grilled King Hawaiian Bun
Chili Roasted Beef with Chopped Cherry Peppers, Sliced Pears and Chimichurri Aioli
Veal and Ricotta Meatball Sliders

Coconut Fried Shrimp Po' Boy with Mango-Papaya Salsa and Spicy Creole Mustard
Peppered Turkey and Bacon with Goat Cheese and Avocado on Grilled Cranberry Bread
V.B.L.T. Crisp Veal Bacon, Grilled Baby Romaine, Heirloom Tomato and Pesto Aioli
Lobster Club with Smoked Bacon and Avocado on Brioche with Saffron Aioli
Smoked Beef Brisket with Fried Green Tomatoes and Creole Mustard on Grilled Cornbread
Cracked Pepper Bacon, Smoked Tomato, Fresh Baby Spinach and Maple Sour Cream
Cider Braised Short Rib with Charred Onions, Pickled Carrots and Sambal Mayonnaise
Spiced Lamb Gyro with Grilled Asparagus, Green Onions, Feta and Lime Tzatziki

P.B.L.T. Braised Pork Belly, Red Leaf Lettuce, Dried Tomatoes and Smoked Garlic Mayonnaise
Country Ham, Grilled Pears, Baby Romaine and White Cheddar and Horseradish Mustard
Open Face Sandwich of Fig Jam, Fresh Mozzarella and Lemon Basil Leaves
Roast Beef with Brie and Thin Sliced English Cucumbers with Purple Horseradish
Braised Short Rib, Blue Cheese and Roasted Garlic on Grilled Brioche
Fried Clam BLT with Smoked Bacon, Grilled Romaine, Tomatoes and Lemon-Chive Aioli
Rosemary Grilled Chicken, Fried Mozzarella, Red Onion and Crisp Iceberg Lettuce on Pretzel Roll
Grilled Bratwurst with Dark Ale-Braised Onions, Red Cabbage Slaw and Whole grain Mustard

SANDWICHES

Grilled Portobello with Gouda, Mint Pesto and Roasted Pepper Coulis
Roasted Chicken with Red Pepper Aioli, Herbed Tomato Relish and Butter Lettuce
Grilled Teriyaki Tuna with Asian Slaw and Spicy Aioli
Slow Cooked Pork, Smoked Provolone, Pickled Pepper Relish
Baked Rosemary Ham with Chèvre and Thin Red Onion Slices
Roasted Sirloin with Béarnaise on a Butter Grilled Croissant Crouton
Open Face Smoked Salmon with Slice Egg, Avocado and Caper-Watercress Cream Cheese
Shrimp Salad on Lemon Pepper Bread
Grilled Sea Bass and Crisp Bacon with Chipotle Mayo, Charred Onions and Ripe Tomato

Carolina Pork BBQ with Spicy Vinaigrette Sauce
Char Grilled Soft Shell Crab
Pastrami Club with Swiss, Spicy Slaw and Russian Dressing
Grilled Shrimp Club
Blackened Catfish with Sweet Pickle Chutney
Smoked Salmon BLT with Bourbon Aioli on Peasant Rye Toast
Meat Loaf Club with Munster Cheese
Grilled Pork Chop with White Bean Ragout and Smoked Paprika Oil

Country Pate' with Peppered Roast Beef on Peasant Bread
Low Fat Club - Grilled Chicken, Canadian Bacon, Lettuce and Tomato, No-fat Dujonaise
Ham, Port-Salut, 1000 Island Dressing
Fried Oyster Club with Country Ham, Red Onion Jam, Lettuce and Tomato on Old Bay Biscuit
Hot Open Face Turkey and Ham on Cornbread with Gravy
Proscuittine, Genoa, Mozzarella, Grilled Mushrooms on an Italian Roll with Olive Oil
Turkey, Crisp Fried Onions, Green Peppers and Swiss on a Hard Roll
Grilled Grouper and Smoked Cheddar on Marble Rye with Honey Mustard

Fresh Salmon with Paper Thin Cucumbers served with a Caper and Onion Relish
Crab Club with Bacon, Avocado, Tomato, Sliced Egg and Key Lime Aioli
Spiral Sliced Ham with Pineapple, Fresh Spinach and Bacon
Seared Salmon BLT with Honey Mustard on Grilled Focaccia
Open face NY Strip with Provolone Cheese, Mushrooms, Crisp Fried Onions
Bison Short Rib Sliders with Root Beer Glaze
Sliced London Broil with Roasted Shallots and Horseradish Mayonnaise
Grilled Shrimp Club served with Spicy Lime Relish

Blackened Catfish with Sweet Pickle Chutney on Marbled Rye
Smoked Trout with Capers and Horseradish on Black Bread
Pepper Crusted Roast Pork with Queso Fresco
Avocado, Ham and Alfalfa Sprouts with Herb Yogurt on Whole Wheat
Open Face Pork Barbecue with Cheddar Cheese on Crusty French Bread
Corned Beef and Pastrami Club with Swiss and Slaw, Russian Dressing
Eastern Shore Hero - Smoked Chicken, Fried Oysters, Cocktail Sauce, Lettuce, Tomato and Onion

SANDWICHES

Roast Pork, Smoked Eggplant and Fontina
Grilled Turkey, Cheddar and Sliced Apple on Pumpernickel
Open Face Brie, Sautéed Shallots and Mushrooms on a Toasted English Muffin
Grilled Salmon, Tomato and Cucumber Slices with Dill Mayonnaise on a Rosemary Roll
Olive Tapenade, Onions, Bacon and Fontina on Toasted Focaccia
Grilled Tuna served on Sesame Brioche
Twice Cooked Pork and Chinese Cabbage with Spicy Hoisin Sauce
Open Face Chicken Breast, Asparagus and Hollandaise on Rye

BLT with Pesto Mayonnaise
Grilled Salmon Salad with Fresh Mint and Tomatoes
Cajun Roast Beef, Marble Cheddar, Chipotle BBQ Sauce, Spicy Apple Slaw
Feta, Cucumber and Gaeta Olive Tapenade in Crusty Pocket Bread
Pan Fried Trout with Bacon and Sage on a Poppy Seed Roll
Broiled Red Snapper on Toasted Sourdough with Sweet Pickle Salsa
Horseradish Crusted Grouper with Wilted Endive and Dill Mayonnaise
Slow Cooked Beef with Sliced Avocado and Tomatillo Salsa

Smoked Salmon, Bacon and Red Onion on a Grilled Croissant with Chive Sour Cream
Fresh Tomato with Hummus and Lemon Olive Oil on Sesame Flatbread
Dry Spice Rubbed Sirloin Strips with Maple Glazed Onions on Garlic Toast
Smoked Sausage with Brazed Red Cabbage and Apples on a Hard Roll
Breast of Chicken with Grilled Orange Slices on Onion Focaccia
Seared Fresh Tuna on Dill Biscuits
Cajun Chicken Breast, Grilled Wild Mushrooms and Sweet Red Peppers
Lobster Salad on Grilled Brioche with Sliced Cucumbers and Fresh Cracked Pepper
Crispy Pork Belly with Smoked Tomato Jam, Grilled Apple and Calvados Molasses Aioli

Cod "Po Boy" with Sriracha Rémoulade, Spicy Slaw and Grilled Scallions
Slow Cooked Pork Shoulder with Smoked Provolone, Onion Slaw and Chipotle BBQ Sauce
Freshwater Char with Boston Lettuce, Summer Tomatoes and a Brown Butter Aioli
Duck Reuben with Red Cabbage Slaw and Cranberry Cheddar on Marble Rye
Curried Chicken Salad with Raisins, Walnuts and Papaya Slices
Roasted Vegetables with Lemon Pesto and Goat Cheese
Caribbean Pork Diablo with Scotch Bonnet Orange Compote on Grill Charred Sourdough
Roast Chicken with Gruyere and an Apple and Fresh Tarragon Slaw

Smoked Ham, Avocado and Sweet Butter on Crisp Baguette
Curried Egg Salad with Dried Currants, Toasted Almonds and Arugula served on a Croissant
Seared Tuna and Napa Slaw with a Sweet Pecan Rémoulade
Chicken Salad with Walnuts, Roasted Tomatoes and Pickled Red Onions
Grilled Chicken, Crisp Bacon, Smoked Tomato and Brown Sugar Dijon
Nicoise - Salmon Salad with Red Potatoes, Baby Green Beans and Capers is stuffed into a Baguette

BURGER AND CHICKEN SANDWICH COMBINATIONS

The number one tip to improve the flavor of burgers and hot sandwiches is to butter grill the bun or bread. Many of these combinations will work well as a topping for either a burger or a grilled chicken breast.

Cooper Sharp Cheddar and Amber Ale Glazed Onions on Grilled Yeast Bread
Green Fried Tomato Slices and Crisp Bacon
Aged Gruyere, Shaved Black Truffles and Seared Foie Gras
Korean with Spicy Pepper Dusting, Korean BBQ Sauce and Kimchee Slaw
Red, White and Blue Burger of Roasted Red Peppers, Vadalia Onions and Blue Cheese
Buffalo Burger with Espresso Ketchup and Red Pepper Slaw
Sautéed Cucumbers, Kalamata Olive Tapenade and Feta Cheese
Bel Paese, Tomato Marmalade and Roasted Garlic Aioli

Far East with Sunflower Sprouts, Sriracha and Kimchee on a Black Sesame Bun
Au Poivre Crusted with Cracked Peppercorns and Finished with a Creamy Mushroom Aioli
Greek Lamb Burger with Kalamata, Lettuce, Cucumbers, Feta and Hummus
Gruyere with Balsamic Red Onions
Roasted Chilies with Mole Aioli
Pressed Cuban Burgers with Salami, Dill Pickles, Shaved Pork and a Mustard-Mayo Spread
Sweet Saffron Onions and Crisp Mushrooms
Zesty Lemon Mayonnaise
Stuffed Prosciutto Burgers with Fresh Mozzarella, Roma Tomato and Sun Dried Tomato Pesto

Tomato Marmalade and Shaved Black Truffle on Grilled Brioche Bun
Caramelized Onion and Jalapeno Relish with Red Pepper Mayonnaise
Grilled California Avocado B.L.T Burgers with Sour Cream
Feta and Sun-Dried Tomato Stuffed Burgers
Smoked Turkey Burgers with Maple-Dijon Sauce
Grilled Portobello with Red Onion Jam
Mango Ketchup and Red Cabbage Slaw

Horseradish with Havarti
Balsamic Caramelized Onions, Arugula and Goat Cheese
Chinese Five Spice Rub and Crunchy Asian Coleslaw
Roasted Corn Relish, Monterey Jack Cheese and Pico De Gallo
Black Bean Burger with Chopped Tomato, Thin Sliced Cucumber and Red Onion with Tzatziki
Vegetarian Lentil Burger with Mango Chutney and Chili Aioli
Spicy Tuna Burger with Pickled Ginger and Wasabi Tossed Scallions on a Sesame Seed Bun
Alaska Wild Salmon Burger with Watercress, Golden Raisin Caponata and Syrah Butter

Masala Burgers with Tangy Tamarind Sauce and Red Onion-Mint Relish
Sliders served on King's Sweet Hawaiian Buns with Blue Cheese Aioli and Arugula
Manchego Cheese, Sofrito and a Sun Dried Tomato-Roasted Garlic Aioli
Boursin and a Red Onion and Orange Confit

BURGER AND CHICKEN SANDWICH COMBINATIONS

Thick Smoked Bacon and Mango Habanero Salsa
Sliced Grilled Lobster with Saffron Mayonnaise
Crispy Chinese Noodles, Red Chili Paste and Ginger Pineapple Compote
Pecan Crusted with Mushrooms and Bleu Cheese
Sun Dried Tomatoes and Balsamic Glazed Onions
Green Olive Tapenade, Sliced Red Onion and Arugula
Southwestern with Queso Fresco and a Tomato and Caramelized Corn Salsa
Cracked Pepper-Crusted with Sweet Saffron Onions and Sliced Avocado

Grilled Portobello, Red Onion Jam and Smoked Mozzarella
Jerk Burgers with Papaya Salsa
Honey-Chipotle Glaze with a Mint-Avocado Salsa
Pork and Chorizo Burgers with Green Chili Mayonnaise
Oven Roasted Oyster Mushrooms, Red Pepper Puree and Fontina
Spicy Andouille, Grilled Sweet Onions and Creole Rémoulade Sauce
Lamb Burger with Goat Cheese and Mint Tzatziki
Roasted Green Chili and Cilantro Ranch Slaw

Fontina with Tomato and Truffle Confit
Chorizo, Caramelized Red Onions, Grilled Anaheim Chilies and a Chimichurri Aioli
Three Peppercorn Crusted Burger
Jerk Seasoned with Smoked Tomatillo Salsa and Spicy Lemon Aioli
Italian Sausage, Roasted Peppers, Grilled Red Onion and Sharpe Provolone
Turkey Burgers with Grilled Pears and Maple-Dijon Sauce
Coconut Basil Chicken Burgers with Fresh Mint and Thai Peanut Pesto
Caramelized Onion, Jalapeno Relish and Red Pepper Mayonnaise

Spicy Cajun Relish with Pepper Jack Cheese
Fresh Mozzarella, Roma Tomatoes and Fresh Basil Leaves
Cajun Seared with Poblano Peppers and Fresh Tomato Chutney
Buffalo Hot Sauce and Blue Cheese
White Cheddar, Arugula and a Caramelized Onion and Apple Compote
Avocado, Bacon and Caramelized Chipotle Onions
Pepperoni, Mozzarella and Pizza Sauce
Grilled Vegetables and Pumpkin Seed Pesto

Brie, Mushrooms and Crispy Onions
Sun Dried Tomatoes, Bel Paese with a Balsamic Reduction on Focaccia Toast
Pepper Jack Cheese, Caramelized Onions and Herbed Aioli
Grilled Pineapple, Teriyaki Glaze, Canadian Bacon, Fresh Spinach
Chipotle-Orange Glaze with Cashew Pesto Mayonnaise
Roasted Garlic, Grilled Red Onion and Port-Salut
Smoked Salmon and Dill Sour Cream

BURGER AND CHICKEN SANDWICH COMBINATIONS

Goat Cheese, Roasted Peppers
Caramelized Apple and Onion Chutney with Port Salut
Wild Mushroom Pesto, Smoked Tomato Slices and Fontina
Caramelized Pears, Gorgonzola and Hazelnut Mayo
Caesar – Romaine, Shaved Parmigianino and Caesar Dressing
Balsamic Reduction, Tomato Cream Cheese and Roasted Mushrooms
Sautéed Cucumbers, Feta Cheese and Tzatziki Sauce
Fresh Basil Leaves, Oven Dried Tomatoes and Smoked Mozzarella

Jamaican Jerk Seasoning with Orange Chipotle Mayonnaise
Crunchy Onion Topping and Herbed Boursin Cheese
Black Jack - Blackened, Jack Cheese, Creole Mustard and Frizzled Onions
Cajun Dusted with Black Bean Spread, Oaxaca Cheese and Grilled Poblano
Ahi Tuna Burger with Preserved Lemon, Fresh Thai Basil and Harissa Aioli
Turkey Burger with Grilled Sage Stuffing Cake, Sautéed Spinach and Cranberry Relish
Portobello, Sun Dried Tomato Pesto, Fresh Buffalo Mozzarella and Basil Leaves
Beef and Mushroom Burger with Fried Mozzarella Slice and Smoked Tomato Ragout

Caribbean Spiced with Sliced Mango, Sweet Onion and Chipotle Honey Mustard
Bacon, Fried Egg and Cheddar on Grilled English Muffin
Double Burger of Beef and Chorizo Patties, Manchego Cheese and Charred Serrano Relish
Mediterranean with Feta, Olive Oil and Oregano Tomatoes, Red Onions and Kalamarta Olives
Grilled Onions, Bourbon Black Beans and Horseradish Cheddar
Garlic Butter Burger topped with Roasted Garlic and Herb Butter
Havarti Cheese, Sliced Fresh Tomato and Tarragon Rémoulade
Grilled Lamb Burgers with Minted Cucumbers and Tomato Marmalade

Coleslaw, Onion Rings and Horseradish Cheddar
Hombre with Smoked Poblano Pepper, Avocado, Enchilado Cheese and Red Pepper Aioli
Gorgonzola, Cremini Mushroom and Crispy Shallots
Baby Spinach, Roasted Beets and Horseradish Aioli
Burgers with Guinness Caramelized Onion Fondue for Dipping
Cambazola Cheese, Brown Sugar Cured Bacon, Arugula and Roasted Garlic Aioli
Bison Burger with Mango Relish, Brie and Baby Spinach
Bel Paese, Smoked Ham and Apple-Rosemary Compote

Seared Salmon Burger with Spicy Cucumber Slices and Pea Sprouts
Pancetta and Caramelized Onion Fondue
Sunshine Burger topped with Fried Egg, Bacon, Crispy Hash Browns and White Cheddar
Smoked Portabellas, Crispy Chives and a Root Beer Finishing Sauce
Bratwurst Burger with Red Cabbage Kraut, Grilled Onions and Spicy Mustard on a Pretzel Bun
Shredded Short Rib, Colby-Jack and Chipotle Ranch Dressing
Caramelized Pineapple Slices and Jerk Seasoning

GRILLED CHEESE

Munster, Country Sausage and Green Tomato
Spicy Buffalo Chicken, Pepper Jack and Blue Cheese
Crab and Bel Paese
Italian Long Hots with Sharp Provolone
Wild Mushroom and Edam with White Truffle Aioli
Brie au Poivre and Roasted Garlic
Smoked Gouda and Goat Cheese on Brioche with Avocado and Sun Dried Tomatoes
Gruyere and Caramelized Onion on Rye
Butterkase with Heirloom Tomato and Caraway
Grilled Cheese with Oven Dried Tomatoes and Parmesan Crust
Braised Short Rib and Bel Paese
Buffalo Mozzarella and Yellow Tomato on Focaccia
Caramelized Pork Belly with Boursin, Chanterelles and Honey Crisp Apple
Pancetta and Fresh Spinach with Asiago
Queso Fresco with Roasted Red Jalapenos

French Onion Grilled Cheese with Beef Braised Caramelized Onions
Caprese Grilled Cheese with Smoked Mozzarella, Roma Tomatoes and Purple Basil
Roasted Butternut Squash, Manchego and Balsamic Grilled Onions
Port-Salut with Red Onion Jam
Scallion Cream Cheese and Hot Pepper Marmalade
Goat Cheese and Kalamarta Tapenade
Irish Cheddar, Bread and Butter Pickles and Chopped Chives on Pumpernickel
Munster and Dried Apricots
Oaxaca Cheese, Charred Poblano and Crushed Tortilla Chips
Boursault with Grilled Shrimp
Mango, Havarti and Watercress
Camembert with Grilled Apples
Brie with Dates and Currants on Banana Bread
Pan Roasted Brussels Sprouts with Country Ham and Smoked Gouda
Sopressata and Sharp Provolone

Tillamook Cheddar and Bourbon Baked Bean Hash
American Cheese, Grilled Hot Dog and Crushed Potato Chips on Pretzel Bread
Smoked Ham, Swiss and 1000 Island Dressing
Cheddar, Feta, Gorgonzola and Caramelized Onion
Scallion Cream Cheese and Dried Beef on Sourdough
Mac and Cheese and Applewood Smoked Bacon Grilled Cheese
Havarti with Grape Jelly
Chèvre and Watercress
Smoked Cheddar with Roasted Pears
Mascarpone and Burnt Sugar
Gorgonzola and Charred Romaine
Grilled Pineapple and Pepper Jack
Three Cheese Grilled Cheese with Lobster
Chèvre with Maple Toasted Almonds

HOT DOG AND SAUSAGE SANDWICHES

Hombre - Chipotle Spiced Refried Black Beans, Three Pepper Slaw and Pepper Jack Cheese Sauce
Carolina - Pulled Pork, Cole Slaw and Carolina BBQ Sauce
Au Poivre - Cracked Black Pepper and Jack Daniels Brown BBQ Sauce
Boston Boy - Baked Beans, Smoked Onions, Gouda and Mustard on Boston Brown Bread Roll
Crazy Mixed Up Dog - Stuffed with Cheese, Wrapped in Salami with Fried Onions and Bacon
Cobb - Bacon, Lettuce, Tomato, Blue Cheese, Avocado, Hard Boiled Egg and Ranch Dressing
Chihuahua - Stuffed with Cotija Cheese and Wrapped in Jalapeno Bacon topped with Pico de Gallo

Tex-Mex - Chipotle Peppers, Pickled Onion, Mole Sauce, Guacamole and Sour Cream
Korean - Spicy Pepper Dusting, Korean BBQ Sauce and Kimchee Slaw
Curryosity - Thick Curry Sauce, Diced Onions and Golden Raisins
Bruschetta - Chopped Tomatoes, Fresh Basil, Fresh Mozzarella
Nacho - Monterey Jack Cheese Sauce, Diced Jalapenos, Black Olives and Crushed Tortilla Chips
Chicago - On Poppy Seed Bun with Sliced Cucumber, Lime Green Relish, Chopped Onion, Sliced Tomato, Dill Pickle Spear, Sport Pepper, Mustard and Celery Salt

Garden - Thin Sliced Cucumbers, Diced Peppers and Shaved Carrots in a Sweet Onion Marinade
Grilled Vegetable - Zucchini, Peppers, Red Onion and Mushroom
The Salsa - Fresh Jalapeno, Chopped Tomatoes, Red Onion and Cilantro with Lime Sour Cream
The Burb -Hot Pepper Jelly, Chopped Scallions and Cream Cheese Spread
Carnitas - Diced Crisp Pork, Grilled Peppers and Onions with Manchego Cheese
Enhanced Chili Dog - Chili topped with a mixture of Diced Poblano, Shredded Cheddar and Crushed Tortilla Chips with a Shake of Ancho Chili Powder

The Philly Joe - Yellow Mustard on a Soft Pretzel Roll
Blue Boy - Blue Cheese, Diced Lettuce and Tomato with Chopped Nuts
Rio Grande - Black Beans, Salsa Verde, Chili Sour Cream
Pilgrim -Turkey Dog with Turkey Stuffing, Dried Cranberries and Apple Cider Mustard
Casablanca - Smoked Paprika Onions, Harissa, Diced Dried Fruit
Greek Isle - Ground Lamb, Feta, Diced Cucumbers and Tzatziki
Bird Dog - Smoked Turkey, Sweet Pepper Relish and Colby Cheese

Three Dog Night - 3 Hot Dogs on Pretzel Roll with Beans, Amber Ale Onions and America Cheese
Waldorf - Dried Cranberries, Thin Sliced Apples, Walnuts and Cider Sour Cream on Challah Roll
Mediterranean - Crumbled Goat Cheese and Sun Dried Tomato Pesto
Buffalo Dog - Buffalo Hot Sauce, Blue Cheese and Diced Celery
Baltimore - Topped with Crab Imperial and Old Bay
The B.L.T. - Wrapped in Bacon with Lettuce, Tomato and Mayonnaise on Toasted Roll
Breakfast Boy - Bacon Wrapped with Hash Browns and Fried Egg
The Dog Corlieone - Italian Sausage, Fennel Onions, Sun Dried Tomato Pesto, Mozzarella
Twisted Citrus - Wrapped in Lemon Pepper Bacon and Topped with Three Citrus Compote
Colonel Cajun - Andouille, Cajun Onions and Shaved Dry Jack Cheese
The Cadillac - White Cheddar, A1 Sauce and Crispy Onion Strings

HOT DOG AND SAUSAGE SANDWICHES

Jersey Sun Rise - Taylor Pork Roll, Fried Egg and American Cheese
Aloha Wake Up - Dusted with Kona Coffee and topped with Diced Crisp Pork and Pineapple Salsa
Country Cousin - Spiced Beans, Diced Smoked Ham, Corn Relish
Dog Von Claaus - Sauerkraut, Munster, Whole Grain Mustard on Pumpernickel Roll
Only Baloney - Wrapped in Lebanon Bologna with Guinness Ale Onions on a Grilled Rye Roll
My Thai - Red Thai Chili Sauce, Chopped Roasted Peanuts, Cilantro and Fresh Mint
Do the Jerk - Caribbean Jerk Sauce, Pineapple-Mango Salsa
The Ballpark - Glazed with Spicy Root Beer and topped with Bacon and Chopped Peanuts
Mac Attack - Topped with Mac and Cheese, Bacon and Red Onions
Havva Hawaiian - Teriyaki Glaze, Grilled Pineapple and Scallion Salsa on a Kings Hawaiian Roll
Tiger Ranch - Chopped French Dip Beef, Smoked Cheddar and Tiger Sauce

MUSTARD AND KETCHUP VARIATIES

A great way to add a little bit of uniqueness is to have a house flavor of mustard or ketchup that customers might associate with your establishment. Even just one well chosen flavored mustard or ketchup can be memorable. If you want to have a few selections available try to keep it to a manageable number. Say four different types of ketchup with your great French Fries. Or an offering of three to five different mustards with a jumbo hot dog. Remember that the mustard selections could be used for other items like huge soft pretzels or as a dip for chicken tenders or like items. Not only are flavored ketchups a great way to make a basic burger better but they can be used as a sauce for cheese steaks or as a steak sauce for your New York strip steak. You will have to manage the assortments of mustards and ketchups so take that into consideration. Proper rotation and condiment handling routines are essential when dealing with multiple selections. An easy way to achieve the flavor profile is to incorporate any flavored oil such as basil oil, cilantro oil or curry oil. Whisk it in and it's ready to go. Some other ideas;

Champagne	Pommery	Red Jalapeno	Habanero Honey	Molasses
Maple	Cranberry	Green Peppercorn	Black Currant	Basil
Hot Paprika	Burgundy	Tarragon	Harissa	Smokey
Horseradish	Caper with Dill	Jack Daniels	Black Peppercorn	Chili
Roasted Garlic	Stone Ground	Dark Rum	Texas Pete	Creole
Orange	Orange Honey	Lemon	Chipotle	Wasabi
Chipotle Lime	Guinness	Tequila Lime	Walnut	Sesame
Balsamic	Sweet Onion	Caramelized Onion	Gingerbread	Old Bay
Smoky Onion	Raspberry Honey	Maple	Black Truffle	Raspberry
Horseradish	Cognac	Irish Whiskey	Hot Pepper Relish	Curry
Cherry Pepper	Black Grape	Orange Ginger	Ginger Chutney	Pinot Noir
Caramelized Ginger	Smokey Mesquite	Roasted Tomato	Smoked Tomato	Mango
Smoked Paprika	Chocolate	Mole	Rosewater	Vodka
Pepper Vodka	Sweet and Sour	Red Curry	Green Curry	Triple Sec
Peanut Butter	Maple Peppercorn	Tangerine	Pomegranate	Dijon
Wild Berry	Cilantro Jalapeno	Blue Cheese	Gorgonzola	Peach
Preserved Lemon	Sweet Paprika	Dark Cherry	Port	Cider

MELTS AND PANINI

Look for additional ideas in the *Sandwich* category that will also make great melts or panini. Another option is to make a pressed sandwich in the style of a Cuban sandwich. This involves using an airy roll and pressing the sandwich with a heated press. This differs from a Panini because this type of press does not provide the toasted line in the bread associated with the panini. If you do not have a press you can use a foil wrapped brick that has been heated on the grill or in the oven as a substitute.

Italian Beef with Braised Escarole, Grilled Onions and Sharp Provolone
Sliced Leg of Lamb, Feta Cheese, Kalamata Tapenade and Mint Pistou
Grilled Portobello, Roasted Eggplant, Fresh Basil Leaves and Bel Paese
Lamb Burger Melt with Hummus, Gjetost Cheese and Niçoise Olives
Island Pulled Pork, Queso Fresco, Grilled Pineapple and Habanero Mayo
Grilled Fresh Tuna, Chèvre Cheese, Marinated Artichoke Hearts and Black Olive Pesto
Chicken Salad with Sweet Onions, Arugula and Asiago
Roast Sirloin, Sun Dried Tomato Pesto, Grilled Portobello and Fontina

Grilled Vegetables with Burrata, Fried Eggplant and Sundried Tomato Pesto
Roasted Chicken, Granny Smith Apples, Caramelized Red Onions and Boursin
Country Ham with Charred Baby Romaine Leaves, Port-Salut and a Wholegrain Mustard Aioli
Guinness Braised Short Rib, Smoked Gouda, Three Pepper Slaw
Italian Roast Pork with Fig Compote, Gorgonzola and Roasted Red Peppers
Wild Mushroom, Brie, Spinach and Mint Pesto
Asian Glazed Tuna with Kimchee Slaw on Toasted Sesame Bread
Smoked Turkey, Oven Dried Tomatoes, Fontina and Basil Pistou

Buffalo Spicy Chicken, Gorgonzola, Red Onions, Green Tomatoes
Mortadella, Roasted Peppers, Fontina
Grilled Chicken, Fresh Mozzarella, Oven Roasted Tomatoes, Fresh Basil Leaves
Charred Beef Tenderloin, Roasted Mushrooms, Baby Spinach, Herb Boursin, Red Onion Jam
Hot Cappicola, Gruyere, Red Onion Jam
Jalapeno Chicken Melt with Grilled Chicken, Smoked Onions, Jack Cheese and Pasilla Chili Mayo
Italian Sausage, Fontina, Grilled Vegetables, Baby Spinach
Marinated Shrimp, Edam, Pickled Peppers and Lemon-Garlic Aioli

Bresaola, Mozzarella and Sundried Tomato Gremolata
Sopressata, Burrata Cheese, Three Olive Tapenade
Whole Roasted Garlic Cloves, Oven Dried Tomatoes, Fontina, Chili Flakes and Fresh Basil
Roast Beef, Port Wine Cheddar, Sautéed Onion and Grilled Romaine
Wild Mushroom, Gorgonzola, Arugula and Sun Dried Tomato Pesto
Grilled Tuna, Sliced Avocado, Wakame, Wasabi Aioli
Roasted Seasonal Vegetables, Goat Cheese and Hummus on Kalamata Olive Bread
Grilled Portabella, Fresh Basil, Roasted Red Peppers, Bel Paese

MELTS AND PANINI

Honey Ham, Sliced Apple, Havarti, Champagne Mustard
Smoked Turkey, Olive Tapenade, Baby Spinach and Feta
Roast Sirloin of Beef, Caramelized Onions, Fresh Basil Leaves, Horseradish Cheddar
Spicy Turkey, Brie, Avocados, Tomatoes
Prosciutto, Roasted Pears, Arugula, Fontina
Pastrami and Gruyere with Caramelized Shallots and Horseradish Crème Fraîche
Prosciutto, Fig, Bel Paese and Grilled Radicchio
Skirt Steak, Charred Onions, Grilled Red Peppers and Extra Sharp Cheddar
Tavern Ham, Spiced Pork, Dill Pickles, Green Onions, Munster and Brown Mustard
Sweet Sopressata, Hot Peppers, Oven Dried Tomato and Smoked Provolone

Goat Cheese, Grilled Vegetables and Black Olive Pesto
Mozzarella, Peperonata and Roasted Pork
Croissant Crab Melt
Artichoke, Grilled Fennel and Fontina
Bresaola, Asparagus, Sliced Tomato and Fresh Mozzarella
Sliced Apple, Caramelized Onion, Taleggio and Walnuts
Grilled Eggplant, Sweet Onion, Roasted Red Peppers and Goat Cheese
Peppered Roast Beef, Wild Mushrooms, Fresh Spinach and Pesto

Grilled Zucchini, Onions and Red Peppers with Fontina and a Romesco Aioli
Black Forest Ham with Cooper Sharp Cheddar, Thin Sliced Red Onion and Cardamom Mustard
Soft Shell Crab, Crisp Romaine and Old Bay Seasoned Grilled Tomatoes on Pressed Sour Dough
Virginia Ham with Muenster, Smoked Tomato and Bacon-Braised Mustard Greens
Proscuittine, Sharp Provolone, Arugula and Grilled Scallions
Sopressata, Fresh Mozzarella and Roasted Peppers with Balsamic Reduction
Smoked Chicken, Edam and Caramelized Shallots
Chicken, Oven-Roasted Tomato, Asiago and Baby Spinach

Grilled Pear, Smoked Ham, Queso Fresco
Three Peppercorn Turkey, Havarti, Sliced Mango and Sun Dried Tomato Relish
Fresh Mozzarella, Grilled Eggplant, Oven Dried Tomatoes and Liguria Tapenade
Fried Eggplant, Artichoke Hearts, Gorgonzola, Roasted Peppers, Balsamic Dressing
Grilled Shrimp, Fresh Baby Spinach and Horseradish Tartar Sauce
Seasoned Grouper, White Cheddar and Crisp Apple Slaw
Walnut Pesto, Fresh Mozzarella, Marinated Onions and Oven Dried Tomatoes
Dry Rubbed Chicken, Queso Asadero, Grilled Tomatillo and Cilantro Pesto

Country Ham, White Cheddar, Grilled Granny Smith Apple and Honey Dijon
Italian Sausage, Roasted Peppers, Grilled Red Onion and Sharpe Provolone
Buffalo Spicy Chicken and Gorgonzola
Tavern Ham, Roast Pork, Caramelized Onions, Muenster, Mustard and Dill Pickle Slices
Grilled Chicken, Fresh Mozzarella, Pesto and Sun Dried Tomato Aioli
Basil Roasted Chicken, Three Olive Tapenade, Baby Spinach and Sharp Provolone

SANDWICH WRAPS

I think the secret to a great wrap is that there is a really flavorful filling. Something that not only adds an unexpected layer of flavor but an additional element of texture. It could be a great chopped olive salad, rice filling or simply lettuce and tomato if they are mixed with a good olive oil and a great seasoning. Cut the filling small and wrap it around something that will help keep it from leaking out like sliced salami or sliced cheese. Varieties of flavored wraps are available or you can use the old standbys; flour tortillas, flatbreads or pitas. Heat the wraps lightly to make them pliable, but be careful that they don't dry out and become brittle.

Blackened Shrimp with Grilled Asparagus, Alfalfa Sprouts and Fresh Pineapple Salsa
Hard Salami, Black and Green Olive Salad, Ripe Tomatoes, Toasted Pine Nut Butter
Roasted Pork, Mexican Cornbread Stuffing, Chopped Green Chilies, Chipotle Sauce, Jack Cheese
Sliced Spiced Beef, Fresh Bean Sprouts, Szechuan Sauce, Vegetable Fried Rice
Seared Ahi Tuna, Cool Cucumber, Pickled Ginger, Crisp Bok Choy, Wasabi Mayonnaise
Roast Turkey, Sausage Dressing, Dried Cranberries, Maple Mayonnaise
Grilled Chicken Club with Bacon, Heirloom Tomatoes Avocado and Caramelized Red Onion
Smoked Shrimp, Spicy Asian Slaw, Sweet Chili Paste, Water Chestnuts
Steak Wrap with Frizzled Onions, Wild Mushrooms and Honey-Horseradish Aioli
Smoked Salmon, Scallion Cream Cheese, Diced Tomato, Watercress
Cappicola, Arugula, Oven Dried Tomatoes, Fontinella Cheese
Fresh Grilled Tuna, Tender Romaine Leaves, Red Onion Compote, Curry Mayonnaise
Sliced Pork, Roasted Peppers, Sharp Provolone
Spiced Skirt Steak, Sliced Avocado, Grilled Peppers, Chipotle Sour Cream
Seared Tuna, Hoisin Sauce, Napa Cabbage, Crisp Red Peppers
Spicy Chicken, Roasted Corn and Black Bean Relish, Shredded Jack Cheese, Crisp Greens
Grilled Salmon, Fresh Spinach, Toasted Pine Nuts, Mint Pesto
Asian Beef, Broccoli Slaw, Oyster Sauce
Andouille, Cajun Rice, Caramelized Onion, Tequila Lime Salsa

Try these Wraps for Breakfast

Thin Sliced Canadian Bacon, Scrambled Eggs, Chopped Scallions
Cinnamon Apples, Crumbled Sausage and Blue Cheese
Scrambled Egg, Sweet Peppers, Fried Potatoes and Smoked Gouda
Ranchero - Eggs, Salsa, Chorizo, Shredded Cheese, Sour Cream, Re-fried Beans, Jalapenos
Scrambled Egg, Chicken Sausage, Spinach, Spicy Salsa and Dried Jack Cheese
Corned Beef Hash, Horseradish Scrambled Eggs
Grilled Steak, Caramelized Onion, Wild Mushrooms and Eggs
Country Ham, Hash Brown Potatoes, Roasted Peppers and Diced Sharp Cheddar
Smoked Salmon, Grilled Asparagus, Dill Hollandaise
Crumbled Cornbread, Jalapenos, Red Onions, Eggs and Smoked Gouda
Grilled Vegetable Frittata, Shaved Parmigianino, Pesto
Roasted Pears, Crisp Bacon, Diced French Toast

Try your Favorite Omelet Combinations Too!

ENTRESS

Beef
Veal
Pork
Lamb
Chicken
Duck
Game
Meatloaf
Casseroles and Pot Pies
Home-Style Entrees
Savory Waffles
Foie Gras
Liver
Sweetbreads

Fish
Lobster
Shrimp
Scallops
Oysters
Crab
Clams
Calamari
Mussels
Vegetarian Entrees
Tex-Mex
Pasta Combinations
Layered and Stuffed Pasta
Ravioli

Chapter Notes, Ideas and Conversions

Main Ingredient	Element 1	Element 2	Element 3	Sauce	Texture

Main Ingredient	Element 1	Element 2	Element 3	Sauce	Texture

Main Ingredient	Element 1	Element 2	Element 3	Sauce	Texture

BEEF

Charred Filet served with Wild Mushrooms and Brie Demi-glace
Ancho Marinated Skirt Steak with Caramelized Corn and Black Bean Risotto
Grilled Tenderloin with Morel and Fontina Fondue
Plum and Sesame Glazed Short Ribs
Prime New York Steak on Bone-Marrow Brioche Bruschetta with Caramelized Shallots
Miso Crusted Tenderloin with Wasabi Butter
Grilled Rib Eye with Yukon Potato Confit, Smoked Tomato Jam and Cabernet Demi-glace
Orange Chili Marinated Flat Iron Steak with Three Onion Home Fries

Wood Grilled Sirloin, Pinot Mashed Red Potatoes and Crispy Fried Shallots
Smoked Strip Loin with Chanterelles, Grilled Baby Bok Choy and a Red Onion-Celery Root Purée
Five Pepper-Crusted Rib Eye with Ancho Chili Sauce
Orange and Saffron Braised Short Ribs
Charred Hanger Steak with Vidalia Onion Compote and Cabernet Shallot Butter
Honey and Chipotle Glazed Rib Eye
Short Ribs with a Chipotle, Tomato and Horseradish Cream
Spicy Dry Rubbed Rib Eye with an Oven Roasted Mushroom and Smoked Tomato Salsa

Charred Filet with a Ginger Marsala Reduction
Bourbon Braised Short Ribs
Grilled Filet Mignon over Spicy Escarole with a Roasted Garlic Confit
Chili-Grilled Flank Steak with Smoked Tomatillo Salsa
Pan Seared Filet of Beef with Brown Butter Poached Shallots
Short Rib, Andouille, Caramelized Corn and Cannelloni Bean Cassoulet
Beef Bourguignon in Buckwheat Crepe with Rosemary Crème Fraîche
Chianti Braised Chuck Roast with Wild Mushroom Ragout

Pasilla Braised Beef with Tomatoes
Grilled New York Strip with Blue Cheese and Black Peppercorn Demi-glace
Beef Wellington with Seared Foie Gras and a Black Currant-Cognac Reduction
Grilled Cuban Rib Eye Marinated in Dijon and Tabasco
Charred Skirt Steak with Spicy Black Bean and Poblano Puree
New York Strip Steak with a Jack Daniel's Three Peppercorn Sauce
Pan Seared Tenderloin with Shallot and Madeira Sauce
Boneless Short Ribs Braised with Tomatillos, Caramelized Onions and Jalapenos

Smoked Beef Brisket with Cambazola Mac and Cheese, Double Au Jus and Grilled Asparagus
Short Ribs with Winter Vegetables, Charred Onion Demi-glace and White Cheddar Curds
Grilled Hanger Steak with Black Garlic and Onion Soubise, Fresh Pea Tendrils and Carrots
Pittsburg Grilled Filet with a Blue Cheese Bread Pudding and Roasted Coffee Pan Sauce
New York Strip with Duck Fat-Red Potato and Swiss Chard Gratin and Black Pepper Sauce
Seared Tenderloin Tips with Ricotta Salata and a Beet and Blood Orange Compote
Ale and Balsamic Braised Beef Stew with Roasted Garlic Mashed and Caramelized Carrots
Skirt Steak with a Grilled Scallion Confit, Wilted Watercress and Burnt Brandy Pan Juices

BEEF

Beef Tenderloin with Shallot Confit and Cabernet Sauce
Pan Roast with a Trumpet Mushroom and Chestnut Risotto
Smoked Rib Eye with Parsnip Puree and a Bitter Orange Compote
Onion Charred Flatiron Steak with Cambazola Cheese Grits and Grilled Red Onion
Porcini-Dusted Filet with Honey Balsamic Cipollini Onions
Fig and Guinness Braised Short Ribs served on Rustic Polenta with Caramelized Brussels Sprouts
Grilled Beef Kebobs with a Mexican Chocolate Mole and Balsamic Glaze Swirl
Braised Short Ribs with Turnip and Root Vegetable Puree and Pan Roasted Onion Gravy

Smoked Brisket with a Red Potato-Porcini and Gorgonzola Hash and Roasted Shallot Demi-glace
Slow Cooked Short Ribs with Bacon and Three-Cheese Herb Gnocchi
Achiote Rubbed Filet Mignon with Charred Serrano Chilies and Red Onion Demi-glace
Grilled Filet Tidbits with a Wild Mushroom and Fontina Fondue
Short Ribs with Bacon-Mustard Greens, Roasted Sweet Potatoes and Blue Cheese Crumbles
Five Spice Short Ribs with Truffle Potato Hash and Honey Roasted Beets
Smoked Rib Eye with Syrah Syrup and Chimichurri
Braised Beef Chuck Roast with Salsify Puree and Smoked Mozzarella

Grilled Skirt Steak Red Curried Vegetables and Vanilla Cucumber Yogurt
Chili Braised Brisket Cipollini Onions and Tangerine Pico de Gallo
Pan Seared Filet Mignon with Green Tomato Jam and a Port Wine Reduction
Grilled Beef Satay with a Bourbon Peanut Reduction
Harissa Braised Beef Short Ribs with Sweet Onion Ragout
Blackened Flank Steak with Cherry Chipotle Barbeque Sauce
Slow Roasted Pot Roast with Savory Bread Pudding and Smoked Tomato Gravy
Spiced Filet Mignon with Scotch Bonnet Marmalade

Braised Boneless Short Ribs on Pan Fried Potatoes with Horseradish Cheddar Sauce
Rib Eye Steak with Black Garlic Mashed Potatoes
Wood Grilled Filet Mignon, Fresh Horseradish and Roasted Onion Cream
Grilled Filet of Beef with Black Currant Syrup and Cambozola Cheese
Braised Beef Short Ribs with Butter Beans and Rosemary Jus
Smoked Paprika Rubbed Skirt Steak
Asian Style Braised Pot Roast with Star Anise, Ginger and Pink Peppercorns
Braised Short Ribs with a Red Curry and Three Onion Ragu

Marinated Skirt Steak with Lavender Jus and Roasted Shallots
Port-Braised Beef Short Rib with Onion and Mascarpone-Whipped Polenta
Braised Pot Roast with Oven Roasted Salsa and Zinfandel Jus
Miso Crusted Prime Rib Eye with Red Miso-Wasabi Butter
Wood Fired Sirloin Steak with Smoked Bacon-Bourbon Demi-glace
Achiote Marinated Skirt Steak with Pasilla Chili Risotto
Chimichurri Rubbed Rib Eye Steak with Smoked Tomato Cream
Marinated New York Steak with Charred Chayote

BEEF

Char Grilled Rib Eye with Chipotle-Honey Ketchup
Beef Short Ribs with Lemongrass, Kaffir Lime and Ginger
Pepper Crusted Sirloin Steak with Charred Tomato Compote and Balsamic Syrup
Port-Braised Short Ribs served on Tomato Pesto Crostini with Cracked Pepper Jus
Grilled Hanger Steak with Roasted Garlic Aioli
Miso Marinated Filet with Rosemary Butter
Grilled T-Bone with Saffron Onions and Mushroom Jus
Beef Tenderloin Medallions with a Black Truffle and Manchego Fondue

Maple Braised Short Ribs with an Aged Balsamic Reduction
Five Spice Strip Steak with a Ginger Soy Drizzle
Pan Roasted Rib Eye Steak with Tangy Purple Horseradish Butter
Chili Seared Sirloin with Fresh Ginger and Charred Scallion Cream Sauce
Steak Southwest - Marinated in Salsa with Grilled Onion Rings
Smoked Beef Tri -Tip with Mustard Greens and Barbecue Jus
Prime Rib with a Roasted Garlic and Horseradish Crust
Filet of Beef Stuffed with Oysters and Wrapped in Bacon

Chianti Braised Short Ribs with Horseradish Gremolata
Delmonico Steak Marinated in Dark Beer
Smoked Short Ribs with Black Truffle Port Wine Reduction
Tenderloin of Beef with Portabellas and Cranberry Demi-glace
Rib Eye Steak with Whiskey-Peppercorn Sauce and Chili Fried Onions
Slow Braised Short Ribs with a Sausage, Horseradish and Red Onion Gravy
Seared Beef and Shrimp tossed with Rice Noodles and a Red Thai Curry Sauce
Slow Cooked Pot Roast with Creamed Caramelized Leeks

Roasted Tenderloin of Beef with Tomato Basil Mayonnaise
Charred Rib Eye Steak with Boursin, Crispy Leeks and Demi-glace
Beef Filet with Smoked Cheddar and Mushroom Duxelles, Baked in Puff Pastry
Herb Cream Cheese Stuffed Filet of Beef with Bordelaise and Crispy Red Onions
Grilled T-Bone Steak Marinated in Red Chili Oyster Sauce
Gorgonzola Crusted Filet of Beef with Dijon Demi-glace
Tournedos Rossini with Seared Foie Gras, Glace de Viand and Madeira Sauce
New York Strip with a Crust of Cracked Peppercorns and Mustard Seed with Tamarind Chutney

Medallions of Beef in a Walnut Cream Sauce
New York Strip with a Fennel Seed and Hazelnut Crust served with a Red Wine Sauce
Pan Seared Sirloin with Jalapeno Butter
Dry Rubbed Flank Steak with Chili Plum Sauce
Grilled Porterhouse with Smoked Tomato Mashed Potatoes and Roasted Autumn Vegetables
Grilled Porterhouse Steak with an Olive and Caper Tapenade
Filet of Beef with Roquefort Burgundy Butter and Crispy Fried Leeks
Seared Filet of Beef with a Cilantro Peppercorn Crust Flamed in Armagnac
Aged New York Strip Steak Saltimbocca

VEAL

Veal Tenderloin with Cannelloni Beans and Roasted Garlic Spinach
Veal Porterhouse grilled over Hardwood Charcoal with 25 Year Balsamic
Pistachio Crusted Veal Chop with Braised Swiss Chard and Apple and Red Fingerling Hash
Veal Tenderloin and Sweetbreads over Watercress Gnocchi with Amaretto Pan Sauce
Porcini Crusted Veal Chop with White Truffle Risotto and Reduced Mushroom Jus
Veal and Fresh Mozzarella Roulades with Roasted Butternut Puree and Red Pepper Coulis
Veal Milanese with Three Cheese Orzo, Broccolini and Tomato Basil Marinara
Veal Medallions Pan Seared with Whiskey and Wild Mushrooms

Grilled Veal Chop with Manchego Grits and Sweet Onion Marmalade
Slow Cooked Veal Ragú with Morels, Shaved Parmigianino and Black Truffle Butter
Sautéed Veal Scallops with Fresh Chanterelles, Marsala and Cream
Grilled Veal Porterhouse with Roasted Corn and Red Potato Hash and a Charred Onion Demi-glace
Braised Veal Cheek "Hunter Style" over Pappardelle Pasta with a Tomato and Oregano Emulsion
Veal Tenderloin with a Lemon and Caper Beurre Blanc
Pan Roasted Veal Chops with Morels and Molasses Butter
Grilled Veal Chop with Porcini and Chanterelle Ragu over Asiago Polenta and Braised Endive

Rosemary-Tomato Braised Breast of Veal over Roasted Garlic Polenta
Osso Buco in Natural Juices with Wild Mushroom Risotto
Veal Scaloppini with Grilled Lobster Medallions and Pinot Grigio Reduction
Veal with Leek and Roquefort Sauce
Grilled Veal Chops and Braised Radicchio with Lemon-Caper Sauce
Veal Scallops with Bacon and Potatoes
Roasted Loin of Veal with Porcini-Marrow Sauce and Pickled Chanterelles
Blackened Veal Chops with Caramelized Fennel and Figs

Veal with Eggplant and Prosciutto
Veal Meatballs and Baby Carrots in Dilled Cream Sauce
Sautéed Veal Medallions with Sun Chokes, Mortadella and Fontina
Red Chile Glazed Veal Chop
Veal Chop with Sautéed Sweetbreads and Maple Syrup Glazed Cipollini Onions
Braised Veal Shank "Bolognese" with White Truffles over Pappardelle
Bone in Veal Sirloin over Creamy Herb and Prosciutto Polenta
Roasted Veal Chop with Wilted Spinach and Pomegranate Jus

Sautéed Veal Medallions with Fresh Mint and Capers
Pan-Roasted Veal with Green Chili and Charred Onion Salsa Verde
Veal Osso Buco with Morels and Smoked Tomatoes
Veal Loin Stuffed with Serrano Ham, Manchego Cheese and Escarole
Sauté Medallions with Cremini Mushrooms, Grilled Scallions and Aged Port Wine Reduction
Roasted Veal Chop with Morels and Favas in an Onion Jus
Bourbon and Chili Glazed Rack of Veal
Grilled Veal Chop with a Roasted Carrot and Chestnut Ragout

VEAL

Basil-Crusted Veal Chops on White Bean Ragout
Lemon, Pancetta and Orzo Stuffed Breast of Veal
Braised Veal Cheeks with Papaya, Mint and Grilled Pineapple over Coconut Risotto
Veal Roulade with Crabmeat, Spinach and Shallot Stuffing, Sauce Perigourdine
Grilled Veal Chop with Madeira Fig Sauce
Veal Loin Stuffed with Roasted Peppers and Goat Cheese
Veal Chops with Creole Mustard Crust
Madeira and Caramelized Onion Braised Veal Cubes over Grilled Polenta

Boursin Stuffed Rack of Veal with a Smoked Tomato Bordelaise
Roasted Loin of Veal with Smoked Garlic and Whole Grain Mustard Gravy
Veal Paillard with Pancetta Poached Collards
Veal Scaloppini with Lemon Zest and Roasted Fennel
Thyme and Madeira Braised Veal Shanks on Mascarpone Polenta
Pan Roasted Veal Chop with Roasted Garlic and Balsamic Pan Sauce
Veal Medallions with Caramelized Apples, Walnuts and Riesling Reduction
Veal Chops Stuffed with Fontina, Spinach and Porcinis

Pan Seared Boneless Veal Loin with a Smoked Tomato-Orange Sauce
Basil and Parmesan Crusted Veal Medallions over Roasted Eggplant Puree
Pan Seared Veal Sweetbreads with Oven Dried Pears and Pear Cider Jus
Dark Rum Braised Veal Shanks with Caramelized Red Onions and Black Beans
Grilled Veal Chop with Gorgonzola and Hazelnut Butter
Medallions of Veal with a Red Onion Marmalade
Pan Seared Scaloppini with Orange Rosemary Sauce
Veal with Tomatoes, Leeks, Cremini Mushrooms and Demi-glace
Sautéed Veal with Artichokes and Lump Crab in Lemon White Wine Sauce

Grilled Veal Chop with Porcine Mushrooms, Pesto and Cream
Veal Rib Eye Stuffed with Camembert and Fresh Chervil
Medallions of Veal with a Chardonnay Butter Sauce
Veal Sautéed with a Sherry Lemon Glaze
Pan Roasted Veal Chop with Smoked Crawfish Butter
Panko Crusted Veal Roulade with Pancetta, Smoked Mozzarella and Mushroom Filling
Veal Sautéed with Wild Mushrooms with a Maple Cream Sauce
Black Pepper Crusted Veal Chops with a Bourbon Peach Barbeque Sauce

Cutlet of Veal with Crab, Shrimp, Smoked Ham and Port Salute
Sautéed Veal with Roasted Apples and Flamed with Applejack
Rollitini of Veal with Artichokes, Oyster Mushrooms and Cream Sauce
Grilled Veal Chop with Honey and Green Peppercorns
Veal Strudel with Grilled Apples and Roasted Pears with Cider Demi-glace
Veal Medallions Marinated in Tamarind and Mango

PORK

Pancetta Wrapped Pork Tenderloin with Honey Roasted Apples
Huckleberry Braised Pork Shoulder with Blue Cheese Pan Sauce
Pan Fried Pork Chops with Sweet Potatoes and Sausage Gravy
Grilled Pork Tenderloin with a Ginger Garlic Sauce
Smoked Pork Rib Roast with Spicy Balsamic Syrup
Bacon Wrapped Loin of Pork with Burgundy Braised Red Cabbage
Slow Roasted Pork Butt with Guinness Roasted Wild Mushrooms and Onions
Baby Back Ribs with a Thai Chili BBQ Sauce

Cola-Baked Fresh Ham with Dark Cherry Compote
Crispy Pork Belly with Watermelon, Red Onion and Cilantro Salsa
Asian Spice Rubbed Ribs with Plum-Ginger Glaze
Maple Cured Pork Porterhouse with Smoked Cheddar Grits
Grilled Pork Loin Chop served with Apple and Roasted Parsnip Puree with Apple Cider Jus
Ancho Rubbed Pork Chops with Black Bean BBQ Sauce
Whiskey-Mustard Glazed Spit Roasted Pork Loin
Smoked Pork Shoulder served over Fried Green Tomatoes with Ham Hock Gravy

Slow Roasted Mongolian Pork with Five Spice Rub and Spicy Kimchee
Herb Crusted Roasted Fresh Ham over Bacon Sautéed Escarole
Pork Osso Buco with Creamy Horseradish Polenta
Pork Belly Skewers with a Spicy Maple Glaze, Cilantro and Meyer Lemon
Pork Tenderloin Glazed with Honey Yuzu served on Ginger Polenta
Marinated Grilled Pork with Roasted Shallots and a Shishito Pepper Chimichurri
Wine Braised Pork Chops with Roasted Tomato Mashed Sweet Potatoes
Wood Grilled Pork Chop with Pork Belly Hash and Caramelized Apple Marmalade

Slow Roasted Shoulder of Pork with Smoked Ham Gravy over Grilled Cornbread Wedges
Suckling Pig Confit with Red Lentils and a Tamarind and Date Compote
Crispy Pork with a White Bean and Garlic Puree
Pork Tenderloin with Balsamic Cipollini Onions and Apple Currant Compote
Rosemary Grilled Pork Chop with Cranberry and Maple Glazed Sweet Potatoes
Three Olive Stuffed Loin of Pork
Double-Cut Pork Chop in a Roasted Tomatillo Adobo Sauce
Roasted Pork Shoulder with Country Ham Grits, Chanterelle Mushrooms and Brussels Sprouts

Caramelized Pork Chops on Wild Rice Pilaf with Bacon Braised Apples and a Aged Cider Sauce
Watermelon and Maple Syrup Glazed Ribs
Bacon Wrapped Pork Loin with Butter Beans and Savoy Cabbage
New Mexican Spice Rubbed Pork Tenderloin with a Bourbon-Ancho Chili Sauce
Pan Roasted Pork Tenderloin with a Caramelized Onion and Dried Cherry Chutney
Crispy Braised Pork Belly with Pickled Peaches
House Cured Pork Loin Chop with Mission Fig Grits, Garlicky Spinach and Fig Balsamic

PORK

Peppercorn Crusted Pork Chop with a Peach-Bourbon Barbeque Sauce
Pan Seared Loin Chops with Orange Chipotle Glaze
Chili-Seared Pork with Grilled Pineapple and Dark Rum Salsa
Pork Medallions with Roasted Garlic Flan and Port Reduction
Porterhouse Pork Chop with Maple Roasted Onions and Burnt Brandy Demi-glace
Barbecued Ribs with Chipotle Honey and Caramelized Shallot Glaze
Slow Roasted Pork with Green Apple and Crisp Bacon Cabbage
Kalamata Olive and Ancho Stuffed Pork Loin

Pork Osso Buco with Wild Mushrooms and Smoked Tomato Bordelaise
Asian Spice Roasted Pork Belly with a Sesame Orange Glaze
Pancetta Wrapped Pork Tenderloin with Gorgonzola and Honey Roasted Pears
Cola-Baked Pork Shoulder with Cherry-Tangerine Glaze
Coriander Crusted Pork Tenderloin over Winter Vegetable Ragout
Grilled Double Pork Porterhouse with Whole Grain Mustard Sauce
Pecan Smoked Pork Tenderloin with Butter Browned Apples and Sweet Vermouth
Grilled Pork Tenderloin Paillard with a Tomato Basil Pan Sauce

Chorizo and Cornbread Stuffed Pork Chop with Smoked Tomato Demi-glace
Caribbean Marinated Pork Chops with Grilled Pineapple and a Dark Rum Glaze
Vanilla and Bourbon Marinated Pork Loin
Cider Glazed Pork Belly with Roasted Tomatillo over White Corn Polenta
Hard Cider Cured Double Thick Pork Chops with Baked Apple and Shallot Confit
Chipotle Marinated Pork Tenderloin with Banana-Tamarind Salsa
Ancho Chili Rubbed Pork Tenderloin with a Cranberry and Apricot Chutney
Grilled Pork Tenderloin with Cranberry Merlot Wine Sauce

Barbecued Country Ribs with a Mint, Mango and Habanero Glaze
Rack of Pork with Chili and Roasted Mushroom Chutney
Double Cut Pan Seared Pork Chop with a Maple and Horseradish Glaze
Pan Roasted Rack of Pork with a Prune and Bourbon Sauce
Chicken Fried Pork with Sweet Jalapeno Sauce
Pan Roasted Pork Tenderloin with Sour Apple Glaze
Grilled Rib Pork Chop with a Bourbon and Gorgonzola Demi-glace
Thai Spiced Pork Tenderloin with an Orange Curry Sauce

Grilled Rack of Pork with Chipotle and Hard Cider Glaze
Grilled Loin of Pork with a Red Chili and Fresh Ginger Puree
Sautéed Pork Tenderloin with Cognac Pan Sauce
Seared Pork Tenderloin with Caramelized Granny Smith Apples and Bourbon Pan Sauce
Honey Mustard Glazed Spare Ribs
Pork Scaloppini with Pistachios, Rosemary and Lemon Butter
Grilled Pork Tenderloin with a Red Chili Paste

PORK

Orange Honey Glazed Loin with Cabbage, Smoked Bacon, Red Onion and Leeks
Pan Roasted Pork Tenderloin with Kiln-Dried Cherries and Natural Jus
Grilled Pork Tenderloin with an Apple Jack Cream Sauce over Sautéed Spinach
Sautéed Pork Tenderloin with Leeks and Caraway
Grilled Pork Chops with a Horseradish Cream
Grilled Pork Tenderloin with Maytag Blue Cheese and Currant Pan Sauce
Pan Seared Pork Chops with Toasted Sesame Ginger Butter
Grilled Pork Tenderloin with Honey and Thyme

Marinated Pork Tenderloins with Sautéed Greens in a Cherry Cider Sauce
Grilled Double Pork Chops with Wilted Greens and a Greek Garlic-Almond Sauce
Grilled Loin of Pork Stuffed with Sausage and Pesto served with Roasted Garlic Au Jus
Onion Smothered Fried Pork Chop with Bacon Gravy on Grilled Jalapeño Cornbread
Cider Brined Pork Chop with Wild Mushroom Bread Pudding and Bourbon Apple Butter
Pork Porterhouse with Persimmon Glaze and Herbed Couscous
Braised Pork Shoulder with a Sweet Potato and Apple Hash and Rainbow Chard
Tenderloin with Hen-of-the-Woods Mushrooms and a Corn and Pepper Relish over Garlic Spaetzle

Roasted Pork Chop stuffed with Gingered Sweet Potatoes and a Charred Onion Sauce
Granola Crusted Pork Chop with Whiskey-Pear Chutney
Pork Tenderloin with a Maple and Raspberry Barbecue Sauce
Grilled Pork Cheek with Figs, Braised Endive and Cider Jus
Blackened Pork Chop with Mustard Greens and Pickled Onions over Grilled Cornbread
Smothered Pork Chops over Bacon Spaetzle with Red Onion Jam
Pomegranate Molasses Glazed Pork Tenderloin with Celery Root Gratin
Bacon Wrapped Pork Loin with Cannelloni Beans and Sour Apple Relish

Grilled Pork Tenderloin stuffed with Spinach, Bacon and White Horseradish Cheddar
Applejack Braised Pork with Ricotta-Apple Dumplings
Dark Rum Marinated Pork Loin wrapped in Banana Leaf and Steamed over Hot Coals
Charred Grilled Loin Slices with a Roasted Tomato and Sopressata Ragú over Toasted Polenta
Crisp Pork Chop with an Apple and Grilled Pear Compote over Ginger Whipped Potatoes
Whiskey Peach BBQ Pork Ribs
Cherry Cider Braised Pork Shoulder with Dried Cherries, Fennel and Fresh Tarragon
Honey and Balsamic Glazed Ribs with Three Pepper Slaw

Maple Braised Pork Shank with Collard Greens and Wild Mushrooms over Thyme Scented Grits
Cinnamon and Pistachio Crusted Pork Tenderloin with Molasses Sweet Potatoes and Broccoli Rabe
Braised Pork Shank with Eggplant Caponata and Sun Dried Tomatoes over Toasted Orzo
Grilled Double Cut Pork Chop with a Maple-Mustard Reduction
Beer Braised Pork Shoulder with Pumpkin Spaetzle and Caraway Roasted Brussels Sprouts
Mustard Seed Crusted Pork Tenderloin with a Roasted Peach and Red Cabbage Confit
Grilled Pork Tenderloin with Smoked Tomato Ragu over Crispy Parmesan Polenta
Coffee Brined Pork Chop served on a Crisp Polenta Cake with Dried Cherry Compote

LAMB

Braised Ragú over Pappardelle Pasta, with Dried Cherries, Caramelized Cauliflower and Gremolata
Grilled Lamb T-bone with Mashed Sweet Potatoes and Charred Onion Vinaigrette
Roasted Lamb Sausage Bolognese over Bucatini with Lemon Zest and Caramelized Carrot Jam
Maple and Red Wine Braised Lamb Shanks
Pan Roasted Lamb Chops with Charred Pepper Risotto and Crispy Wild Mushrooms
Grilled Lamb Rack with a Fig and Mint Compote
Wood-Grilled Lamb Ribs with Curried White Beans and Cilantro Yogurt
Lemon and Butter Basted Roast Leg of Lamb with a Coriander-Mint Gastrique

Grilled Lamb T-Bone with Serrano Pepper Couscous, Pickled Red Onions and Rosemary Oil
Braised Lamb Shanks with Charred Polenta and a Chianti and Gaeta Olive Tapenade
Smoked Leg of Lamb with Roasted Eggplant, Chorizo and Grilled Scallion Cornbread
Lamb Loin with Hibiscus Poached Dates and Nasturtium Butter
Braised Lamb Shank with Oven Roasted Carrots and Yukon Potatoes and a Cranberry Gremolata
Rack of Lamb with Wilted Arugula and a Caramelized Orange Demi-glace
Lamb Shoulder Stew over Butter Beans with Spicy Slaw
Roasted Lamb Saddle with Toasted Pistachio Polenta and a Fennel Demi-glace

Slow Braised Lamb Ragú with Root Vegetables over Buttermilk and Ricotta Gnocchi
Roasted Leg of Lamb with Mint Jus and Lavender Salt
Lamb Sheppard's Pie with Smoked Cheddar and Crispy Onions
Roasted Lamb Loin with Grilled Asparagus and Piquillo Peppers, Olive Vinaigrette
Lamb Chops Au Poivre with Dried Fruit Compote
Porcini Encrusted Lamb Chops with Pomegranate Glaze
Maple Rubbed Roasted Leg of Lamb with Mint and Fresh Pea Risotto
Grilled Paillard of Lamb with Rosemary Roasted Red Pearl Onions and a Syrah Reduction

Grilled Moroccan Spiced Lamb Chops with Orange Blossom Honey Glaze
Grilled Saddle of Lamb with Roasted Eggplant Puree and Merlot Reduction
Pan Roasted Lamb Chops with a Shallot and Apple Butter Chutney
Lamb Cutlet on Minted Fresh Pea Puree with a Garlic Pan Sauce
Braised Lamb Shank with a White Bean and Date Puree
Grilled Lamb Chops Marinated in Spicy Pomegranate Sauce
Leg of Lamb with a Spiced Eggplant and Black Trumpet Mushrooms Ragu
Mustard-Herb Crusted Rack of Lamb with Natural Jus

Balsamic Marinated Rack of Lamb with a Whole Grain Mustard and Rosemary Reduction
Agave and Mint Glazed Rack of Lamb
Huckleberry Braised Leg of Lamb with Gorgonzola Polenta
Grilled Lamb Rack with a Harissa and Lamb Jus
Slow Roasted Leg of Lamb with Merlot Poached Figs
Lamb Chops with Goat Cheese Gnocchi on Wilted Swiss Chard
Fennel Dusted Rack of Lamb with a Spring Onion Flan
Grilled Lamb Loin served over Spicy Stewed Tomatoes with Rosemary Jus

LAMB

Roasted Leg of Lamb with a Boursin Flan, Baby Spinach and Sorrel Emulsion
Seared Lamb Chops with Pomegranate Reduction
Lamb Medallions with Maple Glazed Cipollini Onions and Cremini Mushrooms
Grilled Lamb Porterhouse with Cilantro, Mint and Allspice Butter
Saffron Braised Lamb Shank with a Tomato Confit and Burnt Orange Tapenade
Grilled Rack of Lamb with Roasted Garlic and Roquefort Polenta and Sun-Dried Tomato Jus
Pan Roasted Rack of Lamb with Poached Figs and Vanilla Parsnip Puree
Braised Lamb Shank with Red Chilies, Chanterelles and a Red Wine Sauce

Moroccan-Spiced Leg of Lamb with Caramelized Apple and Black Currant Chutney
Chianti Braised Lamb Shanks with a Toasted Almond Mint Pesto
Rack of Lamb with Pomegranate and Cracked Black Pepper Jus
Pan Seared Medallions of Lamb with an Apricot Brandy-Peppercorn Sauce
Slow Roasted Leg of Lamb with a Red Wine Jus and Tomato Mint Chutney
Moroccan Braised Shank with Golden Raisin and Roasted Pistachio Couscous and Minted Tzatziki
Roasted Leg of Lamb on Grilled Eggplant with Blackberry Lamb Jus
Balsamic Marinated Lamb Chops with a Dijon and Rosemary Reduction

Rack of Lamb with Cilantro Pesto Crust and a Baked Apple Sauce
Tender Sliced Lamb on Grilled Fontina Polenta with Charred Asparagus and Thyme Oil
Whole Grain Mustard and Herb Crusted Rack of Lamb
Grilled Lamb Medallions with a Balsamic Glaze and a Saffron Mint Pesto
Roast Leg of Lamb with Red Chili Crust and Coriander Jus
Saltimbocca of Lamb with Prosciutto and Sage
Slow Roasted Leg of Lamb with Spicy Red Cabbage
Medallions of Lamb with Oven Roasted Fruits

Spit Roasted Rack of Lamb with a Blackberry Mint Glaze
Hazelnut Crusted Lamb Chops served with a Tomato and Olive Ragout
Rosy Pink Lamb Medallions with Braised Fennel and Roasted Pear Puree
Rack of Lamb with a Thai Basil and Mint Reduction
Lamb Chops with Sweet Butter and Fresh Mint
Smoked Leg of Lamb with Cumin Salt Crust
Roasted Loin of Lamb with a Walnut-Roquefort Sauce
Lamb Medallions with Basil Mashed Potatoes and Caramelized Apple Puree

Bacon Wrapped Cubes of Lamb with Cumin, Coriander and Garlic on a Skewer
Country Style Ground Lamb with Fresh Herbs and Spinach in Phyllo
Rack of Lamb with Creole Mustard Crust and a Scallion and Fresh Pear Relish
Roasted Leg of Lamb with Smoked Tomato Confit and Three Olive Tapenade
Char Grilled Lamb T-bone with Blistered Cherry Tomatoes, Gaeta Olives and Lamb Reduction
Pan Roasted Lamb Chops with Port Wine and Dried Cherry Sauce
Medallions of Lamb with Apple Puree and Braised Fennel
Lemon Basil Marinated Leg of Lamb

CHICKEN ENTREES: FILLINGS, TOPPINGS AND SAUTÉS

Chile Dusted Rotisserie with Buttermilk Mashed Sweet Potatoes and a Honey-Butter Broth
Pan-Roasted Breast with Chestnut Spaetzle and Pomegranate Pan Sauce
Rosemary Skewered with Red Pearl Onions and Baby Bella Mushroom Caps, Port Wine Glaze
Sauté over Goat Cheese Polenta with Bacon Braised Arugula and Toasted Pine Nuts
Smoked Chicken Stew served over a Cheddar and Caramelized Onion Biscuit
Cast Iron Roasted with Couscous and a Cured Lemon and Black Olive Tapenade
Spiced Chicken Stew served over Rosemary Spaetzle and topped with Toasted Pumpkin Seeds
Rotisserie with a Honey-Habanero Mop served with Pickled Lemons and Red Onions

Sauté with Roasted Tomatoes and Shaved Fennel over Wilted Spinach
Citrus Marinated and Roasted with Charred Red Peppers and Garlic-Black Bean Mashed Potatoes
Black Olive and Citron stuffed Breast with Oven Roasted Tomatoes and Braised Baby Bok Choy
Hot Coal Grilled Guava Marinated with Charred Red Onions and Smoked Pepper Rice
Chimichurri Marinated Rotisserie with Roasted Garlic Mashed Potatoes
Slow Roasted Thighs with Dried Apricots, Green Olives and Celery
Blackened with an Apricot and Chipotle Compote and Crumbled Goat Cheese
Pecan Crusted with a Jack Daniels-Whole Grain Mustard Sauce

Pan Roasted Stew with Sweet Potato Pudding and Fried Cabbage Confit
Herb Infused Rotisserie with a Blackberry Port Wine Sauce
Smoked Mole with Habanero Black Beans and Cilantro Sour Cream
Jerk Chicken Slow Roasted in a Banana Leaf served with Orange Walnut Rice
Tandoori with a Dried Currant Couscous and Curry Yogurt
Cracked Peppercorn Crusted Breast stuffed with Andouille and Boursin
Curry Rubbed Roasted served with a Sweet Potato and Dried Fruit Spoon Bread
Chicken and Thyme Croquettes with Smoked Paprika Cream Sauce

Cornish Game Hen with Pistachio Spaetzle
Breast stuffed with a Roasted Chestnut and Braised Onion Puree
Sautéed Breast with a Pommery Mustard Cream and Balsamic Reduction
Clay Pot Roasted with Cured Olives, Currants, Almonds and Pan Jus
Pretzel Crusted with Honey Mustard
Olive Oil Poached with a Basil and Roasted Tomato Sauce
Grilled Breast with Foie Gras Butter and a Madeira Wild Mushroom Sauce
Clay Pot Roasted with Braised Chick Peas over Cucumber Couscous with Pomegranate Reduction

Achiote with Spanish Chorizo served over Braised Savoy Cabbage and a Spicy Chicken Jus
Roasted with Crisp Brussels Sprout Leaves over Parmesan Polenta with Toasted Pistachio Oil
Clay Pot Roasted served with Yellow Pepper Couscous, Wilted Spinach and Lemon Harissa Jus
Tamarind Roasted with Three Olives
Roasted over Lemon Poppy Seed Spaetzle with Rosemary Jus
Thighs with Black Mustard Seed Crust
Roasted Half Brushed with Bacon Fat and dusted with Sherry Lemon Salt

CHICKEN ENTREES: FILLINGS, TOPPINGS AND SAUTÉS

Lemon and Rosemary Roasted with Fresh Fennel
Skillet Roasted with Smoked Ham Braised Savoy Cabbage and Hazelnut Oil
Roasted Breast stuffed with Fontina and Artichokes and Wrapped in Prosciutto
Clay Pot Barbecued Breast with Maple Mashed Sweet Potatoes
Stuffed with Goat Cheese, Roasted Peppers and Green Onion
Macadamia Crusted served with Tropical Fruit Salsa and a Passion Fruit Vinaigrette
Ancho Chili Rubbed with Smoked Tomatillo Salsa and Queso Fresco
Preserved Lemon and Pomegranate Roasted with Watermelon Radish and Broccoli Sprout Slaw

Thyme Braised served over Lemon Zest Spaetzle with Merlot-Poached Apples
Grilled Supreme on Sautéed Spinach with White Bean and Chorizo Cassoulet
Cinnamon and Clove Crusted Game Hen
Blackened with Grilled Pineapple and Madeira Plumped Sultana Raisins
Coriander and Cumin Roasted with Onion Pan Jus
Molasses Brined with Grilled Peaches and Sautéed Arugula
Herb Roasted over Mascarpone Polenta and Broccoli Rabe with a Roasted Garlic Sauce
Foie Gras Butter and a Roasted Morel and Madeira Sauce

Stuffed with Apples, Shallots and Almonds
Lemon-Thyme Sauté with Sun Dried Tomatoes, Chanterelles and Boursin
Thighs Stuffed with Roasted Peppers, Prosciutto, and Spinach
Sauté topped with Prosciutto, Fontina and Fried Sage Leaves
Sauté Diablo with Tomatoes and Dark Beer served over Roasted Onion Spaetzle
Skillet Roasted with Smoked Bacon, Grilled Onions and Feta
Roulade with Spinach, Sun Dried Tomatoes and Goat Cheese
Crispy with Wild Mushrooms and Grilled Herb Polenta

Basil Roasted with Preserved Lemon and Pomegranate
Lemon Glazed with Merlot Poached Pears
Grilled with White Bean and Chorizo Cassoulet
Cremini and Manchego stuffed with Maple and Roasted Apple Puree
Lemongrass with Green Soba Noodles and Red Curry
Pan Roasted over Crispy Sliced Sweet Potatoes with Browned Chicken Jus
Crunchy Nut-Crusted served over a Cheddar, Corn and Potato Gratin
Saltimbocca with Garlic, Mushrooms, Prosciutto and Sage

Citron - sautéed and tossed with Lemon, Lime, Grapefruit and Orange Sections
Sautéed with Mushrooms, Shallots and Marsala served over Garlic Spaetzle
Spit Roasted with Chanterelles and Summer Truffles and a Lemon Pan Sauce
Breast on Mushroom Risotto with a White Truffle Shallot Pan Sauce and Grilled Asparagus
Spring Vegetable stuffing with a Chardonnay Sauce
Mole Braised with Caramelized Corn, Grilled Scallions, Queso Fresco and Smoked Red Jalapeños
Breast stuffed with Pine Nuts, Roasted Eggplant and Herb Cheese

CHICKEN FILLINGS, TOPPINGS AND SAUTÉS

Sugar Cane Skewer Coated in Chopped Peanuts and Red Jalapeno Pesto
Hazelnut Crusted Breast with Tomato Béarnaise
Grilled with Plum Chutney
Napoleon with Vegetable Ragout, Gruyere, Garlic Mashed Potatoes and Roasted Pepper Cream
Oven Glazed Almond
Toasted Coriander and Cumin Seed Crusted Breast
Boneless Thighs Stuffed with a Ham, Sweet Pepper, Honey and Onion Compote
Breast stuffed with Grilled Vegetables, Herbs and Brie

Tea and Cassia Bark Smoked with Hunan Red Onion Pickle
Roulade stuffed with Feta Cheese and Pistachios, Red Zinfandel Sauce
Breast Topped with Crab Imperial and Grilled Asparagus
Grilled with Danish Bleu, Fresh Grapes and Tri-Color Apples
Sauté with Grilled Fresh Peaches and Balsamic Glaze
Herb Roasted with Apple-Sage Dressing and Thyme Jus
Scaloppini with Lemon Herb Sauce
Chili Dusted with a Plum and Honey Glaze

Braised with Shiraz, Shallots and Fresh Sage
Maple Glazed with Caramelized Apples and Pears
Mediterranean with Tomatoes, Feta, Lemon Olive Oil and Fresh Oregano
Wasabi Dusted with Cucumber and Mango Chutney
Boneless Thighs stuffed with Figs and Wild Rice
Layered Bake with Spinach, Ricotta, Sun Dried Tomatoes and Fresh Basil
Thai Red Coconut Curry over Sesame Peanut Noodles
Dutch Oven Baked with Pecan Couscous and a Ginger-Lime Cream Sauce

Toasted Sesame with Hoisin and Red Pepper Flake Glaze
Ginger Crusted Teriyaki with Fresh Scallions
Grilled with a Green Peppercorn Hollandaise
Pecan Crusted with a Dijon Mustard Sauce
Breast stuffed with Almonds, Dried Fruits and Lemon Couscous
Sauté with Lime Salsa over Tex-Mex Noodles
Tequila Braised with Black Beans, Poblano and Roasted Corn
Dutch Oven Braised with Fresh Mint, Lime and Cilantro over Steamed Bulgur

Pan Roasted with White Beans, Spicy Sausage and Rosemary
Hot Coal Charred with Coconut with Papaya Salsa
Sautéed with Serrano Peppers, Lime, Cardamom and Sugar Snap-Peas
Sauté with Cumin, Cinnamon and Blood Oranges
Slow Braised with Tomatoes, Capers and Kalamata Olives
Sauté with Pink and Green Peppercorns

DUCK

Rosemary Sea Salt Rubbed and Spit Roasted
Whole Rotisserie Duck basted with a Cane Sugar and Huckleberry Syrup
Duck Confit with Thai Red Rice, Pistachios and Kiln Dried Cherries
Clay Pot Duck in a Pecan Mole Sauce
Roasted with Burnt Orange Sauce
Asian-Spiced Breasts with Ginger-Chili Glaze
Roasted and served over a Grilled Peach and Sweet Corn Puree
Slow Braised with Red Cabbage and Honey Vinaigrette

Crispy Duck on Fried Green Tomatoes with Chorizo Pan Gravy
Lavender and Honey Marinated Roast Duck
Breast with a Black Currant and Balsamic Vinaigrette
Crispy Duck over Sweet Potato Spaetzle with a Ginger and Soy Reduction
Roasted with a Green Peppercorn Demi-glace
Crisp Duck and Scallion Pancake with Ginger Orange Glaze
Sautéed Livers with a Warm Fig and Port Reduction
Crispy Peking Breast over Grilled Baby Bok Choy with Cranberry Hoisin

Molasses Glazed with Watermelon Radishes and Spiced Jus
Roasted with Lingonberry Port Wine Sauce
Pomegranate Glazed Breast with Wilted Mustard Greens
Pan Roasted Breast with Celeriac Puree and a Caramelized Onion-Dark Cherry Compote
Seared Breast with Grilled Figs and Bacon Braised Collards
Yellow Curry over Red Lentils with Crisp Pancetta and Wild Mushrooms
Roasted with Blackberry and Cognac Sauce
Crispy Mace Crusted with Sour Cherry and Orange Ragout

Pan Roasted Breast with a Pinot Noir Glaze
Citrus and Spice Rubbed Duckling with Orange Cranberry Sauce
Seared Breast with a Blueberry Maple Glaze
Grilled Breast with Roasted Figs, Caramelized Shallots and a Balsamic Glaze
Slow Braised with Tangerine and Vanilla Chutney
Pan Seared Breast with a Chive and Shiitake Mushroom Reduction
Seared Breast with Roasted Grapes and Curried Carrot Puree
Pan Roasted Breast with Red Currant Demi-glace

Iron Skillet Roasted with Burnt Orange Demi-glace
Asian-Spiced Dry Rubbed with Ginger-Chili Glaze
Slow Braised Thighs with a Raison, Coconut and Smoked Onion Ragout
Lacquered Duckling with a Coffee and Grand Mariner Glaze
Fig Glazed Breast with Goat Cheese Tartlet and Red Onion Jam
Duck Confit with BBQ Lentils, Golden Bolden Beets and Mustard Greens
Wood-Grilled Breast over Quinoa and Caramelized Corn Hash
Roasted with Sausage and Smoky Lentils

GAME

When menu planning with game, it is important to match the cut of game to the preparation. The more tender cuts can be cooked quickly with dry heat methods, whereas tougher cuts are more suitable for moist heat preparations. Venison is actually any cut from a Deer, Elk or Antelope. Each type of venison has its own distinct characteristics for flavor and tenderness, but for the most part the types of venison are interchangeable.

Slow Roasted Venison Roast with Savory Bread Pudding and Pan Juices
Elk Loin Chops with Rosemary and Balsamic Marinade
Venison Loin with Swiss Chard and Huckleberry Reduction
Braised Rabbit Leg over Rosemary Pappardelle with Portabellas and Roasted Carrots
Prosciutto Wrapped Venison Loin with Black Currant Sauce
Chardonnay Braised Rabbit with Morels and Ramps
Ballottine of Rabbit stuffed with Country Style Rabbit Pate and Wrapped in Prosciutto
Mushroom Stuffed Quail with Calvados Glaze

Slow-Roasted Rabbit with Cornbread and Sausage Stuffing and Crisp Pancetta Gravy
Pan Seared Venison Loin with Roasted Garlic Spaetzle and Black Currant Demi Glace
Crawfish and Cornbread Stuffed Quail with a Smoked Tomato Brown Sauce
Lavender and Honey Glazed Venison Ribs
Grilled Venison Rib Chops with a Merlot, Sweet Onion and Pomegranate Reduction
Braised Rabbit and Coffee Gravy served over Black Pepper Biscuits with Fried Eggs
Blue Corn Pancake filled with Slow Braised Wild Boar and served with a Habanero Chili Sauce
Wild Mushroom and Black Cherry Braised Elk Roast served over Saffron Spaetzle

Bacon Wrapped Grilled Quail with a Golden Raison, Grilled Peach and Toasted Pine Nut Compote
Slow Cooked Rabbit and Bacon Ragout served over Fried Green Tomatoes
Rosemary and Green Peppercorn Braised Venison Shanks served over Cranberry Spoon Bread
Chili-Rubbed Venison Loin with Green Peppercorn Sauce
Pan Roasted Quail stuffed with Foie Gras and Wild Mushrooms, Walnut Pan Jus
Roasted Loin of Venison with a Honey and Apricot Compote
Grilled Venison Medallions with Wild Mushroom Bread Pudding and Dried Cranberry Sauce
Rabbit with Shell Beans and Roasted Tomatillo

Grilled Venison Loin with Rosemary Maple Mustard
Black and Blue Antelope Steaks Au Poivre
Rabbit Chasseur served with Cracked Black Pepper Dumplings
Tangy Chipotle and Orange Barbecued Elk Ribs
Lemon and Honey Glazed Pheasant served with Roasted Garlic Spaetzle
Caramelized Corn Polenta layered with Quail Confit and Fennel Sausage with Port Demi Glace
Grilled Venison and Blueberry Sausage with a Caramelized Shallot Pan Sauce
Slow Roasted Squirrel in Caramelized Onion Sauce

Grilled Venison Chop with Mashed Sweet Potatoes and a Muscat and Fig Reduction
Rabbit and Andouille Gumbo with Grilled Scallion Hushpuppies and Smoked Paprika Sour Cream
Cayenne-Honey Glazed Quail served with Tasso Ham Lentils and Braised Chard

GAME

Elk and Vegetable Pie with Spicy Phyllo Crust
Grilled Quail Marinated in Dark Beer and served with Red Chili Sauce
Blackened Breast of Pheasant with Caramelized Peaches and Roasted Chestnuts
Venison Roast Glazed with Brown Sugar, Dijon Mustard and Cajun Seasonings
Braised Goose with Tangy Port Wine Sauce
Slow Simmered Corned Venison Roast
Hunters Stew with Wild Mushrooms and a Jalapeno Cornbread Crust
Venison Chili with Black Beans and Whole Roasted Garlic Cloves

Roast Goose with Ground Pork and Cranberry Dressing
Doves in Spicy Tomato Sauce over Parmesan Risotto
Cider Braised Venison with a Sliced Sweet Potato Crust
Rabbit with Rosemary over Steamed Red Potatoes and Leeks
Sautéed Dove with Apples and Black Walnuts
Baked Stuffed Quail with Polenta, White Wine and Fresh Herbs
Venison Shanks Braised in a Dry Chianti Sauce
Rack of Venison with Red Zinfandel Sauce and Pear Relish

Smoked Cornish Game Hen with Fresh Thyme Shallot Sauce
Grilled Venison Chop with Roasted Garlic Potatoes, Shitakes and Sweet Onion Chutney
Charred Venison Steaks with Grilled Sweet Peppers, Onions and Portobello
Venison Swiss Steaks with Amber Ale Barley Pilaf and Wilted Greens
White Ale Braised Rabbit Leg stuffed with a Saffron and Pancetta Risotto
Roasted Bison Sirloin with Fiddlehead Ferns, Red Fingerlings and Bordelaise
Pan Roasted Venison Rack with Cauliflower Puree and Trumpet Mushrooms
Buffalo Filet with Mashed Sweet Potatoes, Oven Roasted Carrots and a Chianti-Fig Reduction

Pheasant with a Bacon, Grilled Ramp and Carrot Ragout
Slow Cooked Boar Shoulder with Caramelized Brussels Sprouts and a Chestnut-Chocolate Puree
Crispy Pheasant with Bacon Mashed Cauliflower, Red Pearl Onions and Dark Rum Demi-glace
Pan Seared Venison Saddle with Roasted Garlic Spaetzle, Red Cabbage Kraut and Currant Jus
Cast Iron Pan Roasted Quail with a Chestnut, Bacon and Dried Cranberry Stuffing
Muscat Braised Rabbit with a Fire Roasted Corn and Dried Apricot Ragout
Roasted Venison Saddle with Caraway Fried Cabbage, Red Onion Jam and an Anise Jus
Cider Braised Venison Shanks with Cipollini Onions, Mushrooms and a Thyme-Dijon Reduction

Cassis Glazed Squab with a Roasted Pear, Chestnut and Celery Root Compote
Pan Seared Breast of Pheasant with a Thyme, Red Wine and Brown Butter Pan Sauce
Rabbit Saddle with a Rye Bread, Pistachio and Black Grape Stuffing and a Merlot Pan Sauce
Venison Swiss Steaks with Caraway Scented Spaetzle and Bacon Fried Cabbage
Roasted Quail with White Truffle Polenta and Caramelized Shallot Marmalade
Quail and Dumplings with Baby Fall Vegetables and a Sweet Onion and Mushroom Broth
Crispy Pheasant with Roasted Chestnuts and Bacon Braised Savoy Cabbage
Seared Wild Boar Strip Loin with Braised Rainbow Chard and Golden Raisons

MEATLOAF

Roasted Shallot and Veal with a Wild Mushroom Reduction
Bacon-Wrapped with Brown Sugar-Ketchup Glaze
Chorizo and Pork with Roasted Mushroom Jus
Spicy Sausage with Smoked Provolone
Veal with Madeira Gravy
Vermont Cheddar with Bourbon Barbeque Sauce
Chipotle with Double Smoked Bacon Gravy
Three Cheese

Veal with Gorgonzola and Prosciutto Gravy
Tex-Mex with Chipotle Chili Glaze and Cheddar Mashed Potatoes
Turkey and Wild Mushroom wrapped in Bacon with Smoked Tomato Sauce
Veal and Pork with Sage, Pancetta and a Fontina Cheese Sauce
Turkey with Feta, Sun-Dried Tomatoes and Kalamata Olives
Applewood Bacon and Horseradish Cheddar
Pizza Style stuffed with Chopped Pepperoni and Diced Mozzarella
Three Chili with a Mexican Chocolate Mole Sauce

Served with a White Cheddar and Truffle Fondue
Turkey, Spinach and Feta
Asian Pork and Chicken with Hoisin Glaze
Veal and Basil topped with Fontina
Amber Stout and Cheddar Fondue with Cubed Meatloaf and Pumpernickel for Dunking
Caramelized Apple and Pork with Cinnamon Onion Gravy
Pork and Wild Mushroom with Spicy Italian BBQ Sauce
Smoked Turkey with Oven Dried Tomato and Grilled Onion Gravy

Roasted Vegetable with Walnuts and Balsamic Glaze
Veal with Spinach, Walnuts and Shaved Parmigianino
Black Bean and Roasted Corn served on Spicy Salsa
Peppercorn crusted on a bed of Saffron Onions
Jerk Seasoned with Caramelized Pineapple Glaze
Lamb with Goat Cheese and Mint
Pork, Chorizo and Roasted Poblano with Chili Sour Cream
Turkey with a Maple and Whole Grain Mustard Sauce

Veal, White Cheddar and Roasted Pear
Topped with Fried Green Tomatoes and Ham Hock Gravy
Pesto with Fresh Tomato Sauce
Stuffed with Black Truffles and Portabellas with Burnt Cognac Demi-glace
Blackened with Pepper Jack Cheese

CASSEROLES AND POT PIES

Add appropriate vegetable combinations, mix and match spices, toppings and crusts.

Baked Chicken Pot Pie with Andouille, Wild Mushrooms and a Cheddar Chive Biscuit Crust
Seafood and Andouille Gumbo with a Crust of Roasted Chilies, Cornbread and Colby
Smoked Sea Bass and Winter Vegetables with Crisp Potato Top
Five Alarm Chili with Re-Fried Bean and White Cheddar Crust
Chicken Creole topped with Cilantro and Butter Garlic Crostini
Mom's Turkey Pot Pie Topped with Old Fashion Bread Stuffing
Slow Roasted Pork, Wild Mushrooms and Grilled Eggplant with Gorgonzola Crust
Spinach and Oyster Pie with Fresh Herb Crumble

Lobster Sheppard's Pie with Mushrooms, Leeks, Corn and a Truffle Mashed Potato Crust
Boneless Fried Chicken and Root Vegetable Pie with a Crisp Maple Honey Waffle Cap
Chicken with Porcini Mushrooms, Roasted Pumpkin and Sliced Sweet Potato-Ancho Honey Crust
Braised Elk with Fava Beans, Dried Tomatoes and Thyme-Whipped Yukon Potato Topping
Smoked Chicken Pot Pie Topped with a Sweet Potato Biscuit

Shredded Beef with Tomatoes, Roasted Garlic and
Wild Ramps with a Fingerling and White Cheddar Crust

Ahi Tuna Noodle Casserole with Saffron Cream, Crushed Wasabi Peas, Shiitake and Panko Crust
Short Rib with Fried Cabbage, Roasted Onions, Rosemary-Tomato Brown Sauce, Noodle Topping
Lobster Pot Pie with Tarragon Fennel Cream, Summer Vegetables and Flaky Pastry Crust
Apples, Caramelized Onions and Braised Pork with Thin Sliced Sweet Potato Crust
Barbecued Beef, Grilled Red Onion and Black Bean Bake with Colby and Crisp Tortilla Topping
Curried Lamb Casserole with Crisp Thin Sliced Yukon Potato Topping
Fresh Halibut Pie with Dill and Buttermilk Biscuit Crust
Chicken Pizzaiola topped with Pesto Flavored Phyllo
Ham and Oyster Bake with Saltine Crust Flavored with Cracked Black Pepper
Braised Beef Tips with Blue Cheese, Caramelized Onion and Pumpernickel Crust

Beef and Dark Beer Compote with Yorkshire Pudding Topping
Baby Clam and Vegetable Bake with Roasted Red Potato and Rosemary Crust
Shepherd's Pie topped with Chive and Horseradish Mashed Potatoes
Shrimp and Scallops with Ginger and Crisp Sesame Noodle Topping
Garlic Roasted Chicken and Spinach Pot Pie with Brie Crostini Top
Smoked Duck and Harvest Vegetables with Cranberry Thyme Crust
Artichokes, Mushrooms and Asparagus with Bacon and White Cheddar Biscuit
Oven Roasted Tomato Pie with Fresh Oregano Focaccia Crust

Osso Buco with Polenta and Sun Dried Tomato Crust
Mediterranean Seafood Pie with Crumbled Feta and Puff Pastry Topping
Southwest Pepper Pot with Toasted Tamale Topping
Smoked Ham and Roquefort with Wild Mushrooms and Caramelized Onion Biscuit Topping

HOME STYLE ENTREES

Southern Pot Roast with Smoked Tomato Brown Sauce served with Chili Mashed Potatoes
Baked Sausage Casserole with Flaky Crust
Roasted Garlic Chicken and Dumplings
Beef and Habanero Black Bean Stew
Sliced Country Ham and Roasted Turkey over Grilled Corn Bread with Gravy
Chili Pot Roast with Green Chili Tomato Sauce

Scalloped Potato and Ham Skillet
Macaroni and Cheese Bake with Beef, Tomato and Mushrooms
Country Ham, Wild Mushrooms and Poached Oysters with Dumplings
Fried Chicken on Onion Waffles with Amber Maple Syrup
Chicken and Sausage Stew
Scalloped Potato, Grilled Onion and Country Ham Skillet

Beef and Ale Pie with Caramelized Onions and a Mustard-Caraway Crust
Spicy Sausages and Scallion Mashed Potatoes with Whole Grain Mustard Gravy
Skillet Chicken with Roasted Vegetables and Biscuit Dumplings
Smoked Oyster and Roasted Corn Stew over Pan Fried Sweet Potatoes
Ham and Cabbage with Butter Beans
Pork and Sauerkraut over Caraway Spoonbread

Country Style Salmon Cakes with Scalloped Potatoes
Sour Beef and Slippery Dumplings
Sausage, Potato and Green Bean Stew
Smoked Brisket and Stewed Tomatoes over Toasted Peasant Bread
Crispy Fried Chicken Livers with Spicy Sausage Pan Gravy
Baked Cod Cakes with Home Fried Potatoes

Slow Braised Pork Ribs with Mushrooms, Onions and Limas
Sausage and Roasted Mushroom Sheppard's Pie
Ham and Cheddar Fondue over Savory Bread Pudding
Smoked Tomato Braised Short Ribs with Horseradish Mashed Potatoes
Slow Braised Pork Shoulder with Scalloped Sweet Potatoes
Sliced Pot Roast over Texas Toast

Crispy Fried Chicken with Tasso Gravy and Sour Cream Biscuits
Beef and Lamb Goulash with Smoked Paprika Dumplings
Garlic and Rosemary Braised Lamb Shanks over Pan Fried Potatoes
Iron Skillet Roasted Pork Butt with Apples and Red Cabbage
Hearty Red Eye Sausage Gravy served on Fried Green Tomatoes
Slow Cooked Lamb Stew served over Grilled Irish Soda Bread
Dutch Oven Country Pork Ribs with Fall Vegetables

SAVORY WAFFLES

Flavor the waffle batter with any number of ingredients to add depth, body and character to the dish. Strain or cook out any large amount of moisture before adding it to the batter. If serving with a sauce, consider placing the sauce under the waffle to help keep the waffle crisp. Top your dish with a corresponding crème fraîche, sour cream or savory flavored whipped cream and a flurry of chopped fresh herbs or nuts.

Roasted Corn and Scallion Waffles with Smoked Salmon and Herb Boursin Cheese
Seared Foie Gras on Pecan Waffles with Blueberry Compote and Vanilla Crème Fraîche
Red Curry Waffle topped with Saffron Chicken, Golden Raison Compote and Toasted Coconut
Fresh Thyme Waffle with Smoked Chicken, Caramelized Shallots and Sherry Butter
Malted Waffle Topped with Grilled Shrimp and a White Cheddar Thermidor Sauce
Cracked Black Peppercorn Waffle with Pastrami, Roasted Peppers and a Dijon Mustard Sauce
Rosemary Waffle with Seared Foie Gras, Caramelized Pineapple and a Veal Reduction
Cornbread and Cheddar Waffle with Chili, Roasted Poblano, Pico D Gallo and Cilantro Sour Cream

Rye and Caraway Waffle with Corned Beef, Sauerkraut and Swiss Cheese Sauce
Buttermilk Fried Chicken on Chive Waffle with Maple Balsamic Reduction
Onion and Chive Waffle with Grilled Asparagus, Country Ham and Red Eye Gravy
Buckwheat Waffle with BBQ Chicken, Red Onion, Blue Cheese and Bacon
Roasted Garlic Waffle with Grilled Shrimp and a Lemon-Garlic Butter and Parsley Crème Fraîche
Sun Dried Tomato Waffle with Mushrooms, Grilled Onions and Melted Brie Sauce
Caramelized Corn Waffle with Fried Green Tomatoes and Bacon Gravy
Sourdough Waffle with Cajun Barbequed Chicken, Roasted Vegetables and Pomegranate Syrup

Whole Wheat Waffle with Wild Mushrooms, Goat Cheese and Truffle Oil
Crisp Pancetta Waffle with Roasted Pears, Caramelized Onion, Fig Jam and Gorgonzola
Caramelized Onion Waffle with Arugula, Smoked Salmon and Whipped Scallion Mascarpone
Roasted Garlic Waffle with Crisp Sopressata, Sun Dried Tomatoes and Shredded Fontina
Pepper Jack Waffle with Grilled Vegetables and Chunky Sausage Gravy
Toasted Cashew Waffle with Jerk Pork, Sliced Avocado and Passion Fruit Syrup
Aged Cheddar Waffle with Caramelized Corn Pudding, Rotisserie Chicken and Fried Sweet Peppers
Pecan Waffle with Crispy Duck Confit, Bourbon-Maple Syrup and Fried Sage Leaves

Pumpkin Seed Waffle with Chicken, Grilled Asparagus and Apple Cider Syrup
Three Onion Waffle with Pork Belly, Poached Apples and Balsamic Reduction
Southern Fried Chicken on a Chive and Maple Waffle with Black Pepper Gravy

Green Onion Waffle with Shaved Roasted Lamb, Sautéed Cucumbers and
Greek Olives, Goat Cheese and Tzatziki

Grilled Scallion Waffle with Sliced Sirloin, Roasted Hen of
the Woods Mushroom and Gorgonzola Demi Glace

Corn and Onion Waffle with Flash Fried Crawfish and Sliced
Andouille, Grilled Peppers and Cajun Spiced Demi-glace

FOIE GRAS

Seared on Brown Sugar Brioche with 75 Year Balsamic
Pistachio Crusted with Blackberry Jus
Served with Sliced Strawberries on Three Peppercorn Pound Cake with Balsamic Glaze
Quick Pan Roasted with Black Truffles, Parmesan and Merlot Reduction
Roasted Foie Gras with Caramelized Onion on Gruyère Crostini
Served on Crispy Raisin Bread with Red Onion Marmalade
Sautéed with Peppered Apple Salad and Port Wine Sauce
Pan Seared with Caramelized Pears and a Warm White Balsamic Vinaigrette

Served on Grilled Brioche with Raspberry-Merlot Jam
Seared and served on Crisp Baby Arugula with Espresso Honey
Sautéed with Black Raspberries and Dark Chocolate
Pistachio Crusted with Caramelized Onions and Fig Syrup
Black Truffle Foie Gras Flan with Morel Ragu
Seared with Cracked Pepper over Roasted Grape Risotto
Served with Watermelon Pickle and Grilled Brioche
Seared with Strawberry Rhubarb Compote and Sautéed Watercress

Served with Roasted Autumn Fruits
Sautéed with Blackberries and Dark Chocolate
Foie Gras Mousse on Crispy Raisin Bread
Roasted with Three Onions and Port-Salut on Charred Bruschetta
Pan Roasted with Black Pepper Pound Cake and Cabernet Reduction
Pressed on Crusty Sourdough with Apricot Compote and Brown Butter
Seared Scallops and Foie Gras with Fresh Pear Demi-glace
Foie Gras Flan with a Balsamic and Cabernet Reduction

Served on a Hot Rock with an Aged Sherry-Rhubarb Compote and Crystallized Ginger
Chilled Foie Gras with Walnuts, Strawberries and a Merlot Reduction
Cured and Smoked Foie Gras on Toasted Brioche with Honey and Green Peppercorn Butter
Seared with Roasted Carrot Flan and Red Wine Caramel
Served on Hazelnut Bread Pudding with Maple Glazed Dark Cherries
Pan Seared with Caramelized Apples and Leeks and a Calvados Pan Sauce
Served on Phyllo Crouton with Honey Glazed Oranges
Foie Gras on Wheat and Herb Cracker with Fig Marmalade

Seared with Roasted Banana and Ginger Compote and Toasted Pine Nuts
Served with Grilled Dates with a Carrot-Bacon Jus
With Strawberry Preserves on Grilled Brioche Crouton
Roasted Chestnuts, Black Truffles and a Pear Balsamic Drizzle
Served with Blood Oranges, Roasted Fennel and Sherry Reduction
Pan Seared Foie Gras with Smoked Mushrooms, Cracked Hazelnuts, and a Red Zinfandel Pan Sauce
Seared over Warm Ginger Bread Pudding with Roasted Concord Grapes and Pistachio Brittle

LIVER

Sautéed served with Caramelized Pear and Bacon Mashed Potatoes and a Madeira Pan Sauce
Grilled with an Apple and Asparagus-Potato Hash and Red Onion Jam
Sautéed with a Cabernet Reduction and Crispy Leeks
Pommery Mustard and Roasted Onion Cream Sauce
Sautéed with Pancetta Braised Red Cabbage
Pan Roasted with Shallot Confit and Bourbon Sage Glaze

Served with Canadian Bacon and Three Onions
Sautéed with Mushrooms, Shallots and Spiced Apples
Pan Braised with Onions, Cider Vinegar, Veal Sauce and Sour Cream
Sautéed with Andouille and Wild Mushrooms
Served with Figs, Shallots and Red Wine

Pan Roasted with Caramelized Onions and Grilled Apples over Crisp Country Ham Slices
Sautéed with Bacon, Fresh Sage and Dry Vermouth
With a Shallots and Cider Vinegar Pan Sauce
Served with Sliced Golden Potatoes and Red Onions
Sautéed with Scallions, Parsley, Dijon and White Wine

Sautéed with Sun Dried Tomato Demi-glace
Pecan Crusted with Oranges and Rosemary
Cornmeal Dusted with Red Eye Sausage Gravy
Braised with Brandy, Currants and Golden Raisons
Blackened with Horseradish Spaetzle
Au Poivre with a Red Zinfandel Sauce

SWEETBREADS

Glazed with Lime, Cipollini Onions and Tamarind Glaze
Pan Roasted with Cucumber and Watermelon Relish and Caramelized Garlic Vinaigrette
Cornmeal Crusted with Apple Chutney Red Onion Marmalade and Fennel Vinaigrette
Sautéed and served with Parsnip Purèe and Sage Brown Butter
Pan Fried with Green Apples, Grilled Fennel and Vanilla Maple Syrup
Crispy Crusted with Toasted Pistachios and Grilled Pear Butter
Served with Crab Fondue and Shitake Mushrooms
Crispy with Smoked Potato Gnocchi and Black Trumpet Mushrooms

Served with Sunchoke Panna Cotta and Foie Gras Mousse
Pan Seared with Crispy Brussels Sprouts and a Meyer Lemon and Fig Jam
Smoked with Parsnip Puree, Pancetta and White Balsamic Vinegar
Herb and Panko Crusted with Capers and a Port Wine Reduction
Seared and served over Roasted Butternut Puree with Bacon Lardons and Pumpkin Syrup

FISH

Cedar Plank Sea Trout with Maple Glaze and Dried Mushroom Dusting
Potato Crusted Alaskan Halibut with Citrus Glaze
Crispy Yellowtail Snapper with Kalamarta Olives and Saffron Broth
Pan Blackened Scrod with Horseradish Cheddar Grits and a Tasso and Charred Tomato Sauce
Crunchy Grouper dipped in Corn Flake Batter with a Green Goddess Aioli
Pan Roasted Black Grouper with Red Quinoa and Vanilla-Lobster Broth
Habanero and Brown Sugar Glazed Salmon
Five Spice Mahi Mahi with Vanilla Rum Butter and Green Apple and Red Onion Salsa

Chili Seared Tuna with Pineapple Gastrique and Sweet Soy Sauce
Miso Glazed Red Snapper on Saffron Orzo with a Ginger Vinaigrette
Olive Oil Poached Salmon on Sunchoke Salad with a Tart Meyer Lemon and Parsley Dressing
Saffron Aioli Crusted Redfish with Chorizo, Black Beans and Grilled Scallions
Pan Roasted Halibut with Wilted Chard, Blistered Red and Yellow Grape Tomatoes and Olive Oil
Potato Crusted Rockfish stuffed with Crabmeat and served with a Sherry Wine Aioli
Walnut Coated Catfish served on Charred Polenta with a Spicy Smoked Tomato Sauce
Pan Roasted Halibut with Peach Molasses

Crusted Turbot with a Wild Mushroom and Sweet Corn Flan and Bacon Cider Jus
Blackened Swordfish with Roasted Tomatillo Cream
Wood-Grilled Rainbow Trout with Spicy Peppers and Onions
Crispy Honey-Miso Turbot with Sticky Rice and Ginger-Soy Reduction
Puff Pastry Wrapped Snapper with Orange Beurre Blanc
Pan Seared John Dory with a Fresh Basil Beurre Blanc and a Gaeta Olive and Caper Tapenade
Monkfish with Bacon Braised White Beans and Kale
Tandoori Grouper with Double Yolk Mashed Potatoes and Greek Yogurt

Coconut Crusted Basa with a Fresh Lime and Dark Rum Cream Sauce
Chili Grilled Black Drum with a Black Bean Puree and Crispy Leeks
Sea Trout with Chorizo Braised Red Pearl Onions, Porcini and Parsnips
Walleye Pike with Caramelized Cauliflower Flan and Orange Vinaigrette
Grilled Salmon Filet with Lemon and Ginger Tzatziki
Pretzel Crusted Grouper with a Wasabi Aioli
Banana Leaf Wrapped Trout with Ginger and Scallions
Pan Roasted Grouper with Cipollini Onions and Chorizo

Grilled Cocoa-Chili Rubbed Barramundi
Crisp Fried Red Fish with Spicy Tasso Ham and Mustard Cream
Slow Roasted Cod with Caramelized Parsnips and Red Wine Butter
Pan Seared Sesame Crusted Salmon served over Lemon Orzo with a Soy and Blood Orange Drizzle
Rainbow Trout with a Spinach and Couscous Stuffing and served with a Lemon Beurre Blanc
Atlantic Salmon with Apples, Horseradish and Dijon Mustard
Rice Paper Wrapped Red Snapper with Green Curry Sauce
Butter Roasted Cod with Summer Tomatoes and Fresh Herbs

FISH

Miso and Sake Marinated Kampachi with Blistered Cherry Tomatoes and a Pistou-Dashi Broth
Grilled Tuna with Maple Soy Pepper
Dover Sole with Caramelized Shallot and Morel Confit and Chive Oil

Halibut and Chorizo Kabobs on Toasted Orzo Tossed with
Diced Cherry Peppers, Tomatoes and Arugula

Butter Poached Monk Fish with an Orange and Fresh Fennel Compote
Pan Roasted Red Snapper with Blackberries and Micro Fennel
Red Zinfandel Cured Drum with a Pickled Pepper Relish
Fresh Halibut with Sweet Potato Gnocchi and a Ver Jus Reduction

Peppercorn Crusted Tuna on Sesame-Soy Dressed Greens with Wasabi Peas
Cedar Plank-Roasted Trout served over Red Lentils
Cranberry Maple Glazed Salmon
Sweet and Sour Monkfish with Capers, Golden Raisins and Preserved Lime
Grilled Wild Salmon with Braised Green Lentils and White Truffle Oil
Pan Roasted Cod with Garlic and Chickpea Puree
Alaskan Halibut with Smoked Tomato-Lobster Butter
Coriander Fennel Crusted Tuna with Soba Noodles and a Miso-Lemongrass Broth

Grilled BBQ Spice Rubbed Hawaiian Kampachi with Lime Scented Rice and Watermelon Salsa
Pan Braised Atlantic Cod with a Chorizo, Lobster and White Bean Stew
Pretzel Crusted Halibut with a Dijon and Rosemary Beurre Blanc
Maple Smoked Salmon Croustade with Caramelized Fennel
Coriander Seared John Dory with Syrah Butter and Charred Baby Bok Choy
Vodka Cured Black Bass with Greek Yogurt, Toasted Walnuts, Roasted Shallots and Cured Olives
Pan Roasted Salmon with a Spicy Black Currant Glaze
Black Pepper Seared Albacore with Glass Noodles and Hen of the Woods Mushrooms

Pistachio Crusted Hake with a Lemon-Chive Emulsion
Halibut with Blistered Red and Yellow Grape Tomatoes and a Black Truffle Sherry Vinaigrette
Sea Bass Braised in Sake with Heart of Palm, Young Ginger and Spring Garlic
Olive Oil Poached Halibut with Caramelized Cauliflower Puree, Wilted Spinach and Pistachio Oil
Crispy Rare Salmon with a Dilled Tzatziki and Charred Tomato Vinaigrette
Pan Roasted Wild Striped Bass with Red Chile Sauce and Caramelized Onion Grits
Copper River Salmon with Roasted Pepper Relish
Ginger and Carrot Poached Halibut with Green Garlic Broth

Rockfish Bouillabaisse with Andouille, Charred Onions and Meyer Lemon Aioli
Pan Seared Monkfish with Roasted Chestnut Butter
Seared Arctic Char over Tequila and Lemon Braised Leeks
Char Grilled Haddock over Roasted Vegetable Orzo with a 75 Year Balsamic Drizzle
California Sand Dabs with Avocado and a Chive Nage
Seared Ahi Tuna dusted in Moroccan Spices served with Minted Hummus

FISH

Red Snapper with Meyer Lemon and Fennel
Three Citrus Marinated Wild Salmon with a Lemon and Charred Tomato Beurre Blanc
Mesquite Seared Albacore with Lime-Ginger Guacamole
Olive Oil Poached Halibut with a Roasted Carrot Broth
Seared Red Snapper served with Mango Citrus Slaw and an Orange Vinaigrette
King Salmon with Capers and Nasturtium Butter
Pan Crisped Fresh Cod served on Parmesan Polenta with Wild Mushrooms Broth
Seared Sea Bass with Thin Sliced Cucumbers and a Lemon Parsley Pesto
Fresh Cod Poached in a Bacon, Smoked Sausage and Tomato Broth
Pan Roasted Trout with Heirloom Tomato and Basil Pistou

Blackened Swordfish with Summer Peach and Sweet Onion Compote
Pan Roasted Red Snapper with Red Chili and Smoked Tomato Barbeque Sauce
Cornmeal Crusted Atlantic Kingfish with Roasted Poblano and Grilled Peach Puree
Seared Black Drum with a Dark Beer and Ancho Sauce
Serrano and Honey Glazed Grouper with a Spicy Black Bean and Tomatillo Salsa
Pan Roasted Monkfish with Coconut and Ginger Sambal
Pistachio Crusted Mahi-Mahi with Oranges and Lemon Oil Vinaigrette
Honey-Wasabi Glazed Sea Bass over Saba Noodles in a Miso-Lemongrass Broth

Oven-Roasted Yellowtail Snapper with Shrimp-Rosemary Beurre Blanc
Grilled John Dory with Sorrel Coulis
Olive Oil Poached Tuna with a Carrot-Cumin and Orange Glaze
Hawaiian Sunfish with Scallion Confit and Three Citrus Vinaigrette
Oven Roasted Pan Size Rockfish stuffed with Crab and Drizzled with a Macadamia Beurre Blanc
Orange Roughy with Orange Vinegar, Plumped Raisins, Toasted Pine Nuts and Glazed Onions
Lemon Pepper Catfish with Three Peppercorn Vinaigrette over Crisp Chinese Noodles
Black Bass on a bed of Fish Fumet Scented Wild Mushrooms and Cucumbers

Grilled Northwest Salmon with an Ancho Chili, Lemon and Honey Glaze
Pan Roasted Halibut with Vanilla and Orange Braised Fennel
Rum and Pepper Painted Tuna - Brush on sauce of Rum, Cloves, Brown Sugar, Soy and Cayenne
Pecan Crusted Trout with a Orange Rosemary Butter Sauce
Pan Fried Pompano with Risotto of Wild Mushrooms and Beurre Noisette
Sea Trout Stuffed with Shrimp Mousse over a Leek-Shiitake Confit
Orange Roughy with Lobster Medallions and a Shrimp Pepper Sauce
Black Peppercorn Crusted Haddock smothered with Tomatoes, Red Onions and Capers

Sole on Vanilla Parsnip Puree with a Champagne Beurre Blanc
Seared Alaskan Halibut with Chili-Mint Vinaigrette
Iron Skillet Roasted Grouper with a Caramelized Shallot and Smoked Tomato Velouté
Pistachio Crusted Catfish with a Blood Orange Beurre Blanc
Grilled Mahi-Mahi with Caramelized Pineapple and Red Onion Salsa
Chamomile Smoked Wild Salmon with Lemon Oil
Pacific Sablefish with Burnt Agave Nectar, Ancho Chili Sea Salt

FISH

Wild Mushroom Crusted Rainbow Trout with a Brown Butter Sauce
Black Sesame Seared Ahi with a Sweet Chili Soy Vinaigrette
Peppercorn Crusted Flounder with Port Wine Poached Fruit Coulis
Pan Fried Red Snapper with Coriander Seed and Whole Cumin Crust
Blackened Hawaiian Kampachi with Pomegranate Glaze
Black Tea Crusted Salmon with Caramelized Pineapple a Mango-Jalapeno Vinaigrette
John Dory with a Saffron and Lobster Broth

Grilled Atlantic Halibut with White Truffle Oil
Seared Yellow Fin Tuna in a Poblano Ginger Brown Butter
Crispy Crusted Catfish with a Lemon, Dill and Cauliflower Puree
Seared Barramundi with Chanterelles, Grilled Mangos and a Corn and Black Bean Salsa
Herb and Potato Crusted Walleye with Fresh Lemon Pan Sauce
Red Curry Seared Mahi-Mahi with Pickled Ginger on Wakame
Grilled Grouper over Sticky Ginger Rice with Pineapple Papaya Salsa and Plum Beurre Blanc
Grilled Redfish with a Caramelized Garlic and Truffle Coulis

Macadamia Crusted Grouper with a Coconut Ginger Curry Sauce
Grilled Pompano with an Ancho, Lemon and Molasses Glaze
Sashimi Tuna with a Serrano Chili and Roasted Lemon Ponzu Sauce
Fennel Crusted Sea Bass with Balsamic Braised Red Cabbage
Cashew Crusted Wahoo with Lime Butter
Dry Rubbed Mesquite Grilled Red Drum with Pistachio and Roasted Shallot Vinaigrette
Bluefish with a Jicama, Red Pepper and Sweet Onion Relish and Passion Fruit Soy
Pan Seared Spice Rubbed Mahi-Mahi

Blackened Perch with Andouille Infused Creole Sauce
Black Sesame Crusted King Salmon with a Ginger Scallion Relish
Tandoori Roasted Striped Bass with Harissa and Toasted Quinoa
Grilled Halibut with Bacon and Lentils
Hazelnut Crusted Trout with Orange Rosemary Sauce
Filet of Sole with a Julienne of Leeks and Smoked Salmon
Pompano with a Caper, Kalamata and Sun Dried Tomato Compote
Sea Bass grilled over Fennel Branches

Asian BBQ Wahoo with a Green Curry Sauce
Blackened Tilapia with Grilled Tomato and Jalapeno Relish
Seared Sea Bass with Basil Roasted Artichokes
Grilled Tuna served over a Sage Scented White Bean Ragout
Herbed Shad Roe en Papillote
Pan Braised Halibut Topped with Tender Endive and Plum Tomatoes
Peppery Pomegranate Glazed Grouper with Black Rice
Turbans of Sole with Lemon Rice Stuffing
Poached Skate Wings with Steamed Littleneck Clams
Pan Roasted Monk Fish with a Lobster and Wild Mushroom Butter

FISH

Prosciutto Wrapped John Dory with a White Wine Cream Sauce
Hazelnut Crusted Rainbow Trout with an Orange and Fresh Fennel Salsa
Old Fashioned Salt Cod Cakes with Bacon, Tomatoes and Rémoulade Sauce
Salmon wrapped in Chinese Cabbage with a Spicy Mustard Glaze
Seared Tuna with Triple Sec Orange Sauce served over Crisp Sesame Noodles
Sautéed Dover Sole with Almond Butter
Chilean Sea Bass with Orange Hollandaise
Cornmeal Crusted Catfish with a Dijon and Green Peppercorn Sauce

Grilled Alaskan Halibut with a Fig and Mango Compote
Jerk Seasoned Grouper with a Roasted Banana Curry Sauce and Toasted Coconut
Wild Pacific King Salmon with a Dried Cherry and Red Wine Glaze
Sesame Crusted Ahi Tuna with Asian Vegetable Stir-fry, Scallion Sticky Rice and Three Pepper-Soy
Grilled Catfish with Tiny Green Beans, Pan Fried Potatoes and Spring Herbs
Marsala Braised Black Bass served over a Black Lentil and Roasted Butternut Squash Confit
Charred Mahi-Mahi over Egg Noodles with Rice Wine Sauce
Tilapia with a Pineapple Basil Sauce

Red Drum with Shrimp and Chipotle Pepper Sauce
Wild King Salmon with Pan Roasted Parsnips and Spinach Flan
Seared Hoki with Crisp Potato Fondant, Vegetable Ragout and Lemon Thyme Emulsion
Cashew Crusted Alaskan Halibut with a Morel Mushroom and Parmesan Risotto
Sesame Ahi Tuna with a Roasted Tomato Ragout and a Toasted Soy and Wasabi Reduction
Grouper Stacked with Crab Meat, Chardonnay Cream, Sautéed Spinach and Crisp Potatoes
Tomato Braised Monkfish over White Beans, Red Onion and Pine Nuts with Kalamata Butter
Rainbow Trout Stuffed with Spinach, Mushrooms and Brie

Corn Crusted Ocean Perch with Chive Mashed Potatoes, Spinach and Thyme Beurre Blanc
Flounder Stuffed with Scallop Mousse and finished with Cucumber Dill Sauce
Baked Lemon Sole with Watercress Mousse and Onion Confit
Grilled Yellow Fin Tuna with a Warm Oriental Vinaigrette
Turbot with Curly Endive and Morels
Sour Cream and Mustard Crusted Catfish
Fresh Halibut with Sun Dried Tomatoes and Black Olives
Pan Seared Fresh Cod with Curried Mushrooms and a Sweet Soy and Orange Glaze

Bluefish with Wild Rice and Mushroom Stuffing and a Dujonaise Crust
Pacific Salmon in Potato Crust with Olive Pesto
Grilled Fresh Atlantic Cod with Tomato Marmalade and Tarragon
Curry Seared Red Drum with Mint Butter and Fresh Thai Basil
Cedar Plank Roasted Trout with a Citrus Horseradish Crust served with Spicy Slaw
Pan Roasted Kingfish with a Ripe Tomato Relish
Herb Baked Pan Size Rockfish
Grilled Halibut with Savory Cabbage, Bacon, Heirloom Beans and Dill

LOBSTER

Lobster and Charred Pasilla Chili Cioppino over Buttered Sourdough Crostini
Cashew Crusted Tail with a Tamarind Glaze
Banana Leaf Wrapped Lobster with Spring Vegetables, Cilantro and Lime
Lobster Cocktail with Avocado and Spicy Lime Vinaigrette
Lobster and Brie Cheese Fondue served over Crunchy Grilled Bruschetta
Broiled Split Lobster Basted with Bourbon Butter
Butter Poached with Green Curry Dipping Sauce
Pan Roast with Spicy Brandy and Tarragon Cream served on Red Rice Cakes

Sauté with Grilled Mangos, Basil Oil and Avocado Cream
Butter Roasted with a Truffle Potato Galette, Grilled Beets and a Cognac Lobster Sauce
Sauté over Vanilla Scented Risotto with Tarragon Roasted Carrots and Grapefruit Confit
Surf And Turf with Spicy Lobster Dumplings and Sweet Chili Braised Short Ribs
Chilled Maine Lobster with Avocado and Hearts of Palm and White Truffle Aioli
Butter Poached Tails with Roasted Salsify, Wilted Spinach and a Madras Curry and Carrot Puree
Pan Roasted with Grilled Scallions and Double Mustard Cream

Lobster Sausage with Lime Butter and Sautéed Spinach
Lobster Martini with Grilled Lobster, Lobster Ceviche and Cilantro Vinaigrette
Pan Roasted with Orange-Chipotle Butter
Lobster Rolls with Red Curry Aioli
Sauté with Sweet Ginger and Chinese Black Vinegar
Sautéed Maine Lobster with Sweet Corn and Rosemary Oil
Stir-Fried Szechuan Lobster with Spicy Red Chili Sauce
Lobster Corn Dog with Tamarind BBQ Sauce

Scampi with a Roasted Garlic Chardonnay Sauce
Grilled Lobster in a Spicy Stone Ground Mustard Cream Sauce
Jerk Seasoned with Mojito Syrup
Grilled with Roasted Shallots and Herbed Goat Cheese and Finished in a Tomato Cream Sauce
Sauté with Oranges, Grapefruit and Pistachio Dust
Maine Lobster Crêpes with Mascarpone and White Truffles
Lobster and Roasted Chili Paella with Saffron-Coconut Rice
Garlic Chili Glazed Lobster Tails

Lobster Strudel with Roasted Carrots, Leeks, Caramelized Apples and Fennel Cream Sauce
Lobster Corn Dogs with Cajun Honey Mustard
Steamed in Saffron and White Wine and Finished with Cream
Pan-Roasted with Seared Chanterelles and Grilled Apples
Puff Pastry topped Lobster Pot Pie with Roasted Vegetables and Morels
Mushroom, Smoked Tomato and Lobster Ragu over Black Pepper Pappardelle
Grilled Lobster with Macadamia Nut Butter
Sauté with Caramelized Shallot and Golden Tomatoes
Coral Butter Poached Lobster

LOBSTER

Baked Whole Lobster with Roasted Garlic Hollandaise
Prosciutto Wrapped Lobster Brochettes with Tomato Jam and Balsamic Glaze
Coconut Crusted Lobster with a Tangerine and Horseradish Dipping Sauce
Grilled Lobster Skewers brushed with a Garlic, Lime and Dark Rum Glaze
Sauté served over Lemon Verbena Risotto with Three Citrus Zest
Chilled Claws with Toasted Pistachio Aioli
Sauté with a Spicy Green Tomato Jam and Bacon-Lemon Vinaigrette
Cast Iron Seared with Salt Porcini Polenta and Spicy Baby Arugula

Muscat Poached with Pumpkin Puree and a Sage and Hazelnut Brown Butter
Seared with Three Orange Oil
Red Curry Lobster with Braised Fennel, Baby Radish and Ginger Madeleine
Hazel Nut and Orange Zest Crusted Lobster with Saffron Rice
Pan Roasted with Lobster Coral Risotto and Black Truffle Oil
Lobster with Vanilla Vodka and White Truffle Oil over Toasted Orzo
Bacon Wrapped Lobster with a Ginger and Balsamic Reduction
Sautéed over Toasted Lemon Bread Crumbs with Fig Vinegar

Grilled with Scallion Rémoulade and Green Papaya Slaw
Chilled Lobster with Key Lime Mustard Sauce
Panko Crusted Medallions with Grilled Scallion Aioli
Lobster steamed in Banana Leaf with Preserved Meyer Lemon, Diced Chilies and Mint
Lobster and Black Bean Cake with Salsa Verde and Yellow Pepper Coulis
Sauté with Roasted Sweet Corn and Tropical Fruit Salsa
Red Curry Lobster with Roasted Chili and Lime
Honey and Adobo Glazed Lobster

Lobster, Passion Fruit and Serrano Ceviche
Sauté over Almond Basmati Rice with Orange Cognac Sauce
Grilled with Thai Sweet Chili Garlic Butter
Three Peppercorn Crusted Lobster Tails Au Poivre
Baked Split Lobster with a Shallot, Lemon and Brandy Cream
Green Curry Seared Lobster with a Mango and Sweet Onion Compote
Poached in Cascabel Chili Butter
Steamed Maine Lobsters with a Spicy Mustard and Sweet Ginger Soy dipping Sauce

Iron Skillet Roasted with Roasted Bananas and Brown Butter
Cumin Grilled Lobster with Red Curry Rémoulade
Grilled Lobster Cake with Tropical Fruit Salsa
Sauté with Wok Fired Asian Vegetables and Warm Spicy Vinaigrette
Agave Syrup Glazed Lobster over Caramelized Pineapple and Orzo Pilaf
Cashew Crusted Lobster with Pineapple Dipping Sauce

SHRIMP

Pan Roasted Shrimp Cocktail with Salsa Verde
Prosciutto Wrapped with Blackberry Raisin Compote and Espresso Oil
Wok-Fired with Anaheim Peppers, Pineapple and Coconut Sugar on Lemongrass Jasmine Rice
Parmesan Fried with Spicy Fra Diablo Sauce on Garlicky Arugula
Sangria Glazed with Three Citrus Rice
Shrimp and Grits with Dirty Andouille and Charred Peppers
Wasabi, Lime and Cilantro Shrimp Cocktail
Bacon Wrapped Grilled Shrimp with a Chipotle Honey Dipping Sauce
Chorizo Oil Poached over Preserved Lemon Orzo

Ancho Dusted and Grilled with a Mild Chili Cream Sauce
Shrimp Cocktail with a Blood Orange, Mango and Scallion Salsa
Spice Seared served on Grilled Cornbread Wedges with Tomato-Horseradish Butter
Grilled with a Spicy Molasses Mustard Dip
Spiced Poached with Roasted Tomatillo Salsa
Grilled Jumbo Shrimp with a Chipotle Honey Dipping Sauce
Spicy Pan Seared with a Lemon-Thyme Emulsion
Thai Red Curried with Kaffir Lime and Lemongrass Oil

Herb and Cornmeal Fried on Tasso Ham Grits
Citrus Poached Shrimp Cocktail with Tequila and Meyer Lemon Cocktail Sauce
Crisp Fried Shrimp Cakes with Mango Salsa and Spicy Chili Aioli
Fennel Scented Prawns with Shiitake Mushrooms on English Pea Risotto with Lemon Oil
Tempura Shrimp with Black Bean Sauce and Golden Pineapple Salsa
Grilled with Curry and Roasted Peanut Sauce
Poblano Peppers Stuffed with Chorizo, Shrimp and Saffron Rice
Spicy Shrimp and Red Eye Gravy over Jalapeno Grits

Palm Sugar Dusted with Caramelized Ginger Barbeque Sauce
Coconut Shrimp with a Roasted Banana Curry Sauce
Grilled Bacon-Wrapped with a Buffalo and Blue Cheese Dipping Sauce
Crisp Fried with Orange Chipotle Hollandaise
Curry Seared with a Mint and Thai Basil Salsa
Blackened Shrimp Kebobs with a Root Beer Barbeque Sauce
Pistachio Crusted with Lime and Papaya Salsa
Grilled Shrimp and Chorizo Skewers with Spicy Gazpacho

Chili Dusted with Poblano and Sausage Gravy over Mexican Rice
Shrimp and Mozzarella Strudel with a Smokey Tomato Sauce
Pan Roasted on Five Chili Grits with Roasted Garlic Oil
Shrimp with Kalamata, Sun Dried Tomatoes and Feta over Orzo
Grilled with Spiced Pistachio Mole
Thai Curry with Cilantro-Lime Couscous
Shrimp with Jalapeno and Caramelized Corn Pilaf

SHRIMP

Peppercorn Crusted over Smoked Cheddar Grits
Tequila Marinated and Grilled with Smoked Poblano and Cilantro Sour Cream
Flaming Ginger Shrimp
Bacon Wrapped with an Orange Chipotle and Honey Glaze
Sauté with Dry Vermouth, Red Chilies and Lime
Shrimp with Fried Brussels Sprout Leaves, Roasted Chestnuts and Brown Butter
Seared with Garlic, Tomatoes, Cured Olives, Pesto and Red Pepper Flakes
Grilled with Smoked Tomatoes, Wilted Arugula and Fried Italian Hot Peppers

Shrimp Tacos with Pesto and Grilled Vegetable Salsa
Tempura Shrimp on Thai Green Curry with Mache and a Caramelized Mango and Banana Chutney
Coconut Shrimp served with a Fire Roasted Red Pepper Sauce
Buffalo Fried with Horseradish Slaw
Shrimp with Asian Spices, Black Beans and Oven Dried Tomatoes
Sautéed with Prosciutto, Leeks, Roasted Plum Tomatoes and Lemon Cream
Sautéed with Garlic, Basil and a Lemon Chardonnay Sauce
Shrimp and Crab Wellington Sauce American

Caribbean Jerk Shrimp with Crispy Plantains, Macadamia Nuts and Passion Fruit Chutney
Shrimp and Crab Cannelloni
Shrimp and Scallop Sauté with Bacon and Tomato Sage Cream over Pasta
Smoked Shrimp on Caraway Bread Pudding with a Red Wine and Roasted Beet Coulis
Grilled with a Habanero and Pumpkin Seed Chimichurri
Smoked Prosciutto wrapped with Lemon-Mint Crème Fraîche
Coconut Shrimp with Caramelized Pineapple Jam and Fresh Scallions
Shrimp grilled on Rosemary Branches with Roasted Red Pepper Coulis

Popcorn Shrimp tossed with Dry Jack Cheese, Chives and Truffle Oil
Crispy with Mango Marmalade and Roasted Poblano Coulis
Pan Roasted Prawns with a Wild Mushroom Ragout and a Sun Dried Tomato Vinaigrette
Chili Seared with Queso Blanco and a Tomatillo Relish
Maple Glazed with Smoked Cheddar and a Scallion and Red Onion Salsa
Green Curry Seared with Mango Coulis
Angry Shrimp - Sriracha Glazed Shrimp tossed with diced Habañeros, Jalapeños and Chili Flakes
Prawns stuffed with a Caramelized Onion and Spinach Mousseline with a Roasted Pepper Coulis

Miso Marinated with Pickled Mango
Spicy Sriracha Shrimp with Diced Chilies and Wasabi Ranch
Shrimp Tempura with Pickled Onions and a Sweet Soy Drizzle
Coconut Beer Batter Shrimp with a Sweet Orange and Horseradish Dipping Sauce
Sautéed with Kalamarta, Toasted Garlic, Dried Chili Flakes and Feta
Shrimp and White Cheddar Grits with Crisp Bacon Lardons and Sweet Onion
Crispy Shrimp with Tamarind BBQ Sauce and Chive Rémoulade

SCALLOPS

Seared with Crispy Bacon and Spiced Carrot Beurre Blanc
Scallop and Asparagus Pan Roast with Shaved Fennel and Lemon Olive Oil
Scallops with Melted Leeks and Horseradish Gremolata over Chive Gnocchi
Pernod Poached with Pea Shoots and Sweet Corn over Orzo
Seared with Fried Brussels Sprouts and Toasted Pomegranate Seeds over Basmati Rice
Andouille Stuffed Sea Scallops with Tarragon Cream Sauce
Pan Seared with a Blood Orange Reduction
Seared on Savory Bread Pudding with Horseradish Cream Sauce

Grilled with a Wild Mushroom and Smoked Tomato Compote
Seared with Brown Butter and a Roasted Apple and Fig Compote
Red Curry Seared with Thai Sticky Rice and Papaya Slaw
Blue Cheese Crusted with Roasted Pears and Pomegranate Syrup
Chili-Orange Glazed with Wakame
Scallops with Roasted Tomato Coulis and Béarnaise Drizzle
Dill Fried with Lemon-Shallot Hollandaise
Pomegranate Glazed Lemon Pepper Scallops

Diver Sea Scallops with a Smoked Tomato Fondue
Grilled on Roasted Asparagus with a Caper and White Balsamic Reduction
Green Curry Seared with Black Bean Dal, Crispy Scallions and Mint Raita
Poblano Crusted with Roasted Parsnip Flan and Caramelized Pear Reduction
Blackened with a Pomegranate Reduction and a Cilantro Mint Salsa
Seared with Spicy Watermelon Salsa
Grilled with an Apple Cider Reduction
Scallops with Pistachio Pistou and Lemon Vinaigrette

Crispy Cornmeal Crusted with Green Chili Chutney
Spicy Scallops with Caramelized Plantains
Miso-Glazed with a Mirin Reduction
Brioche Crusted with a Warm Sesame Vinaigrette
Bay Scallops with Smoked Salmon Cream
Pistachio Encrusted over Papaya and Tangerine Puree
Half Shell Scallops with a Coriander and Lemongrass Vinaigrette
Ancho Crusted with a Green Onion Sauce

Sautéed with Tarragon Cream over Tomato Pasta Nests
Grilled with a Red Curry Aioli and Meyer Lemon Confit
Seared Diver Scallops with Fried Capers and Sherry Lemon Vinaigrette
Cornmeal Crusted with Roasted Corn and Caramelized Shallot Relish
Sautéed with Sweet Peas, Blistered Grape Tomatoes and Béarnaise
Sangria Glazed Grilled Scallops
Pan Roasted with Basil Butter Sauce
Scallops with a Hazelnut and Port Cream Sauce

SCALLOPS

Espresso Crusted with Morel Cream Sauce
Caramel Glazed with Vanilla Butter
Prosciutto Wrapped with Fontina Fondue
Cumin Dusted with Roasted Red Pepper and Tahini Vinaigrette
Blackened with a Tamarind and Caramelized Pineapple Salsa
Scallop Ceviche with Melon, Habanero and Mint
Scallops with a Champagne-Vanilla Butter Sauce

Pistachio Crusted with Brown Butter
Pan Roast with Pork Belly and Roasted Root Vegetables
Bacon-Wrapped with Jalapeno Glaze and Mango Salsa
Potato and Herb Crusted with Smoked Gouda Fondue
Honey Grilled with an Apple Cider Beurre Blanc
Sauté with Smoked Tomato Saffron Sauce
Scallop and Chorizo Kabob
Scallops with Fresh Vegetables and Ginger Cream
Scallops, Chorizo and Smoked Duck on a Rosemary Skewer
Grilled Sea Scallops Moistened with a Roasted Onion and Sherry Vinaigrette over Rice Noodles

Caramelized Diver Scallops on Thyme Pesto Polenta Scented with White Truffle Oil
Porcini Crusted with Crisp Red Rice Cake and Tomato-Saffron Broth
Grilled with a Roasted Carrot and Ginger Beurre Blanc
Sautéed with Rice Pilaf and Sweet Pepper Coulis
Champagne Poached with Red Pepper and Cucumber Relish
Crispy with a Papaya and Mango Salsa and Toasted Almond Oil
Orange Glazed with Sweet Potato Confit
Grilled with Molasses Dijon Barbeque Sauce

Seared with Whole Mustard Seed, Dijon and Tarragon Butter
Sautéed with White Beans and Rosemary over Angel Hair and Cream Sorrel Sauce
Seared with Caramelized Fennel and Crisp Potatoes drizzled with Black Truffle Oil
Salt Roasted with Bacon Braised Collards and Mascarpone Grits and a splash of Lemon Olive Oil
Orange Chili Glazed with Crispy Pork Belly, Wild Mushroom Ragout and Ginger Malt Vinaigrette
Sautéed with Melted Leeks, Broccolini, Potato Hash and Romesco Sauce
Chili Dusted with Gingered Tangerines

Cast Iron Seared with Morel Polenta, Sap Sago Cheese and Baby Arugula
Seared with Roasted Pumpkin Puree, Fried Sage, Toasted Hazelnuts and Brown Butter
Green Curry with Vanilla Braised Fennel, Baby Radishes and Crystallized Ginger Madeleine
Pan Seared with Coffee Vodka, Porcini, Cocoa and White Truffle Oil over Porchetta Pasta
Orange Chili Glazed with Ginger-Malt Vinaigrette
Sautéed with Garlic Romesco over wilted Broccoli Rabe
Scallops with Roasted Corn and Smoked Bacon over Skillet Browned Sweet Potatoes
Roasted with Red Quinoa, Black Barley and Lemon Verbena

OYSTERS

The fall and winter are the best time for oysters. I receive and serve oysters all year round, but the old saying that you should only eat oysters in the months that had an "R" in them has some merit. Also, these are the cooler months and harvesting and shipping oysters during the warm periods can be a tricky task. Cooler weather helps keep the shellfish cold during the harvesting process and during the trip from the boat to the dock.

Here on Maryland's Eastern Shore, I am often told stories of bringing in a barrel of oysters before Thanksgiving and storing it in the shed where the outside weather keep them cooled to the ideal temperature. They were perfectly chilled when there was a small amount of ice forming on the lip. The oysters held well and were eaten through Christmas and the New Year.

A great way to market oysters is as an **Oyster Roast.** A manageable start is to offer six or seven different selections. As an entrée, let the guest select three choices from the list and serve six of each selection. Complete the meal with the normal servings of soup, salad, vegetable and starch. Suggest that two guests share six different types. As an appetizer portion serve two each of their three selections. As a grand feast have a buffet style Oyster Roast with an ambitious assortment of preparations. Although most purists will want their oysters opened to order, if you anticipate a large turnout, you can open and even pre-top the shellfish. After opening, oysters do lose moisture quickly so keep opened ones covered with plastic wrap. If you can only open a limited number to order, save them for the ones eaten raw. For preparations such as oysters poached in champagne and herbs, I add the poaching liquor to the oyster on the half shell and poach them quickly in the oven. If you use the deep side of the shell, it holds the oyster and the flavorful liquid. Remember, a great oyster is a fat oyster!

OYSTERS

Half Shell with Tomato and Cucumber Relish
Oyster Beignets with Raspberry Ginger Marmalade
Oyster Shooters with Pepper Infused Vodka, Chopped Tomato, Lemon and Chives
Wood Grilled and with Spicy Barbecue Sauce and Bacon
Masa Dusted and Fried with Poblano and Red Onion Marmalade
Half Shell with a Saffron Champagne Mignonette
Tempura Battered with Candied Ginger and Sambal Aioli
Oyster Stew with Andouille and Roasted Pepper Puree
Baked with Bacon and Cognac Butter
Cornbread Crusted with Prickly Pear Vinaigrette

Oysters with Parsley and Capers tossed with a Lime Vinaigrette and served with Smoked Chili Aioli
Crunchy Panko Fried with Spicy Mango-Pineapple Relish
Cornmeal Crusted with a warm Bacon and Orange Dipping Sauce
Half Shell with Shaved Prosciutto and Coarse Cracked Pepper
Crisp Oysters with a Truffle Aioli
Cornmeal Fried with Bacon and Onion Jam
Oyster Etouffee served on Spicy Wild Mushroom Grits

OYSTERS

Oven Fired Oysters with Shaved Tasso Ham served over Spinach with Sun Dried Tomato Cream
Half Shell with Black Pepper Ponzu
Fricassee of Oysters with Bacon, Andouille, Leeks and Wild Mushrooms in Puff Pastry Shell
Oysters with Sour Apple and Sweet Onion Mignonette
Chilled Oysters with Tomatillo, Red Onion and Lime Salsa
Oysters with Apple Shallot Mignonette
Lemon Chilled with Spicy Wakame
Gold Tequila and Jalapeno Oyster Shooters
Half Shell with Meyer Lemon, Cilantro and Cucumber Mignonette
Crunchy Panko Fried with Bacon Aioli

Half Shell with Slivers of Asian Pear and Yuzu Ice
Cornmeal Crusted with Habanero Pepper and Sweet Pickle Mayonnaise
Mirin and Passion Fruit Vinaigrette
Half Shell with Malt Vinegar and Caramelized Onion
Mango and Pineapple Relish
Pan Fried with Creamy Horseradish
Baked with Prosciutto and Bulb Fennel Compote
Aged Sherry and Shallot Vinaigrette

Pickled Cucumber and Fresh Mint
Crisp Bacon and Fontina Cheese
Fresh Grated Horseradish and Smoked Ham
Half Shell with Blush Vinaigrette
Topped with Crab Imperial
Baked with Dijon and Herbed Bread Crumbs
Broiled with Rosemary Butter
Oysters with Lemon, Fennel and White Wine

Oysters Poached in Champagne
Half Shell with a Shallot-Apple Cider Mignonette
Grilled with Spicy Tarragon Butter
Scalloped Oysters in Cream
Grilled with Cracked Black Pepper and Tarragon Butter
Cornmeal Crusted with Green Chili Sauce and Ancho Sour Cream
Jalapeño Lime Oysters on the Half Shell
Classic Mignonette - Shallots, Scallions, Tarragon, Vinegar, Chives, Cracked Black Pepper

Baked with Artichokes, Chopped Spinach and Portabellas
Oysters Simmered in Roasted Shallot Beurre Blanc with Paper Thin Truffle Shavings
Oysters with Curried Crème Fraîche
Poached in White Wine with Creamy Mustard
Oysters Ceviche with Habanero, Tomato and Lime
Smoked Oysters with Spicy Three Chili BBQ Sauce

OYSTERS

Fried with Horseradish Cream and Roasted Tomato-Caramelized Corn Salsa
Crisp Fried with Red Chili Vinegar
Ancho-BBQ with a Honey Aioli
Broiled with Country Ham and Celery Cream
Jalapeno and Cornmeal Crusted and Fried with Smoked Tomato-Rémoulade Sauce
Oysters with Black Truffle Broth
Bloody Mary Shooters with Citrus and Roasted Garlic Gremolata
Crispy Oysters with Serrano Honey Aioli

Creamed with Andouille on Toasted Cornbread
Sauté with Wild Mushrooms and Rosemary Butter
Saffron Poached with Leeks and Mushrooms
Half Shell with Fennel-Coriander Mignonette
Baked in a Fennel Prosciutto Cream
Oysters with Lemon and Shallot Dressing
Oyster Cheese Gratin with Crumbled Bacon and Crisp Cracker Crust
Half Shell with Roasted Shallot and Three Peppercorn Mignonette

Grilled with Lemon Dill Vinaigrette
Chardonnay Poached with a Black Pepper Crème Fraîche and Caviar
Chipotle BBQ with Spicy Garlic Butter
Half Shell with Champagne and Chervil Vinaigrette
Half Shell with a Lemon Wasabi Sorbet
Oysters rolled in Smoked Salmon with a Yuzu Soy Sauce
Buffalo Style Breaded with a Red Hot Sauce flavored Ranch Dressing
Cornmeal and Sesame Crusted with a Ginger and Red Onion Jam

Pan Fried with Lemon Butter Sauce
Half Shell with a Fresh Fennel and Leek Relish
Half Shell with Pepper Vodka Cocktail Sauce
Baked with Crab and a Port Wine Reduction Drizzle
Baked with a Artichoke, Spinach and Smoked Gouda Fondue
Champagne Vinegar and Grated Fresh Horseradish
Chorizo and Chick Pea Batter Fried with Scallion Sour Cream Dip
Half Shell with Charred Serrano Chili and Malt Vinaigrette

Half Shell with Chilled Lump Crab and Lemon Crème Fraîche
Firecracker Oysters with Apple Cider Vinaigrette and Red Pepper Flakes
Oyster Pancakes with Caramelized Corn and Black Bean Salsa
Oyster Fritters with Sriracha Honey
Buttermilk Fried with a Pickled Okra Tartar Sauce
Crisp Fried on Smoky Grits with Chili Vinegar
Oysters with a Pernod Sorbet and Chive Crème Fraîche
Half Shell Oysters with a Green Tomato Relish

CRAB

Crab is one of the great delicacies. Its fresh sweet flavor can easily stand on its own and you must take precaution not to overpower its delicate flavor. This does not mean that accompanying sauces and ingredients can't bring that burst of flavor or character. I worked and lived on Maryland's Eastern Shore for many years and I will always prefer high quality fresh crab meat when available. There is a lot of quality pasteurized crabmeat becoming more and more available. One of its high points is the consistently large pieces of meat. In many of these products you will find the huge lumps throughout the entire can. This differs of course of the fresh product in which a pound of fresh crab meat will have been packed with large lumps on top and still high quality but smaller pieces of meat underneath. Some of the pasteurized crabmeat now available is somewhat drier and lacks the favor of fresh crab but it does have a few good points. The pasteurized meat's texture seems to hold together better and is great for sautéing. Also pasteurized is much easier to store and handle. Fresh crabmeat holds its high quality for only about three days at most and only if truly picked fresh. Pasteurized can be kept much longer and is there when you need it.

CRAB

Crabtini - with Jumbo Lump Crab, Diced Avocado, Pico de Gallo and Chili Sour Cream
Quick Fried Dungeness Crab with Spicy Chili and Peanut Sauce
Butter Poached Crab on Lemon Orzo with White Truffle Oil
Crab Cake Crusted with Yukon Gold Potatoes served with Spicy Slaw and Avocado Salsa
Jumbo Lump Crab Cakes with a Caribbean Jerk and Red Pepper Puree
Crab Sauté with a Roasted Corn and Citrus Sauce
King Crab tossed in a Coconut Sugar Glaze with Fresh Pineapple over Mint Jasmine Rice
Pan Roasted Crab Cake with Tomato Relish and a Balsamic Reduction

Blue Crab Fingers with a Ginger Beurre Blanc
Lightly Battered Soft Shell Crab with Chive Oil
Pineapple and Mango Crab Cake with Spicy Aioli
Steamed Alaskan King Crab Legs with Champagne Mustard Butter and Crostini
Risotto of Crisp Soft Shell Crab, Roasted Corn and Grilled Scallions
Panko Crusted Crab Cake with Mango Slaw and Harissa Aioli
Chili Dusted Soft Shell Crab with a Poblano and Roasted Tomatillo Salsa
Saffron Butter Poached King Crab with Fresh Scallion

Soft Shell Crab with Kaffir Lime and Lemongrass Butter
Maryland Blue Crab Cake with a Pink Peppercorn and Tarragon Aioli
Dungeness Crab Sauté with Fuji Apple Slaw and Watercress Vinaigrette
Crispy Soft Shell Crab with a Fresh Fennel Peperonata
Crab Cake with a Carrot, Coriander and Scallion Beurre Blanc
Grilled Crab Cake with a Mango and Sweet Chili Coulis
Pan Roasted Crab with Roasted Pepper Butter
Crab Cake with Tomato-Ginger Vinaigrette

CRAB

Sautéed Lump Crab with Roasted Corn Relish, and Chipotle Aioli
Grilled Scallion Crab Cake with Creole Sauce
Pan Roasted Crab Cake with Salsa Verde and a Poblano-Red Pepper Coulis
Pan Seared Crab topped with a Roasted Shallot and While Wine Beurre Blanc
Pecan Crusted Soft Shell Crabs with Whiskey Lemon Butter
Dungeness Crab with a Roasted Artichoke Rémoulade
Crab Cakes with a Spicy Lime Salsa and Cilantro Aioli
Red Crab Sauté with a Chervil Butter Pan Sauce

Dungeness Crab with Spicy Mango Coulis
Butter Poached Alaska King Crab with a Gala Apple Relish and Vanilla Lobster Emulsion
Crab Cake with Lime-Cilantro Aioli
Roasted Corn and Crab Pudding
Jumbo Lump Crab Sauté with Sweet Peas and Tomato Bits with Lemon Crème Fraîche
Dungeness Crab sprinkled with Saffron Salt and served with Chive Aioli
Black Sesame Crusted Soft Shells with Piquillo Peppers and Sweet Herbs

Pan Roasted Dungeness Crab with a Chive Oil and Orange Beurre Blanc
Grilled King Crab with Harissa Aioli
Pan-Fried Crab Cakes with Scallion Beurre Blanc
Crabmeat Sautéed with Parma Ham on Puff Pastry with a Champagne Mustard Hollandaise
Sautéed Soft Shell Crabs with Olive Oil, Capers and Dry Vermouth
Chilled Crab with Lemon-Chipotle Mayonnaise
Jumbo Lump Crab Cakes with Roasted Chili Tartar Sauce
Tempura Soft Shells with Lemon Fennel Chutney

Cashew Crusted Soft Shell Crabs
Pan Fried Crab Cakes with Smoked Sweet Pepper Butter Sauce
Cracked Crab with Chili Mango Sauce
Blackened Soft Shell Crabs
Crab Cakes with Lemon Thyme Beurre Blanc
Sautéed Soft Shell Crabs with Candied Ginger Lime Sauce
Crab and Wild Mushroom Sauté on Crusted Parmigianino Polenta with a Lemon Olive Oil Drizzle
Pretzel Crusted Crab Cake with a Spiced Raisin Chutney

Coconut Crab Cakes served with a Spicy Harissa Sauce
Crab Sauté with Caramelized Corn, Roasted Shallots and Diced Jalapeños
Spicy Crab Cakes with a Blood Orange Coulis
Chilled Crab with Tomatillo and Rice Vinegar Salsa
Panko Crusted Soft Shells with Braised Chive Scented Leeks and Chipotle Aioli
Scallion and Red Crab Pancake with a Sweet Soy and Sesame Butter
Pan Seared King Crab with Green Papaya, Lemongrass and Mint
Tempura Soft Shell Crab with a Honey-Chili Glaze
Grilled Soft Shells with Captain Morgan Spiced Rum Mango Sauce

CLAMS

Dutch Oven Clam Bake with Bacon, Chorizo and Roasted Corn
Steamer Clams Stuffed with a Meyer Lemon and Caramelized Onion Breadcrumb Stuffing
Fried with a Roasted Garlic, Blue Cheese and Hot Sauce Dip
Clam Pan Roast with Shitakes, Truffles and Thyme
Little Neck Clams on the Half Shell with Champagne-Green Peppercorn Mignonette
Clams with Pancetta and Roasted Garlic
Vermouth Steamed Clams with Artichoke Confit

Sautéed Little Necks with Garlic, White Wine, Cilantro and Lime
Pan Roasted with Chorizo, Oranges and Saffron
Grilled on the Half Shell with Crisp Pancetta and Caramelized Shallots
Cherrystone Clams and Andouille in a Saffron and White Wine Broth
Little Neck Clams on the Half Shell with Grilled Scallion and Red Pepper Relish
Clam Pan Roast with Bacon, Garlic and Chilies
Half Shell with Meyer Lemon and Chive Vinaigrette

Steamed with Capers, Red Onions and Brown Butter
Clams in a Walnut and Smoked Tomato Sauce with Fresh Basil over Orzo
Steamed with Chilies, Cilantro and Fresh Mint
Clams with Fermented Black Bean and Caramelized Ginger Sauce
Steamed in Thyme Broth with Lemon Dumplings
Steamed in a Grilled Scallion and Wild Mushroom Broth
Pan Roasted with Italian Sausage and Sun Dried Tomatoes

Grilled Clams with Spicy Chili Vinegar Dipping Sauce
Steamed in a Smoky Tomato Broth with Chorizo and Grilled Scallions
Roasted with Chimichurri Sauce and Sweet Onion and Grilled Pepper Relish
Half Shell with Roasted Tomatillo and Salsa Verde
Littlenecks stuffed with Garlic Sausage, Roasted Fennel and Caramelized Leeks
Pan Roasted with Smoked Chilies and Bacon
Broiled with Charred Chilies and Cajun Butter

Manila Clams Sautéed with Spicy Kimchee and served over Fried Rice
Clams Stuffed with Shrimp and Grilled Scallions and served with a Citrus Rémoulade
Pan Roasted with Black Beans, Sweet Onions, Sausage and a Vermouth Butter Sauce
Clams stuffed with Tasso Ham, Sweet Peppers and Onions with a Cilantro Crème Fraîche
Sautéed with Star Fruit, Thai Basil and Rice Wine
Littleneck Clams with a Smoked Paprika and Olive Oil Broth over Fire Charred Bruschetta
Roasted Clams in a Garlic and Fennel Broth

Steamed in Nut Brown Ale with Oranges and Grilled Leeks
Sautéed with Fennel and Green Tomatoes over Linguini
Littlenecks tossed with Sesame Butter, Mint, Thai Basil and Diced Chilies
Clams with Pancetta and Sun Dried Tomatoes over a Bed of Spinach Angle Hair

MUSSELS

Mussels with Tomato Chorizo Broth over Orzo Pilaf
Cast Iron Roasted with Crumbled Italian Sausage, Sun Dried Tomatoes and Chianti
Mussels with Leeks and Caramelized Garlic Cream
Slow Simmered with Sun Dried Tomatoes, Fresh Basil and Meyer Lemon
Mussels in a Caramelized Shallot and Poblano Broth with Chive Oil
Steamed with Sake and a Sweet Miso and Scallion Sauce
Simmered with Bacon, Apple Cider and Fennel
Thai Mussels with Coconut Milk, Roasted Chilies, Thai Basil and Mint

Tender Mussels sautéed in a Pernod Cream Sauce served over Saffron Pasta with Caviar
Steamed with Fresh Bulb Fennel and Limoncello
New Zealand Green Tip Mussel Pan Roast with a White Wine and Saffron Broth
Slow Simmered with Roasted Tomatoes and Fresh Basil
Mussels with Summer Tomatoes, Fresh Tarragon and Meyer Lemon Cream
Mussels "Paella Style" steamed with Sofrito, Spanish Chorizo and Black Trumpet Mushrooms
Pale Ale Steamed Mussels served with Sourdough Bruschetta
Smoked Mussels with a Roasted Tomato and Red Onion Chutney

Mussels in a Spicy Black Bean Sauce
Steamed in Tarragon Dijon Emulsion
Mussels in Basil, Olive Oil, Garlic and Tomato Broth Served over Crostini
Sautéed with Olive Oil Prosciutto, and Roasted Peppers
Slow Simmered in a Cured Olive Tapenade
Steamed with Chicory and Scallions
Smoked Mussel Fritters with a Roasted Red Pepper and Sun Dried Tomato Aioli
Emerald Tip Mussels with Grilled Fennel and Dark Beer Broth

Mussels with Red Chili Flakes, Roasted Garlic, Muscat and Cream
Steamed in White Ale with Sliced Shallots, Celery Root and Fresh Bay Leaves
Simmered with Gewürztraminer, Shaved Fresh Fennel and Thyme
Mussels with a Smoked Tomato and Curry Broth
Mussels in a Saffron and Burnt Brandy Broth with Coconut Milk
Simmered with Hard Cider, Blue Cheese and Granny Smith Apples
Steamed with Bouillabaisse Butter and served over a Charred Baguette
Mussels with Nut Brown Ale, Orange Zest and Roasted Leeks

Mussels simmered with Garlic Sausage, Root Vegetables and Parsnip Cream
Mussels with Grilled Scallions and Horseradish served with Red Onion Jam Crostini
Coconut Green Curry Mussels with Diced Green Chilies and Cilantro
Mussels in Kimchee and Pickled Onions
Margarita Mussels simmered in Tequila, Lime, Cilantro and Red Jalapenos with Sea Salt Crostini
Mussels in Chili and Sun Dried Tomato Broth

MUSSELS

Saffron Cream Sauce over Angel Hair Pasta
Mussels with Fresh Ginger, Red Curry Paste and Coconut Milk
Mussels with Vermouth and Green Onions
Steamed in a Tomato and Roasted Fennel Broth
Baked Mussels Stuffed with Smoked Salmon and Dill Breadcrumbs
Smokey Skillet Roasted
Steamed with Chorizo, Cilantro, Lime and Dark Beer
Chilled Marinated Mussels in a Rice Wine and Sesame Vinaigrette

Steamed in a Grilled Onion and Poblano Broth
Thai Red Curry Mussels simmered in Coconut Milk
Steamed with Black Peppercorns and Garlic with Smoked Red Pepper Coulis
Mussels and Littleneck Clams with an Andouille and Fennel Broth
Sautéed with Bacon in a Creole Mustard and Cognac Cream Sauce
Baked Stuffed Mussels with Bacon, Shallots, and Apples
Mussels in a Smoked Tomato and Roasted Garlic Broth
Steamed in Tequila, Lime and Adobo

Sherry Ginger Marinade Mussels
Steamed in Cumin, Fennel and Ouzo
Smoked Mussel Ceviche
Mussels in Fresh Ginger, Lemongrass and Thai Basil Broth
Mussels with a Pernod Cream Sauce
Emerald Tip Mussels with Sausage and Scallion Stuffing
Simmered with Chorizo in a Peppery Broth served over Orzo
Steamed in Saffron and White Wine and Finished with Cream

Mussels simmered in a Vodka and Green Curry Broth
Sautéed with Oranges, Fennel and Mint
Pan Roast with Lemongrass, Kaffir Lime and Coconut Milk served over Jasmine Rice Cake
Steamed Moroccan Style with Harissa and Roasted Tomatoes
Mussels with Caramelized Ginger and Mint over Cellophane Noodles
Pan Roasted with Chorizo, Scallions and Jalapeños and finished with a Tequila Pan Reduction
Slow simmered with Crumbled Italian Hot Sausage, Tomatoes and Escarole
Mussels with Andouille, Roasted Corn and Sweet Red Peppers

Mussels simmered in Ginger Beer with Wild Mushrooms and Toasted Pine Nuts
Mussels with Kaffir Lime and Green Curry over Saba Noodles
Mussels with Gewürztraminer, Fresh Snipped Chives and Crème Fraîche
Mussels simmered with Blood Oranges, Chipotle and Dark Beer
Coconut Green Curry with Cilantro, Lime and Diced Chilies over Crispy Sweet Potato Straws
Cold Mussels with a Fresh Lemon, Garlic and Parsley Chimichurri
Steamed with Pancetta, Smoked Tomato, Toasted Garlic and Broccoli Rabe
Red Curried Mussels over Sweet Potato Matchsticks

CALAMARI

Crispy Calamari tossed with Pickled Cherry Peppers, Arugula and Lemon Aioli
Parmesan-Panko Crusted with a Spicy Sun Dried Tomato Sauce
Calamari with Roasted Garlic, Gaeta Olives, Capers and Golden Raisons
Crispy served with a Spicy Red Onion Rémoulade
Salt and Cracked Black Pepper Calamari with a Cucumber and Jalapeno Salsa
Calamari with Smoked Tomatoes, Lemon and Fried Capers
Calamari with Fried Chilies and Sweet Papaya Dip
Fried with Pepperoncini and Lime

Habanero and Panko Crusted Fried Calamari served with a Sweet Onion and Honey Dipping Sauce
Blue Corn Fried with a Cranberry Chipotle dipping Sauce
Calamari stuffed with Lamb Sausage, Black Garlic and Currants
Horseradish and Panko Crusted served over Ratatouille
Crispy Calamari with White Truffle Aioli and Chopped Fresh Herbs
Spicy Calamari tossed with Feta, Kalamata Olives and Lemon Olive Oil
Polenta Dusted with a Spicy Charred Onion Marinara
Crisp Calamari with Orange Chili Oil, Pasilla and Caper Sour Cream

With Fried Squash Blossoms, Gaeta Olive Tapenade, Caramelized Artichoke Petals and Garlic Aioli
Pretzel Crusted Fried Calamari with a Brandy and Molasses Mustard
Crispy Calamari with Wasabi Honey
Buttermilk Fried with a Chipotle and Smoked Tomato Sauce
Grilled Calamari smothered in a Roasted Garlic and Meyer Lemon Scampi Sauce
Cornmeal Crusted with Jalapeños, Pickled Carrots and a Creole Rémoulade
Fried Calamari dusted with Wasabi Powder and Meyer Lemon Infused Sea Salt
Crispy Calamari with a Cilantro-Brown Sugar Aioli and an Ancho and Tomato Chutney

Calamari with Spinach and a Saffron Cream Sauce
Fried Calamari over Wilted Escarole with Roasted Red Peppers and Lemon Zest
Spicy Calamari with Garlic Sriracha and Chopped Mint and Green Chilies
Grilled with Roasted Cauliflower Tabouleh, Mint and Thai Basil
Ginger Calamari over Wakame with Wasabi Aioli and a Sweet Soy Drizzle
Crispy Calamari with a Black Bean Chili Sauce
Calamari with Fried Parsley and a Sun Dried Tomato Sauce
Crisp Rice Crusted with Spicy Slaw and a Chili Vinaigrette

Lightly Fried with a Meyer Lemon Citrus Dipping Sauce
Crispy with Saffron Yogurt and a Charred Tomato and Onion Compote
Calamari Fra Diavolo sautéed with Hot Peppers, Oven Dried Tomatoes and Roasted Garlic
Crispy Calamari with Spicy Chili Oil and a Coconut and Cilantro Aioli
Garlic Grilled Calamari
Calamari with a Lemon and Cracked Black Pepper Aioli
Fried Calamari tossed with Lime Aioli, Hot Banana Peppers and Chopped Parsley
Sautéed with a Spicy Cured Olive Pomodoro Sauce

CALAMARI

Crispy Calamari Steaks with Sweet Soy Scented Greens and a Vietnamese Dipping Sauce
Ginger Dusted Fried Calamari with Seaweed Salad and Chili Garlic Sauce
Panko Fried with a Smoked Tomato and Harissa Sauce
Fried with Crispy Lemon Rings and Bourbon Cocktail Sauce
Fried with a Roasted Shallot Cocktail Sauce
Panko Crusted with a Smoked Paprika Aioli
Cracked Peppercorn Dusted with a Spicy Lemon-Tomato Coulis
Pan Seared, Green Curry Marinated served over Red Lentil Stew

Crispy Fried with Diced English Cucumbers, Toasted Garlic and a Cubanelle Rémoulade
Wasabi Dusted and Fried tossed with a Citrus and Toasted Soy Vinaigrette
Tempura Battered with a Sweet-Sour Aioli
Grilled with a Spicy Caper Tapenade
Chili Dusted Fried Calamari with a Spicy Mango Mole Sauce
Flash Fried with Pickled Red Peppers and Lime
Calamari with a Drizzle of Sun Dried Tomato Oil and served with Parmesan Peppercorn Aioli
Lightly Fried with a Green Goddess Tartar Sauce

Crispy Calamari with a Roasted Banana and Miso Dressing
Graham Cracker Fried with Spicy Tomato Aioli
Crispy Calamari with Citrus and Ancho Sour Cream
Chili-Lime Fried with Roasted Tomatillo Salsa
Cornmeal Crusted Fried Calamari with Meyer Lemon Butter and Crushed Red Pepper Flakes
Sautéed Calamari served over Wilted Swiss Chard and Chickpeas with Saffron Aioli
Tempura Battered Calamari with a Lime-Soy Vinaigrette and Wasabi Dipping Sauce
Blue Corn Crusted Calamari with Meyer Lemon and Chipotle Tartar Sauce and Green Chili Oil

Calamari with Cherry Pepper Butter
Calamari with Harissa and Sweet Chili Sauce
Ginger Calamari with Ponzu Sauce
Tempura with a Sweet Thai Chili Aioli
Crispy Calamari with Sun Dried Tomato and Roasted Pepper Concassé
Served with Caramelized Onion Rémoulade
Five Spice Crusted Calamari with Chipotle Dipping Sauce

Fried with Fresh Basil and Green Onion Aioli
Calamari with a Roasted Piquillo Pepper Dipping Sauce
Spicy Fried with Chili Oil and a Lime and Cilantro Relish
Buttermilk Marinated with a Lemon and Roasted Poblano Aioli
Spice Dusted with Roasted Pepper Crème Fraîche
Sautéed with Sliced Green Olives, Diced Hot Peppers and Chopped Scallions

Crispy Ginger Fried and tossed with Diced Papaya and Chopped Peanuts served
with a Lime Chili Dipping Sauce

VEGETARIAN

I'm not going to make a distinction here between vegan, non vegan, dairy, egg and so forth. You will want to make those decisions for your operation depending on your particular customer's wants and needs. Many operators feel that offering a simple plate of whatever vegetables available for that day may be a suitable solution to vegetarian requests but by having a true selection of vegetarian entrees you can show that you welcome this group of customers and their non-vegetarian friends. Try to include at least one complex carbohydrate in your entrée to fulfill the balance needed for a complete meal. Whole grains are a good source of complex carbohydrates and these would include brown rice, buckwheat, amaranth, wheat germs and so forth. A convenient way to bring these whole grains to the table is to use whole grain pastas, breads, wraps or even burrito shells and whole wheat chips for nachos in a dish. Whole grain cereals might be used as a crust or coating for a deep fried selection. Legumes are another good source of complex carbohydrates as well as many starchy vegetables.

VEGETARIAN

Oatmeal Crusted Vegetable Cakes served on Roasted Red Pepper Puree with Harissa Aioli
Quinoa Stuffed Cabbage with Rosemary Tomato Sauce
Nutmeat and Brown Rice Loaf with Braised Red Chard, Mashed Rutabagas and Savory Herb Gravy
Goat Cheese, Roasted Vegetable and Tofu Burrito with Red Pepper Sauce and Avocado Mousse
Coconut Curry Cauliflower over Brown Basmati Rice Pilaf with Raison and Fig Compote
All Bran Crusted Ginger Tofu with Coconut Jasmine Rice, Blood Oranges and Baby Broccoli
Moroccan Winter Vegetable Stew over Sweet Potato Couscous with a Cucumber and Cilantro Raita
Eggplant Roulades stuffed with Wild Mushroom Duxelles and Brown Rice

Lentil and Chanterelle Ragu with Roasted Chestnuts, Mustard Greens and Black Truffle Butter
Smoked Tofu Vegetable Chili over a Red Bean and Golden Yukon Hash
Crispy Sun Dried Tomato Polenta Cakes with Wild Mushroom and Roasted Garlic Compote
Curry Spiced Lentil and Quinoa Cake with a Poblano Cream Sauce
Spaghetti Squash with Black Bean Meatballs in a Smoked Tomato and Red Bell Pepper Sauce
Phyllo Dough Strudel of Black Lentils, Pecans, Mushrooms, Fresh Herbs and Fontina Cheese
Seared Baby Artichokes with an Orange Red Miso Glaze, Seared Tofu and Truffle Oil
Grilled Artichokes and Roasted Fennel served over Barley and Red Chard Risotto with Toasted Nuts

Far East Hot Noodle with Napa Cabbage, Broccolini and Shitake Mushrooms topped
with Crushed Peanuts and Thai Basil

Spicy Gratin of Chickpeas, Red Lentils, Mushrooms and Caramelized Onions between
layers of Roasted Eggplant and Garlic Mashed Potatoes with a Crust of Goat Cheese Breadcrumbs

Sloppy Joe of Minced Vegetables in a Spicy Oven Dried Tomato Sauce served
with White Cheddar in a Whole Wheat Bread Bowl

Roasted Carrot Amaranth Risotto with Goat Cheese and Fresh Tarragon
Truffle, Red Lentil and Chanterelle Ragout on Onion Polenta with Pine Nuts and Thyme
Three Bean Griddle Cake with Harissa Braised Collards and Tamarind-Rainbow Lentil Sambal

VEGETARIAN

Black Sesame and Cornmeal Crusted Oyster Mushrooms with a Spicy Red Bean-Poblano Sauce

Five Layer Stack with Whole Wheat Tortillas, Caramelized Plantains, Smoky Black Bean Puree,
Oven Dried Tomatoes, Habanero Salsa Verde and Cashew Sour Cream

Smoked Tofu Vegetable Chili over a Kidney Bean and Golden Yukon Hash
Edamame Gnocchi with Wild Mushrooms, Roasted Carrots and a Sweet Miso Pesto
Semolina Griddle Cakes with Collards, Tamarind-Red Lentil Puree and Spicy Coconut Chutney
Crisp Tofu with Horseradish Mashed Sweet Potatoes, Grilled Asparagus and a Cabernet Reduction
Grilled Portobello stuffed with Pistachio Mint Bulgur and a Lemon Apricot Vinaigrette
Seared Red Rice Cake and Red Coconut Curry with Caramelized Pineapple and Toasted Peanuts
Tofu and Eggplant Ravioli with Grilled Seasonal Vegetables and a Cashew Cream Sauce
Artichoke, Roasted Fennel and Seitan Sausage over a Barley, Shallot and Walnut Risotto

Maple Glazed Smoked Tempeh with Grilled Asparagus, Garlic and
Horseradish Mashed Sweet Potatoes

Peanut Crusted Black Bean Falafel Cakes with Feta and a Chili-Cucumber Greek Yogurt
Cannelloni stuffed with Grilled Fennel and Roasted Chestnuts with a Smoked Mushroom Jus
Sweet Peppers Stuffed with Couscous and Asparagus
Sliced Potato and Caramelized Vegetable Lasagna with Farmer Cheese and Creole Sauce
Lentil Stew with Chick Peas and Fall Vegetables over Grilled Polenta
Whole Wheat Pasta Shells stuffed with Savory Cabbage and Leeks
Garden Eggplant with Grilled Peppers, Fontina and a Yellow Tomato Concassé
Seared Black Rice Cake with Green Coconut Curry, Roasted Root Vegetables and Lemongrass Tofu

Grilled Artichokes with an Orange Miso Glaze, Seared Tofu and Truffle Oil
Spinach and Brown Rice Cakes with Black Bean Salsa
Smoked Paprika Tofu with Roasted Eggplant, Celery Root Matchsticks and Braised Mustard Seeds
Manicotti with a Mushroom, Spinach and Toasted Hazelnut Stuffing
Cannelloni Beans, Roasted Garlic, Fennel Seitan Sausage, Fried Sage and Meyer Lemon Olive Oil
Brown Rice Tempura Vegetables with Spicy Hoisin Sauce
Wild Mushroom, Asparagus and Whole Wheat Pastry Napoleon
Leek and Portabella Pie in a Whole Wheat Crust with Red Pepper Coulis

Baked Polenta with Grilled Vegetables and Fontina with Tapenade over Sesame Buckwheat Noodles
Grilled Corn Cakes with Fried Cabbage and Fennel Seed
Roasted Vegetable Hummus tossed with Garlic Spaetzle
Muesli Crusted Croquettes of Broccoli and Quinoa with Harvest Vegetable Puree and Mushrooms
Fresh Fennel, Seitan Sausage and Poblano Pepper Creole served over Toasted Amaranth
Grilled Asparagus and Mustard Green Spring Roll with Sun Dried Tomato and
Gaeta Olive Tapenade with a Pine Nut and Garlic Gremolata

Deep Fried Whole Wheat Wrap of Falafel and Black Beans served with
Lettuce, Tomato, Cucumbers and a Chili-Feta Aioli

TEX-MEX

Most of these can be interchanged as Burritos, Enchilada, Tacos, Chimichanga and Quesadillas and many will also work as fillings for Chilies Rellenos. An important detail for the Tex-Mex menu is to add some flash to your side dishes. If it is going to be "rice and beans" offer great rice and beans. Add real value and show some interest by including non-traditional accompaniments such as honey fried plantains or spicy Tex-Mex seasoned corn on the cob that's been wrapped in bacon. Check the vegetable, potato and rice categories of this guide on pages *142,148 and154* and find something that fits your style and food cost allowance.

Four Layer Stack of Chorizo, Smoked Tomatoes, Cheesy Texas Toast, Roasted Peppers
Roasted Duck Tostada with Goat Cheese and Cucumber-Banana Pepper Relish
Lobster Tacos with Charred Tomatoes, Cubanelle Relish and Lemon Cilantro Dressing
Seared Scallop and Charred Asparagus Quesadilla with Avocado and Ginger Salsa
Five Alarm Chili served with Grilled Jalapeño Polenta Wedges
Spicy Duck Enchiladas with Salsa Verde and Scallion Sour Cream
Spicy Beef Tongue Taco
Ancho Chicken and Charred Tomato Chimichanga

Citrus Pork Caritas with Queso Blanco, Roasted Corn Arepas and Avocado
Surf And Turf Tacos with Chili Rubbed Steak and Butter Poached Lobster, Lime-Avocado Cream
Grilled Vegetable Burrito with Tomatillo Mole Sauce and Enchilado Cheese
Roast Chicken Quesadilla with Tomatoes, Avocado Relish, Cotija Cheese and Cilantro Sour Cream
Chili-Maple Grilled Sweet Potato Tacos with Roasted Vegetables and Ancho Crema
Pulled Pork Braised in Negro Modelo with Manchego, Roasted Tomatillo and Avocado Mousse
Flash Fried Popcorn Shrimp with Queso, Lettuce, Pico de Gallo, Cilantro Ranch in a Jalapeno Wrap

Red Snapper Tacos with Caramelized Pineapple Salsa
Grilled Piquillo Peppers with Chorizo and Melted Manchego
Fish Tacos with Picked Red Cabbage, Queso Fresco, Diced Tomatillo and Chipotle Lime Aioli
Skirt Steak Asado with Chimichurri and Roasted Plantains
Pork Quesadilla with Oaxaca Cheese, Shredded Spicy Cabbage and a Fig-Habanero Sauce
Sweet Potato Tamale with Crushed Pecan Butter
Chipotle Braised Short Ribs with Roasted Tomato Gravy and Asadero Cheese
Orange and Sherry Marinated Shrimp Cocktail with a Habanero Aioli

Chorizo and Goat Cheese Tamale with Thyme and Brown Butter Roasted Vegetables
Charred Serrano and Chicken Quesadilla with Smoked Tomato Relish and Cilantro Sour Cream
Short Rib and Wild Mushroom Empanadas
Grilled Shrimp Tacos with Corn and Avocado Relish and Meyer Lemon Crème
Churrasco Style Skirt Steak with Grilled Asparagus, Roasted Portobello and Chimichurri
Chili Roasted Chicken Enchilada with Smoked Poblano-Tomatillo Sauce and Melted Queso
Ahi Tuna Empanada with Bacon, Scallions, Chèvre and Avocado Mousse

Cornmeal Crusted Chilies Rellenos stuffed with Roasted Eggplant and
Manchego Cheese with a Smoked Pepper Sauce

TEX-MEX

Pork and Chorizo Pot Stickers with a Grilled Fruit and Honey Chutney
Southwest Chicken Wrap with Warm Queso, Grilled Onions, Pico de Gallo and Southwestern Ranch

Achiote Chicken Taquitos with Fire Roasted Salsa and a
Charred Vandalia Onion and Caramelized Sweet Corn Compote

Spicy Potato Tacos with Carnitas
Short Rib Mole with Chopped Peanuts and Grilled Scallions
Shrimp, Caramelized Onion and Cilantro Pesto Tamale
Crisp Tortilla Stack of Melted Pepper Jack, Roasted Poblano, Smoked Tomatoes, Breaded and Fried
Jalapeno Slices and Drunken Black Beans topped with Chili Sour Cream

Chiles Rellenos with Smoked Shrimp and Queso Fresco
Chorizo and Crab Tamale with Lime Guacamole
Grilled Shrimp Quesadillas with Caramelized Peach Salsa
Spicy Shrimp Tostada with Roasted Tomatillo Sauce and Goat Cheese
Butter Poached Lobster, Grilled Pear and Brie Quesadilla
Chili Rellenos stuffed with White Cheddar, Black Beans and Fresh Cilantro
Wild Mushroom and Crab Tamale with Adobo Chili Salsa

Grilled Lobster Enchilada with Mangos, Roasted Red Peppers and a Tequila Cream Sauce
Chili Crusted Chicken Burrito with Sharp Cheese, Roasted Tomatoes and Tomatillo Salsa
Braised Brisket Enchiladas with Three Pepper Rice, Poblano Chili Sauce and Queso Asadero
Grilled Halibut Tacos with Chipotle Sour Cream, Mango Salsa and Jalapeno Olive Tapenade
Roasted Pork Quesadilla with Green Apples, Queso Fresco, and Ancho Salsa
Asada Burrito with Wild Mushrooms, Caramelized Onions, Pepper Jack and Queso Fresco
Duck Confit Quesadilla with Spicy Blackberry Relish and Mint Sour Cream
Dry Rubbed Chicken Quesadilla with Tomato Relish and Ranch Crème Fraîche

Blackened Salmon Chimichanga with Pepper Jack, Avocados and Tomatillo-Black Bean Salsa
Sweet Potato, Roasted Corn and Grilled Pear Empanadas
Chipotle and Wild Mushroom Braised Short Ribs
Crisp Potato and Chorizo Tortilla
Shredded Pork Taquitos with Roasted Tomatillo Salsa and Goat Cheese
Charred Corn Guacamole with Chips
Slow Roasted Pork and Black Bean Chili with Green Onion Corn Cakes
Tex-Mex Meatloaf with Red Chili Glaze and Cheddar Mashed Potatoes

Poblano Chili and Maple Glazed Beef with Fried Plantains
Lobster and Roasted Garlic Burrito with Colby, Smoked Peppers and Ancho Salsa
Crab Quesadilla with Tropical Fruit and Fresh Cilantro
Grilled Lobster Tacos with Serrano and Avocado Relish
Roasted Poblano stuffed with Shrimp and Goat Cheese with a Pumpkin Seed Crust

Braised Lamb Short Rib Quesadilla with
Modelo Roasted Onions, Queso Blanco and Piquillo Pepper Vinaigrette

PASTA COMBINATIONS AND TOPPINGS

Change the entire texture of a pasta dish by changing the type of pasta. Flavored pastas not only add another layer of taste but offer the opportunity to add color to the dish.

Black Pepper Fettuccini with Fresh Spinach in a Truffle Alfredo Sauce
Pappardelle with Braised Short Ribs, Roasted Corn and Caramelized Carrots in a Rosemary Beef Jus
Bucatini with Chorizo, Smoked Tomato, Caramelized Leeks and Charred Red Peppers
Sage and Hazelnut Gnocchi with Wild Mushrooms and Prosciutto in Brown Butter
Pepperoncini, Gaeta Olives and Feta with Oregano and Olive Oil Sautéed Cucumbers over Linguini
Blackened Shrimp and Pasta in a Smoked Tomato and Roasted Poblano Cream Sauce
Fusilli with Lamp Bolognese and Goat Cheese

Crab and Emmental Alfredo with a Mushroom and Tomato Ragout
Thai Dusted Shrimp with Grilled Portobello and a Red Curry Sauce on Rice Noodles
Sun Dried Tomato Fettuccine with Lobster, Snap Peas and Tomatoes in Brandy and Lobster Butter

Roasted Pumpkin Tortellini with Mushroom and
Toasted Pumpkin Seeds in a Red Peppercorn Beurre Blanc

Cracked Black Peppercorn Gnocchi with Morel Mushrooms and Mascarpone Cream
Butternut Squash and Gorgonzola Mezzaluna with Brown Butter and Sage
Orecchiette with Seared Shrimp and Grilled Vegetables tossed in a Goat Cheese Béchamel

Shredded Duck with Toasted Pine Nuts, Wilted Arugula, Caramelized Brussels Sprouts and Pancetta
Fresh Fettuccini with Red Wine Braised Rabbit, Sun Dried Tomatoes and Wild Mushrooms
Tagliatelle with Slow Braised Pork, Porcini, Radicchio and Marsala
Lemon Thyme Gnocchetti with Cabernet Braised Beef
Jalapeno Agnolotti with Blackened Mahi-Mahi and Manchego Cheese
Rigatoni with Pancetta, Spicy Sausage, Caramelized Onion and Sage in Roasted Garlic Olive Oil
Lemon Zest Fettuccini with Salmon, Heirloom Tomatoes and Tarragon Steamed Artichokes

Agnolotti with Caramelized Corn and a Bacon Cream Sauce
Rigatoni with Chorizo Bolognese, Arugula and Queso Fresco
Ricotta Gnocchi tossed in a Fall Vegetable Ragout with Toasted Pistachios
Sweet Potato Tortellini with Chianti Braised Beef, Roasted Cipollini, Parmesan, Horseradish Cream
Bacon and White Cheddar Tortellini with a Rosemary Demi-glace
Black Pepper Fettuccini with Smoked Salmon and a Dill Nutmeg Cream
Saba Noodles with Chicken, Chilies, Scallions, Roasted Peanuts and a Kung Pao Sauce

Pappardelle with Red Wine Oxtail Ragout, Wild Mushrooms, Shaved Parmesan and Truffle Oil
Grilled Beef with Sun Dried Tomatoes, Seared Chanterelles and Roasted Garlic Cream
Fettuccini with Braised Buffalo Short Rib, Porcini Mushrooms and Smoked Tomato Pan Sauce
Blackened Chicken, Bacon Braised Escarole, Grilled Onions and Truffle Butter
Sesame Noodles, Wood Ears, Grilled Scallions and Roasted Bok Choy with a Garlic Ginger Broth
Whole Wheat Penne with Spiced Sausage, Arugula and Dried Cranberries

PASTA COMBINATIONS AND TOPPINGS

Linguini with Grilled Shrimp, Smoked Tomatoes and Fennel Sausage
Butternut Tortellini with Chanterelles in a Red Peppercorn and Sage Beurre Blanc
Sour Cream Alfredo with Roasted Garlic, Grilled Chicken, Cracked Black Peppercorns and Broccoli
Crisp Salami, Sun Dried Tomatoes and Roasted Red Onions with Cubed Sharp Provolone
Thin Pasta Ribbons with Dungeness Crab, Butter Braised Fava Beans, Lemon and Garlic
Spicy Prawns, Goat Cheese and Red Pepper Flakes
Spinach, Prosciutto, Toasted Almonds and Shaved Parmesan with Garlic Infused Olive Oil

Roasted Apples, Gorgonzola and Caramelized Onion with a Reduced Balsamic Sauce
Smoked Salmon Gnocchi, Mustard Seed Vinaigrette and Pecan-Apple Relish
Dry Rubbed Chicken, Grilled Sweet Peppers, Fresh Cilantro and Tequila Lime Cream Sauce
Chianti Braised Veal, Smoked Tomato, Caramelized Onion
Rigatoni with Roasted Eggplant Puree
Blackened Chicken with a Cajun Alfredo Sauce
Bucatini with Smoked Pancetta, Fresh Tomato and Chili Flakes

Creamy Baked Fettuccine with Asiago and Thyme
Sweet Garlic and Goat Cheese Penne
Spaghetti with Monkfish and Hot Peppers
Tagliatelle with Pancetta and Parsnips
Roasted Red and Yellow Cherry Tomatoes with Angel Hair Pasta and Fresh Herbs
Baked Goat Cheese Tortellini with Radicchio
Black Truffle Fettuccini with Shaved Asiago, Wilted Spinach and White Truffle Oil

Spinach and Smoked Tomato Fettuccini with Fontina
Straw and Hay with Salmon Caviar
Tagliatelle Ribbons with Mushroom and Leek Ragu
Three Vegetable Penne with Tarragon-Basil Pesto
Fettuccine with Oyster Mushrooms, Sweet Garlic, and Arugula
Spaghetti with Anchovies, Dried Chili and Thyme Pesto
Wide Pasta Ribbons, Grilled Shrimp, Pesto, Vodka and Cream

Confit of Duck and Oven Dried Tomato over Spinach Fettuccini
Tagliatelle with Pan Roasted Morels, Sage, Roasted Garlic and a White Truffle Cream Sauce
Pasta with Fresh Favas and Pancetta
Spaghetti with Broccoli Rabe, Toasted Garlic, Parmesan and Cappicola
Quill Pasta with Rosemary Lamb Sausage, Grilled Red Chard and Ricotta
Sweet Potato Gnocchi with Pancetta, Sherry and Cream
Linguini with Sautéed Shrimp, Blistered Cherry Tomatoes, Sno-peas and Pernod

Lemon Pepper Fettuccini with Seared Scallops, Country Ham, Asparagus and Arugula Pesto
Ricotta Cavatelli with Crisp Prosciutto, Roasted Eggplant, Artichokes and Tomato Rosemary Cream
Cilantro Chicken with Charred Peppers and a Chipotle-Tomato Sauce
Roasted Pumpkin Tortellini with Walnuts, Spiced Apple Puree and Sage Oil

PASTA COMBINATIONS AND TOPPINGS

Rigatoni with Fresh Mozzarella, Grilled Portobello, Roasted Carrots and Wilted Spinach
Black Pepper Gnocchi with Smoked Tomato Braised Beef and Wild Mushrooms
Cappellini with Sautéed Scallops and Fresh Arugula Tossed in a Spicy Tomato Sauce
Oak Grilled Chicken, Pesto, Roma Tomatoes, Broccoli, Pine Nuts, Kalamata and Chèvre
Grilled Shrimp, Applewood Smoked Bacon, Fresh Sage and Lemon Cream
Shrimp, Garlic, Tomatoes, Kalamata Olives and Feta
Scallops and Crawfish with Andouille, Tasso Ham, Creole Tomatoes, Onion and Peppers

Crab with Roasted Eggplant, Caramelized Onion and Romano Cheese
King Crab, Broccoli Rabe and Fresh Tarragon Cream
Spinach Fettuccini with Mushrooms and Gorgonzola Demi-glace
Charred Lobster and Shrimp Alfredo
Linguini with Chili Tossed Pawns, Mussels and Calamari and a Roasted Garlic and Parsley Broth
Chicken and Leek Tortellini with Caramelized Cauliflower Puree and Herb Jus
Fresh Basil Gnocchi with a Broad Bean Butter Sauce

Smoked Chicken, Walnuts, Fresh Herbs and Olive Oil
Grilled Scallops with Watercress and Sage Butter
Fettuccine with Ribbons of Lamb, Wild Mushrooms and Mustard Cream
Oysters, Pistachios, Andouille Sausage in a Smoked Chili Cream
Gnocchi with Wilted Chard, Smoked Tomatoes and White Truffle Oil
Shrimp and Scallops with Bacon and Tomato Sage Cream
Oysters Poached in Cream and Herbs over Nests of Tomato and Spinach Pasta

Sorrel Smoked Tuna, Cured Olives and Lemon Zest
Black Pepper Fettuccine with Leaves of Fresh Salmon and a Dill Butter Sauce
Angel Hair with Porcine and Cream
Tagliatelle with Mascarpone and Lemon Zest
Three Cheese Tortellini with Wild Mushrooms, Roasted Peppers and Sweet Peas
Angel Hair with Shrimp, Crab and Lobster in a Saffron Broth
Lemon Fettuccini with Fresh Summer Tomatoes and Chunks of Brie tossed with Spinach

Tomato Pasta with Crab, Fresh Rosemary and Shaved Parmigianino
Fresh Spinach, Red Onions and Radicchio in Chive Oil
Lemon Pepper Fettuccine with Rainbow Trout and Chardonnay Sauce
Sautéed Shrimp with Basil, Grilled Eggplant and Garlic Infused Olive Oil
Blackened Chicken with Mushrooms and Fresh Cilantro

Grilled Shrimp and Plum Tomatoes with Fresh Mozzarella and Red Pepper Flakes
Ziti with Sautéed Escarole, Olive Oil, Red Beans and Black Olives
Cappellini with Bay Scallops and Roasted Shallots Napped in Whole Butter
Pan Roasted Chicken, Portobello, Caramelized Red Onion and a Toasted Garlic Cream
Black Pepper Fettuccine with Chicken, Broccoli and Fresh Dill Sauce

LAYERED AND STUFFED PASTAS

Wild Mushroom and Pecorino Lasagna
Crab and Havarti Cannelloni
Lasagna of Summer Truffles with Garden Peas
Roasted Butternut Squash and Fresh Rosemary Lasagna
Spinach and Morel Lasagna Roll-ups with Gorgonzola Cream Sauce
Lobster Lasagna - Lobster Meat, Fresh Vegetables, Grilled Polenta, Garlicky Marinara
Three Pesto Layered Lasagna
Portobello Lasagna with Spinach and Smoked Tomatoes and Basil Cream Sauce

Salmon Lasagna - Layers of Oven Blanched Yukon Gold Potatoes, Salmon
and Champagne Beurre Blanc

Veal and Roasted Vegetable Lasagna with Bel Paese and Mascarpone
Spinach and Artichoke Ravioli Lasagna
Wild Mushroom Manicotti
Sausage and Roasted Eggplant Stuffed Shells in a Tomato-Basil Cream Sauce
Veal, Swiss Chard and Fresh Herb Cannelloni with a Smoked Mozzarella Béchamel
Grilled Asparagus and Fresh Mozzarella Lasagna
Cannelloni Verde with Yellow Tomato Sauce and Basil Oil

Veal Stuffed Jumbo Shells with Wild Mushroom Béchamel
Asparagus and Prosciutto Cannelloni baked in a Creamy Parmesan Sauce
Sweet Pea Puree, Ricotta and Mascarpone filled Manicotti
Duxelles stuffed Rigatoni with a Smoked Tomato Sauce
Roasted Duck and Mascarpone Cannelloni in a Brown Butter Sauce
Walnut, Broccoli and Gorgonzola Lasagna
Crab and Ricotta Salata Cannelloni with Old Bay Tomato Sauce
Grilled Shrimp and Roasted Eggplant Lasagna with a Herbed Boursin Béchamel

Blackened Chicken and Sliced Smoked Sausage Lasagna with a Dry Monterey Jack Cream Sauce
Italian Sausage and Caramelized Onion Cannelloni with Pesto Béchamel
Roasted Vegetable Stuffed Shells topped with Bel Paese and Crisp Prosciutto
Lasagna of Sliced Oven Dried Tomatoes, Wilted Arugula and Smoked Gouda
King Crab and Grilled Fennel Stuffed Shells in Roasted Pepper Puree
Chorizo and Cremini Mushroom Lasagna with Asadero Cheese and Roasted Chili Tomato Sauce
Rigatoni Stuffed with Roasted Lamb and served with a Lemon Rosemary Butter Sauce
Pumpkin and Devon Blue Cheese Stuffed Shells with a Red Pepper Beurre Blanc

Roasted Root Vegetable and Fontina Lasagna with Braised Oxtail Ragu
Charred Chilies Lasagna with a Tequila-Lime and Jalapeño Cream Sauce
Grilled Lobster and White Truffle Lasagna with Lemon Zest Béchamel
Shells Stuffed with Artichokes, Feta and Kalamata Olives and finished with Brown Butter
Roasted Chicken and Rosemary Cannelloni with a Morel Veloute
Caramelized Onion and Shiitake Cannelloni napped with Veal Glaze
Summer Tomato Lasagna with Fontina and Basil Pistou

RAVIOLI

In menu planning few opportunities arise that allow you to add such a wide variety of flavors to your menu at such a high profit ratio as the use of ravioli. Besides the traditional fillings, ravioli are a great way to utilize small amounts of leftover product.

For example, try chopping lean scraps of beef tenderloin left over from fabricating and trimming. Lightly sauté the beef with Thai spices. Mix it with chopped grilled scallions and an egg with a little breadcrumb to help bind the mix. Fill and prep the ravioli, and serve them in a ginger consommé with a splash of sesame oil. Or maybe the items that were prepped as back-ups for the taco bar went unused. Combine shredded Monterey Jack, shredded cheddar, sliced black olives and diced Jalapenos. Fill the ravioli and quickly deep fry them. Serve them over a warm salsa. The combinations are endless. Savory pates or forcemeat also work great. Vegetable fillings can be either pureed or coarsely chopped. Cook the vegetables down and be attentive to the moisture content in the fillings. Add a little egg and bread crumbs to bind fillings. Dry fillings can be moistened with a sauce or small amounts of seasoned butter. Always test the filling by cooking off a small amount and adjusting the seasoning before filling all of the ravioli.

- Ravioli can be used for any course. Offer different size portions of the same ravioli for appetizer or entree on the same menu. Try two or more fillings as combinations on the same plate or put two contrasting flavored and colored sauces on the same plate.
- Use small size ravioli in soups or on salads.
- Filled ravioli made of sweetened dough, white or dark chocolate leaves or ravioli shaped cookies lend themselves well for dessert presentations.
- You can make your own pasta or use frozen dough. Wonton skins make great ravioli. Just moisten the edges with water to seal.
- Ravioli can be blanched, shocked and held for quicker service. Drop them in boiling water or stock to reheat. You can also reheat by sautéing them in a compound butter or a pan sauce. Caramelized shallot and mushroom raviolis would go well when warmed in a sauce made from deglazing the pan used to sauté a veal dish. What a natural side dish for the veal.
- If you are deep frying your ravioli, take the opportunity to add some flavoring by sprinkling with a spice blend as soon as they are cooked.
- As a finishing touch top you presentation with a slice of compound butter just before service. There are many compound butter selections available in this guide on page *175*.

RAVIOLI

Porcini Mushroom Ravioli with Wild Mushroom-Parmesan Broth and Italian Parsley
Sweet Potato Ravioli with Brown Butter Cream
Short Rib Ravioli with Double Beef Consommé and Shaved Pecorino
Salmon, Mascarpone and Mint Ravioli with Lemon Zest Butter
Shrimp and Scallop Ravioli with Yellow Pepper Romesco
Roasted Corn Ravioli with Oyster Mushrooms, Grilled Scallions and Smoked Gouda Cream
Artichoke Ravioli with Duck Sausage and Fontina Fondue
Goat Cheese and Caramelized Onion Ravioli with an Apricot and Balsamic Reduction

Gorgonzola and Toasted Walnut Ravioli with a Chive Cream Sauce
Braised Leek and Smoked Chicken Ravioli with a Herb Cream Sauce and Crisp Pancetta

RAVIOLI

Duck Liver Ravioli Poached in Duck Consommé with Fennel Brown Butter and Sherry Vinegar
Caramelized Shallot and Turnip Green Ravioli with White Truffle Oil
Roasted Carrot and Goat Cheese Ravioli with Sun Dried Tomato Pesto
Shrimp, Cilantro and Mascarpone Ravioli with Mint Butter
Butternut Squash Ravioli with Cinnamon Butter and Bittersweet Chocolate
Wild Mushroom Ravioli with Eggplant and Goat Cheese
Lobster and Mascarpone Ravioli with Pine Nuts and Roasted Tomatoes in a Vermouth Cream
Spinach Ravioli with Gouda and Fresh Herbs

Cracked Peppercorn Ravioli stuffed with Chorizo and Manchego Cheese
Oxtail Ravioli with a Dry Sherry and Caramelized Carrot Broth
Shaved Parmesan Ravioli with Pan Roasted Artichokes in a Smoked Tomato Coulis
Mushroom and Truffle Ravioli with a Sun Dried Tomato and Fresh Basil Cream
Smoked Duck and Boursin Ravioli with Fried Sage and Brown Butter Sauce
Crab Ravioli with Caramelized Corn, Roasted Artichokes, Crispy Pancetta and Mushroom Cream
Swiss Chard Ravioli with Ricotta, Lemon Zest and Asiago in a Spicy Thyme Sauce
Mushroom and Roasted Garlic Ravioli in a Sun Dried Tomato and Vodka Cream Sauce

Braised Short Rib Ravioli with a Tomato Bordelaise and Herbed Sour Cream
Goat Cheese Ravioli with Fresh Mint Butter
Crab and Shallot Ravioli in Champagne and Saffron Cream
Spiced Pumpkin Ravioli with Brown Butter, Fried Sage and Crushed Pecans
Wild Mushroom Ravioli with Porcini-Truffle Essence
Braised Leek Ravioli with a Fresh Pepper Sauce
Goat Cheese and Caramelized Onion Ravioli with Toasted Pine Nuts and a Sherry Cream Sauce
Lobster Ravioli with a Champagne-Ginger Reduction

Rosemary Ravioli filled with Wild Mushrooms and Lamb with a Thyme Jus
Lobster Ravioli with Cognac Butter
Crab Ravioli with a Caramelized Corn and Crisp Pancetta Cream Sauce
Smoked Mozzarella Ravioli with Oven Roasted Vegetable Ragout
Shrimp Ravioli with Caramelized Carrot Puree and Yuzu Butter Sauce
Spiced Pumpkin Raviolis with Maple Butter and Crumbled Toasted Almonds
Macadamia Nut and Lobster Ravioli with Red Curry Sauce
Veal Ravioli with Morel Demi-glace and Shaved Parmigiano-Reggiano

Black Bass Ravioli with Olive Pesto
Duck Confit and Mashed Potato Ravioli with White Truffle Sauce
Lamb stuffed Ravioli with a Gorgonzola and Rosemary Cream
Artichoke Ravioli with Kalamata Olives and Roasted Red Pepper Coulis
Smoked Tomato Ravioli with Balsamic Brown Butter
Butternut Ravioli with Tarragon and Toasted Hazelnuts
Lobster Ravioli in a Fennel and Chervil-Infused Nage
Bay Scallop Ravioli with Red Pepper Cream Sauce and Grilled Asparagus Tips
Goat Cheese Ravioli with Creamy Walnut Sauce

RAVIOLI

Smoked Gouda Ravioli with Grilled Chicken, Cilantro Pesto and Toasted Walnuts
Parmesan dusted Fried Ravioli with Spicy Marinara Cream Sauce
Boursin and Vegetable Ravioli in a Citrus-Tomato Broth with Fresh Herbs
Lobster and Fontina Ravioli with White Truffle Butter
Smoked Salmon Ravioli with Sour Cream and Dill
Ravioli of Fava Beans, Fresh Oregano and Ricotta
White Bean Ravioli with a Butter and Caper Sauce
Goat Cheese and Sun Dried Tomato Ravioli with a Walnut and Truffle Pesto

Goat Cheese Ravioli with Artichoke Hearts, Sun-Dried Tomatoes and Kalamata Olives
Potato, Leek and Bacon Ravioli in a Fresh Herb Broth
Roasted Portobello and Caramelized Onion Ravioli
Cheddar Ravioli with Fried Cabbage and Bacon
Lamb Ravioli in Mint Demi-glace
Lobster Ravioli in a Fennel and Chervil Beurre Blanc
Smoked Duck Ravioli with Brown Butter, Tarragon and Sun-Dried Tomatoes

Veal Ravioli in a Brown Three Onion Broth
Chèvre Cheese Ravioli with Dried Orange and Hazelnut Dust
Crispy Crab Ravioli with Lemon Oil
Spinach Ravioli with a Pecorino, Toasted Walnut, and Ricotta Filling
Ricotta and Black Pepper Ravioli with Scallops and Green Herb Pesto
Shrimp and Portobello Ravioli in a Garlic Butter Sauce
Spicy Sweet Potato Ravioli with Crayfish

Smoked Salmon Ravioli with Grilled Asparagus and Lemon Cream
Shiitake Ravioli in a Caramelized Corn and Roasted Shallot Sauce
Roasted Parsnip Ravioli on wilted Purple Kale with Thyme Broth
Wild Mushroom Ravioli with Truffle Mascarpone
Crab Ravioli in a Brie, Asparagus and Sweet Corn Butter Sauce
Ravioli of Chicken and Roasted Eggplant
Seafood Ravioli with Fra Diablo Sauce

Roasted Pork Ravioli with a Chipotle Espagnole
Shrimp Ravioli with Parmigianino and Sherry Cream Sauce
Black Lobster Ravioli with Sun-Dried Tomatoes and a Lemon Butter Sauce
Scallop Ravioli with Melted Leeks
Watercress Ravioli with Cinnamon Butter
Portabella Ravioli with a Gorgonzola Cream Sauce
Smoked Trout Ravioli in Caper and Red Onion Beurre Blanc

Bel Paese and Watercress Ravioli Napped with Tarragon Butter
Roasted Pumpkin and Blue Cheese Ravioli with Sweet Red Pepper Coulis
Ricotta Ravioli with Creamy Pesto and Chopped Black Walnuts
Caramelized Corn Ravioli with Butter Poached Lobster and a Sweet Corn Emulsion

RAVIOLI

Roasted Chestnut and Lobster Ravioli with Celery Root Cream
Sweet Potato Ravioli with Whole Butter and Fresh Ginger over Smothered Leeks
Smoked Chicken and Chive Ravioli with a Curry Cream Sauce
Tossed Green Salad with Tiny Toasted Gorgonzola Ravioli
Veal and Sun Dried Tomato Ravioli in Madeira Demi-glace
Butternut Squash Ravioli with Cilantro Butter
Smoked Duck and Artichoke Ravioli with a Green Peppercorn Sauce
Toasted Walnut and Brie Cheese with Fresh Herbs

Crab Ravioli Veronique with White Grapes and a Royal Glasage
Grilled Vegetable and White Cheddar Ravioli with a BBQ Demi-glace
Smoked Duck Ravioli with a Red Asiago Sauce
Goat Cheese and White Truffle Ravioli with Roasted Tomato and Fresh Basil
Shrimp Ravioli with Fresh Thyme Sauce
Smoked Salmon and Black Olive Ravioli with Chive Flavored Broth
Fennel Ravioli with Roasted Vegetables and Saffron Sauce

DESSERT RAVIOLI

Cut dessert ravioli from sheets of chocolate, marzipan or any flavor or color of rolled fondant. Traditional dough that has been flavored will work for some fillings. If you want the dough to be sweet try either crystallized sugars for texture or liquid sugars such as honey or molasses. Fruit flavors can also be introduced here using purees, fruit powders or jelly and jams. To finish dessert raviolis, sprinkle on flavored sugars or cocoa. Don't be afraid to mix some light savory flavor with the sweet.

White Chocolate Ravioli with Dark Chocolate filling and Fresh Fruit Sauce
Lemon Zest Ravioli with an Orange Mousse filling and served with Fresh Basil Ice Cream
Chocolate Chip Ravioli stuffed with Peanut Butter Mousse
Strawberry Ravioli with Black Pepper Ice Cream
Pumpkin Honey Ravioli with Apple Cider Crème Fraîche
Hazelnut Ravioli with a Caramel Cream Sauce
Ricotta and Blueberry Jam Ravioli on a Lemon Crème Anglaise

Toasted Almond and Mascarpone dusted with Dark Cocoa and served with Espresso Ice Cream
Grilled Peach Ravioli with Pralines and Ginger Syrup
Ravioli of Roasted Banana stuffed into Peanut Butter Fondant with Chocolate Sauce
Dried Cherry and Ricotta filled Ravioli with a warm Fig Compote
Dark Chocolate Ravioli with Walnut filling and Reduced Cabernet Drizzle
Mascarpone and Fresh Mint Ravioli with Brown Sugar Lemon Sauce

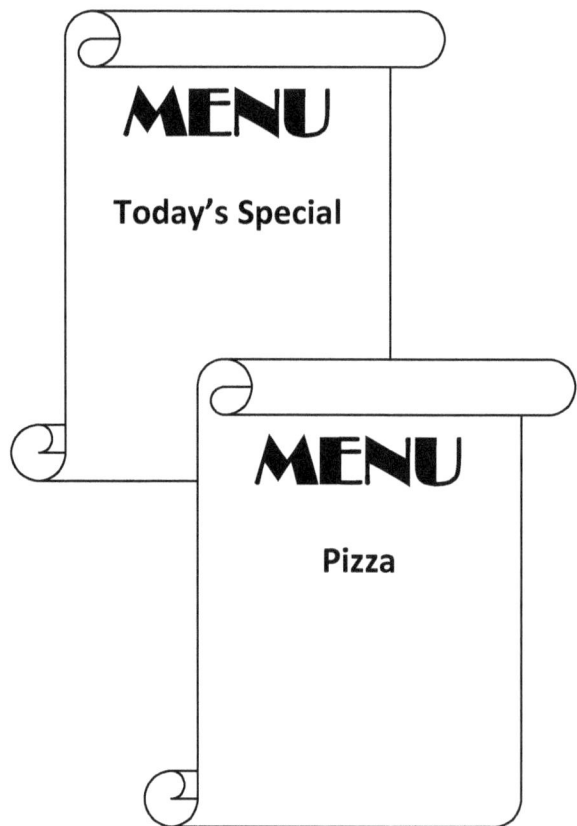

MENU

Today's Special

MENU

Pizza

PIZZA

Chapter Notes, Ideas and Conversions

Main Ingredient	Element 1	Element 2	Element 3	Sauce	Texture

PIZZA

Sliced Italian Sausage with Herb Roasted Potatoes, Roasted Garlic and Smoked Provolone
Spicy Chicken and Black Beans with Salsa and Jalapeno Jack Cheese
Prosciutto, Gaeta Olive, Oven Roasted Plum Tomato, Capers and Bel Paese
Fontina Cheese, Chopped Walnuts, Fresh Sage and Olive Oil
Grilled Shrimp, Smoked Gouda, Red Onion and Fresh Cilantro
Artichokes, Ricotta, Roasted Peppers and Olive Oil
Plum Tomatoes, Grilled Scallops and Grated Asiago
Smoked Salmon and Brie with Red Onions and Capers

Grilled Chicken and Wild Mushrooms with Spinach and Gorgonzola
Country Ham, Crab Meat and Fresh Mozzarella
Spiced Shrimp, Smoked Cheddar, Portabella and Scallions
Ground Lamb, Pistachios, Greek Olives and Herb Feta
Avocado and Chopped Macadamia Nuts with Grilled Pineapple and Brie
Slow Roasted Jerk Pork with Charred Scallions and Queso Fresco
Honey and Jerk Glazed Chicken with Red Onions, Colby-Jack and Roasted Peppers
Fontina, Ricotta, and Parmesan with Wilted Arugula and Roasted Garlic

Dry Rubbed BBQ Chicken with Smoked Gouda, Black Beans and Caramelized Onions
Fennel Crusted Lamb with Fresh Tomatoes, Kalamata Olives, Red Onions and Goat Cheese
Cilantro Black Beans, Chipotle Cheddar, Monterey Jack and Caramelized Corn Salsa
Tequila-Lime Chicken with Sharp Cheddar, Grilled Onions, Diced Serrano and Queso Fresco
Thai Spiced Chicken with Havarti, Crushed Peanuts, Ginger, Cilantro, Mint and Chilies
Goat Cheese with Grilled Eggplant, Roasted Red and Yellow Peppers and Caramelized Shallots
Tandoori Chicken with Mango, Chèvre and Caramelized Onion
Green Curry Chicken with Golden Raisins, Goat Cheese and Toasted Coconut

Slow Roasted Chipotle Pork with Fire Roasted Chilies, Horseradish Cheddar and Enchilada Sauce
Pears, Apples, Fontinella, Caramelized Shallots and Devon Blue
Grilled Shrimp with Roasted Garlic, Edam, Fresh Parsley and Caramelized Lemons
Wild Mushrooms, Caramelized Shallots, Fontina and Sun Dried Tomato Pesto
Carne Asada Beef with Roasted Tomatillo, Grilled Poblano and Jack Cheese
Pineapple, Sesame Chicken and Munster
Grilled Eggplant, Fontina and Lemon Olive Oil
Black Beans, White Cheddar, Scallions, Cilantro Crème Fraîche

Artichokes, Basil and Summer Tomato
Scampi - Grilled Shrimp, Garlic, Lemon Zest
Marsala Chicken with Fresh Mozzarella, Wild Mushrooms and a Brown Tomato Marsala Sauce
White Pizza with Roasted Garlic and Herb Seasoned Toasted Onions
Canadian Bacon, Kiwi, Pineapple and Port-Salut
Dried Mushroom Crusted Chicken with Caramelized Onion, Shitakes, Mozzarella and Gorgonzola
Grilled Vegetables and Goat Cheese

PIZZA

Pesto, Smoked Plum Tomatoes and Ricotta Salata
Sautéed Endive, Pancetta and Fontina
Sliced Tomatoes, Prosciutto, Black Olives and Fresh Mozzarella
Garlic Roasted Chicken with Boursault, Wild Mushrooms and Walnut Pesto
Grilled Eggplant, Sun Dried Tomato Sauce, Broccoli Rabe, Goat Cheese and Mascarpone
Rosemary Chicken, Wilted Spinach, Chèvre Cheese and Caramelized Onion
Seared Beef Tenderloin, Smoked Gouda, Caramelized Shallot White Sauce and Balsamic Drizzle
Roasted Eggplant, Sun Dried Tomatoes and Feta Cheese with Cracked Black Pepper

Tropical Mango with Roasted Bananas and Monterey Jack
Grilled Steak, Shallots, Smoked Tomato, Pepper Jack and Cilantro-Chipotle Pesto
Garlic Grilled Chicken, Herb-Roasted Gold Potatoes, Fresh Oregano and Boursin
Curry Rubbed Tandoori Chicken, Mango and Red Onions, Sweet Chili Sauce and Manchego
Grilled Pork, Pasilla Peppers, Caramelized Corn, Enchilado Cheese, Mint and Lime
Sliced Beef, Charred Chilies, Onions, Cilantro Pesto, Monterey Jack, and Roasted Tomatillo Salsa

Spicy Orange-Ginger and Sesame Marinated Chicken, Scallions and
Grilled Pineapple, Roasted Cashews and Colby Jack

Stilton, Slice Pears and Dried Cranberries
Chorizo and Shredded Pork with Jack Cheese and Sweet Peppers
Fresh Mozzarella, Granny Smith Apples and Caramelized Red Onion
Mushrooms, Walnuts and Blue Cheese
Roasted Garlic and Sweet Bell Peppers with Bel Paese
Smoked Duck, Gouda, Red Onions and Wild Mushrooms
Piccata Sautéed Chicken with Caramelized Lemons, Capers and Fontina Cheese
Asparagus and Bacon with Gruyere

Oven Baked Tomatoes and Cappicola with Boursin
Grilled Chicken with Fresh Scallions and Cured Olives
BBQ Chicken and Cheddar Cheese with Grilled Green Onions
Smoked Salmon and Brie
Herb Grilled Chicken Breast, Foie Gras, Roasted Peppers and Goat Cheese
Caramelized Scallops, Basil Mascarpone, Prosciutto and Toasted Parmesan
Thai Chicken with Grilled Bok Choy and a Roasted Peanut Sauce
BLT with Bacon, Lettuce, Tomato and Fresh Mozzarella

Sliced Yukon Gold Potatoes, Pepper Jack, Cheddar and Green Onion
Chicken and Roasted Vegetables with Sun Dried Tomatoes, Walnut Pesto and Muenster
Thin Bermuda Onions, Vine Ripe Tomatoes, Diced Smoked Bacon, Parsley, and Parmesan
Orange Zest, Sun Dried Tomatoes, Greek Olives, Chipotle Peppers

Add any of the following to the crust just before the final proofing
Cracked Black Pepper - Poppy, Sesame or Fennel Seeds, Curry Powder, Roasted Garlic, Chili
Powder, Chopped or Ground Nuts - Diced Chilies, Caramelized Onion, Chives or Fresh Herbs.

VEGETABLES AND STARCHES

Assorted Vegetables
Potatoes
French Fries
Mashed Potatoes
Rice
Risotto
Mac and Cheese
Other Starches

Chapter Notes, Ideas and Conversions

Main Ingredient	Element 1	Element 2	Element 3	Sauce	Texture

VEGETABLES

Nothing says "bored chef" more than their vegetable side dish selections. A compound vegetable side dish is an excellent way to step up the entrée and add the perception of value to your meal. If you are serving two vegetables on the same plate with the entrée, one of the vegetable selections should be a basic preparation so as not to compete with the entrée and the compound vegetable selection. To step-up a basic vegetable preparation such as steamed fresh green beans, add a slice of compound butter just before serving. Allow it to warm for a few seconds under the heat lamp to slightly melt it while keeping its shape.

Wood Roasted Asparagus with Romesco and Meyer Lemon
White Beans, Roasted Garlic and Spicy Fennel
Sautéed Broccoli with Chestnuts and Black Truffle Butter
Green Beans with Blistered Cherry Tomatoes, Feta and Red Wine Vinegar
Braised Lentils with Escarole and Spicy Sausage
Baby Artichokes with Garlic Breadcrumbs and Sherry Reduction
Sweet Corn with Sage Pesto
Fire-Roasted Corn and Grilled Mushrooms tossed with White Truffle Oil

Green Beans, Melted Tomato and Herbed Brie
Pan Roasted Sunchoke with Balsamic Drizzle
Roasted Rainbow Carrots with Dried Cherries and Toasted Walnuts
Red Lentils with Spicy Escarole
Grilled Radicchio with Lemon Olive Oil, Balsamic and Fennel Salt
Creamed Spinach, Roasted Tomato and Smoked Cheddar Gratian
Butternut Squash with Caramelized Onions, Bacon and Fried Sage
Charred Asparagus with Hazelnut and Onion Romesco

Grilled Artichoke with a Garlic and White Balsamic Cream Sauce
Summer Squash Gratin with Caramelized Corn, Poblano and Queso Fresco
Sautéed Broccoli with Currants and Pine Nuts
Crispy Stuffed Squash Blossoms with Herbed Boursin
Green Beans with Sugar Grilled Lemons and Toasted Pumpkin Seeds
Roasted Pumpkin Cubes with Gorgonzola and Pine Nuts
Wood Roasted Cauliflower with Spicy Chili Vinegar
Beluga Lentils, Spiced Eggplant, Charred Red Peppers and Sherry Shallot Vinaigrette

Caramelized Cauliflower with Morel Mushrooms
Spinach and Baked Carrots with Black Strap Molasses Vinaigrette and Toasted Pumpkin Seeds
Cipollini Onions with Crisp Croutons and Shaved Gruyere
Braised Leeks with a Port Wine Glaze
Grilled Eggplant with Fresh Mozzarella, Hummus and Toasted Pine Nuts
Onion and Fresh Fennel Confit over Green Lentil Stew
Oven Roasted Beets with Hazelnuts and Tangerine Vinaigrette
Garlicky Grilled Baby Broccoli with Poblano and Cider Vinegar
Green Beans with Chili Flakes and Toasted Almonds

VEGETABLES

Crispy Polenta-Parmesan Battered Artichoke Fritters with Citrus Basil Aioli
Roasted Cauliflower with Mint
Sautéed Squash with Fennel, Kalamata Olives and Toasted Almonds
Grilled Mushrooms with Scallions, Taleggio and Smoky Almond Pesto
Asparagus, Sieved Egg and Sherry Emulsion
Spaghetti Squash and Farro with Warm Pomegranate Vinaigrette
Truffle Braised Belgian Endive
Whole Steamed Artichoke with Orange Cinnamon Aioli
Roasted Beets tossed in an Orange Vinaigrette with Dried Cranberries and Goat Cheese
Caramelized Corn Gratin with Parmesan Crust

Broccolini with Lemon, Dill and Balsamic Butter
Porcini Mushrooms and Roasted Pumpkin Panna Cotta
Eggplant, Spinach and Ricotta Crepes
White Bean, Gaeta Olive, Sun Dried Tomato and Meyer Lemon Ragout
Grilled Artichoke with Fontinella and Capers
Fried Green Tomatoes with a Garlic Cayenne Sauce
Zucchini, Smoked Tomato and Fresh Oregano
Bacon Braised Turnips

Roasted Brussels Sprouts with Smoked Ham and Caramelized Shallots
Parmesan Dusted Polenta
Tender Beets, Hazelnut Vinaigrette and Pickled Red Onions
Caramelized Cauliflower, Golden Raisins, Toasted Almonds and Curry Spice
Sautéed Green Tomatoes, Sweet Corn and Warm Ancho Chili Vinaigrette
Pan Roasted Brussels Sprouts with Pancetta and Balsamic
Braised Fennel with Preserved Lemons and Gaeta Olives
Broiled Cauliflower with Morel Mushroom Ragout
Roasted Asparagus Fritters with Green Goddess Aioli

Sweet Corn with Roasted Garlic and Fresh Tarragon
Parsnips and Caramelized Carrots with Dates and Ginger
Grilled Eggplant stuffed with Brie and Herb Breadcrumbs
Creamed Spinach with Caramelized Vidalia Onions
Oven Roasted Hen of the Wood Mushrooms with Crispy Shallots and Béarnaise
Basil Roasted Asparagus
Lavender Steamed Green Beans with Sweet Butter
Passion Fruit Glazed Carrots with Fresh Thyme and Cracked Pepper

Blistered Cherry Tomatoes with Shaved Parmesan and Chive Oil
Sautéed Spinach with Shallots and Toasted Pumpkin Seeds
Roasted Asparagus with Hazelnut Romesco
Baby Spinach with Black Strap Molasses Vinaigrette
Fire-Roasted Corn with Crisp Bacon and Rosemary Cream

VEGETABLES

Broccolini with Parmesan Anchovy Vinaigrette
Tiny Spring Beets, Blue Cheese, Hazelnut Brittle, Golden Raison Balsamic
Grilled Artichokes with Smoked Paprika Aioli
Asparagus Curry with Toasted Pistachios and Currants
Steamed Artichoke with Meyer Lemon and Crushed Hazelnut Dressing
Cornmeal Fried Ripe Tomatoes with a Lemon Butter Capers Sauce
Brussels Sprouts with Toasted Pecans and Pomegranate Seeds
Glazed Baby Carrots with Chorizo and Brown Sugar Butter

Root Vegetable Pot Pie with an Herbed Cheddar Crust
Deep Fried Fresh Fennel with Pecorino Cheese Dusting
Baby Broccoli with Roasted Garlic, Olive Oil and Chili Flakes
Sautéed Escarole with Sun Dried Tomatoes and Roquefort Cream
Grilled Autumn Vegetables with a Whole Grain Mustard Sauce
Artichoke, Shiitake Mushroom and Three Pepper Confit
Butter Braised Savory Cabbage with Caramelized Carrots and Fines Herbs
Celery Root and Roasted Pear Puree

Brussels Sprouts with Parmesan and Balsamic Glaze
Curried Onion Rings
Pistachio Crusted Goat Cheese and Sun Dried Tomato Cakes
Portabella Mushroom and Oven Dried Tomato Ragout Au gratin
Sugar Snap Peas with Fresh Mint
Grilled Fennel and Asparagus Hash
Sautéed Escarole with Chick Peas and White Raisons
Asparagus with Lime Cilantro Butter

Sautéed Green Tomatoes with Herbs and Onions
Spinach and Gruyere Tart
Roasted Parsnip and Fuji Apple Puree
Broccoli Rabe with Sweet Garlic Sauce
Balsamic Roasted Vegetables
Zucchini and Asparagus with Leek Vinaigrette and Pistachio Oil
Brussels Sprout Petals with Pickled Cranberries and Coriander
Braised Spinach with Toasted Almonds

Artichoke with Caramelized Meyer Lemon with Fresh Herbs
Grilled and Marinated Artichoke with Citrus Mascarpone Aioli
Edamame Tossed with Sea Salt
Curry Roasted Cauliflower with Dill Yogurt
Black Trumpet and Oyster Mushrooms with Almonds
Braised Fennel with Pistachios and Caramelized Apples
Vanilla Parsnip Puree

VEGETABLES

Tempura Zucchini Flowers with Three Cheese Filling
Brussels Sprouts with Roasted Cashews
Grilled Pumpkin, Bacon and Tomato Kabobs
Caramelized Corn Pudding
Cannelloni Beans with Toasted Sesame and Sage
Tri-Color Beets with Orange and Cloves
Red Cabbage with Leeks and Sausage
Green Tomatoes sautéed with Chipotle Peppers

Roasted Asparagus with Crumpled Blue Cheese
Fried Cabbage with Four Onions
Home Style Creamed Onions with Caramelized Celery
Whole Carrots Braised in Sherry and Consommé
Grilled Asparagus with Smoked Paprika and Jalapeño Butter
Sliced Radishes with Green Beans
Squash and Broccoli with Ginger Butter
Asparagus with Tomato and Pepper Salsa

Carrots Dijon
Stuffed Artichokes
Fresh Lima Beans with Bacon, Shallots and Rosemary
Stewed Tomatoes with Basil
Cheese Battered Zucchini and Eggplant
Cheddar Scalloped Baby Onions
Cumin Scented Tomatoes with Olive Oil
Grilled Asparagus with a Pecorino and Roasted Shallot Cream Sauce

Fresh Beets with Lemon and Cracked Pepper
Broccoli with Bacon and Chestnuts
Brussels Sprouts with Tangerines and Sesame Seeds
Stuffed Acorn Squash with Red Pearl Onions and Honey
Green Curry Ratatouille
Bourbon Braised Onions
Roasted Parsnips with Rosemary
Braised Celery with Mushrooms

Carrot Pudding
Grilled Corn on the Cob with Blue Cheese Butter
Oven Roasted Artichokes with Thyme and Marjoram
Sautéed Grape Tomatoes with Basil and Prosciutto
Grilled Vegetable Kabobs with Honey Mustard Glaze

VEGETABLES

Grilled Zucchini with Spicy Pepper Butter
Roasted Cauliflower with Caraway
Petite Bell Peppers stuffed with Sun Dried Tomatoes and Pine Nuts
Sautéed Red Onion Slices with Shredded Prosciutto
Spicy Fried Cauliflower with a Roasted Garlic and Smoked Tomato Cream Sauce
Jalapeno Creamed Corn
Curry Roasted Eggplant with Onions
Broccoli with Lemon Sauce

Caraway Sauerkraut
Crispy Brussels Sprouts with Balsamic Reduction
Red Cabbage with Onions, Sausage and Apples
Maple Glazed Carrots with Pecans
Creamed Onions with Poblano Chilies
Spicy Carrots with Roasted Asparagus
Baked Eggplant with Bacon and Onions
Broccoli with Toasted Almonds and Fresh Fennel

Grilled Artichoke with a White Balsamic Aioli
Brussels Sprouts with Chestnuts
Braised Onions with Nut Topping
Grilled Artichoke and Mushroom Kabob
Apple Glazed Carrots
Black Beans with Thyme
Spinach with Garlic, Yellow Raisins, Pine Nuts
Fresh Lima Beans with Bacon, Shallots and Rosemary

Wild Mushroom and Asparagus Napoleon
Brussels Sprouts with Caraway
Baked Onions Au Gratin
Braised Belgium Endive with Walnuts
Mashed Yellow Turnips with Cracked Black Pepper
Grilled Blue Corn Cakes with Fried Cabbage
Eggplant Roulades Stuffed with Wild Mushrooms
Grilled Acorn Squash with Oranges, Walnuts, Golden Raisins and Fresh Nutmeg

Herb Roasted Onions
Sauerkraut with Mushrooms and Peas
Parsnips with Fennel Seed and Red Pepper Flakes
Oven Roasted Fresh Beets with Horseradish
Chickpeas with Sun Dried Tomato Pesto
Bell Peppers with Anchovies, Shallots and Feta
Fried Brussels Sprouts with Black Garlic and Mushrooms

VEGETABLES

Broccoli with Spicy Tomato Chutney
Baby Carrots with Figs and Lemon Zest
Roasted Asparagus with Cannelloni Beans and Rosemary
Spring Onion Flan
Honey Roasted Parsnips
Guinness Roasted Wild Mushrooms and Onions
Lemon Braised Leeks

Mushroom and Feta Wontons
Carrots Cointreau
Roasted Vegetable Hummus tossed with Garlic Spaetzle
Green Beans with Raspberry Vinegar
Baked Onions with Herb Crumb Topping
Fresh Broccoli with Capers and Olives
Wild Mushroom Frito Misto
Skillet Corn Fry with Garlic and Green Onions

Minted Green Beans with Red Onion
Brussels Sprouts with Walnut Oil and Lime Zest
Sautéed Red and Yellow Cherry Tomatoes
Grilled Leeks with Hazelnut Vinaigrette
Sweet Corn with Champagne Cream
Roasted Brussels Sprouts with a Creole Mustard Sauce
Rainbow Carrots with a Sherry Glaze and Spiced Walnuts
Grilled Green Beans with Spicy Miso Mustard and Black Sesame

Curry Cauliflower with Cilantro Relish
Grilled Japanese Eggplant with a Sweet Miso Sauce and Toasted Sesame Seeds
Sweet Corn Crème Brûleè
Braised Collard Greens with Smoked Chicken and Dried Cranberries
Brussels Sprouts with Ham, Golden Raisins and Brown Butter
Sautéed Spinach with Dijon Butter
Spicy Glazed Asparagus with Crispy Bacon
Braised Leeks with Dried Cherries and Toasted Pecans

Stir Fried Asparagus with Lemon Grass and Fresh Mint
Flash Fried Sno Peas with Fish Sauce Vinaigrette
Edamame with Smoked Sea Salt
Dark Rum Glazed Plantains
Edamame seasoned with Lime, Coarse Salt and Chili Pepper Flakes
Broccolini with Red Pepper Flakes and Golden Raisons
Grilled Eggplant Rounds with Tomato Mint Chutney

POTATOES

Boursin Scalloped Potatoes with Crispy Shallot Crust
Yukon Fingerlings with Lemon, Fresh Herbs and Crème Fraîche
Crisp Potato Cakes with Black Pepper and Bleu Cheese Aioli
Mojito Mashed Sweet Potatoes
Spicy Potato and Cheese Fritters with Jalapeño Crema and Chipotle Ranch
Smoked Marble Potatoes with Caramelized Sliced Onions
Red Curry Potato Cakes with Cucumber Yogurt Raita
Chipotle Roasted Potatoes with White Balsamic Tartar Sauce

Smoked Chili Scalloped Sweet Potatoes
Roasted Japanese Purple Yams with Crème Fraîche and Grilled Scallions
Potato and Sage Fritters
Baby Sweet Potatoes with Dried Cranberries and Maple Walnut Butter
Mashed New Potatoes with Fresh Mint
Smoky Sweet Potatoes
Crisp Vinegar and Salt Grilled Potatoes

Chili Dusted Sweet Potato Chips
Oven-Roasted Potato, Caramelized Onion and Sharp Cheddar Gratin
Roasted Chestnut and Yukon Gold Puree
Red Potato and Caramelized Fennel Galette
Cumin and Sesame Roasted Potatoes
Mashed Sweet Potato Casserole Topped with Caramelized Bananas
Sliced Zucchini and Potato Gratin
Creamy Potatoes with Wild Mushrooms

Duck Fat Fingerlings with Pancetta Lardons
Crispy Sweet Potato Strings with Spicy Habanero Maple Syrup
Blue Cheese Potato Cakes with Parsley Aioli
Rosemary Skillet Yukon Gold Hash with Bourbon Butter
Red Bliss, Yukon Gold and Purple Fingerling Hash
Fennel Fried Potatoes with Balsamic Drizzle

Grilled Vegetable and Potato Lasagna
Red Potato and Scallion Ragout
Brandy and Orange Mashed Sweet Potatoes in Orange Cups
Oven Crisped Red Skins with Shaved Truffle and Fresh Rosemary
Double Baked Potatoes with Danish Blue Cheese and Fresh Chives
Grilled Potatoes with Eggplant and Cumin
Chili Sweet Potato Hash
Oven Potatoes with Curry and Red Pepper Flakes
Potato Pancakes with Herb Roasted Feta
Creamy Mashed Potatoes with Crispy Brown Onions

POTATOES

Rosemary and Cracked Pepper Roasted Potatoes
Baked Carrots, Red Potatoes and Sausage
Grilled Potato Slices with Sour Cream Dressing
Marbled Potato Gratin
Mashed Sweet Potatoes with Orange Essence
Pan Fried Potatoes with Saffron and Toasted Almonds
Yukon Gold Potatoes Poached in Chicken Stock and Fresh Herbs
Oven Grilled Potatoes with Lemon Zest

Cumin-Roasted Fingerling Potatoes
Sweet Potato Puree with Fresh Ginger
Tangerine Sweet Potato Casserole
Curry Fried Potatoes
Roasted Red Potatoes with Rosemary
Sweet Potato Chips with Seafood Seasoning Shake
Roasted Potatoes with Asiago
Cider Mashed Yams

Red Potatoes with Feta, Olives and Mint
Warm Curry Potato Salad
South of the Border Potato Pancakes
Braised Potatoes with Thyme
Fried Potatoes with Toasted Almonds and Garlic
Sweet Potato Cakes with Cranberry Salsa
Smoked Yukon Gold Potato and Honey Puree
Roquefort Scalloped Potatoes

Yam Wedges with Sweet and Spicy Harissa
Lavender Pommes Frites
Roasted Sweet Potatoes with Toasted Oat and Brown Sugar Streusel
Sweet Potato and Horseradish Cheddar Gratin
Ham and Chive Potato Croquettes with Herbed Cheddar Fondue
Sweet Potato Cakes with Charred Red Pepper Cream
Roasted Fingerling Potatoes with Sliced Radishes
Lamb Fat Potato Chips with a Black Pepper and Bacon Aioli

Crispy Fried Fingerlings with Saffron Aioli
Smoked Ham and Shredded Onion Potato Cake
Caramelized Onion and Sweet Potato Soufflé
Green Chili Hash Browns
Tomato filled with Duchess Potatoes
Crisp Potato Pancake with Poblano
Gorgonzola Twice Baked Potato
Bacon Roquefort Red Potato Gratin

FRENCH FRIES AND ACCOMPANIMENTS

Unlimited possibilities here by topping with any type of cheese and further enhanced by finishing with flavored oil. There are various ketchup suggestions on page   that can make your offerings unique to your establishment. Also try any of the Wing or BBQ sauce selections on page *177*, almost any brown sauce or demi-glace or one of the compound butters. Make your fries an appetizer event by offering three selections of dipping sauces with each order or treat the fries in same the way you would nachos adding either conventional or non typical toppings in several layers. There are also many unique containers available for table and take-out service.

Rosemary Sea Salt
Buffalo Bleu Fries with Blue Cheese Chunks, Hot Sauce and Celery Salt
Parmesan Fries with Black Truffle Oil
Sun Dried Tomato Powder and Shaved Romano Cheese
Smoked Salt Dusting with Roasted Garlic and Shallot Dip
Sweet Potato Fries with Harissa Aioli
Fresh Rosemary and Truffle Oil
Porky Fries with Pulled Pork, Enchilado Cheese and Bourbon Sauce

Green Chili Hollandaise
Steak Fries tossed with Hot Pork Fat, Sea Salt and Cracked Black Pepper
Thai Chili Oil
Smoked Tomato Demi-glace
Green Curry Sauce
Black Truffle Aioli
Spicy Sweet Potato Fries with Charred Green Chili and Apple Cider Aioli
Crisp Fries tossed with Fresh Herbs and Parmigianino

Chive-Malt Vinegar Crème Fraîche
Sweet Potato Fries topped with Grilled Shrimp and Melted Brie
Five Chili Mole Sauce
Thai Seasoned with Sweet Thai Chili Dipping Sauce
Tossed with Cilantro, Mint and Diced Jalapenos
Dried Mushroom Powder
Scotch Bonnet Tartar Sauce
Cheese, Bacon and Tomato

Shoestring Fries with Smoked Brisket, Horseradish Cheddar, Scallions and Sour Cream
Crisp Fries tossed in Garlic and Herb Butter
Yucca Fries with Poblano Chili Powder and Lime Cilantro Aioli
Chili Dusted Sweet Potato Fries with Cilantro Ranch
Crispy Veggie Fries with Wasabi Ranch Dressing
Chickpea Fries with Spicy Tzatziki
Toasted Fennel Hollandaise
Chipotle and Lime Sour Cream
Tossed with Smoked Paprika and Lemon Zest
Chili Dusted Fries with Smoked Jalapeno Ranch
Cheese Steak Fries with Shaved Rib Eye, Grilled Peppers, Onions and Cheese Whiz

FRENCH FRIES AND ACCOMPANIMENTS

Sweet and Hot Fries - Crispy Fries tossed in Seasoned Rice Wine Vinegar and Crushed Red Pepper
Sea Salt, Fried Fresh Thyme and Gorgonzola Crumbles
Colby-Jack and Diced Jalapeño Fondue
Spicy Salsa Verde
Sweet Potato Fries with Melted Marshmallow Fluff and Chopped Pecans
Garlic Parmesan Fries served with a Smoky Marinara Sauce
Smoked Paprika Aioli
Sweet Potato Fries with Cumin Lime Ranch Dressing

Green Peppercorn Hollandaise
Meyer Lemon and Dill Aioli
Spicy Fries with Honey Citrus Crème
Crisp Pancetta with Caramelized Shallots and Shaved Parmigianino
White Cheddar and Chipotle Cheese Sauce
Dusted with Blackened Seasoning and a Crab Rémoulade Dip
Sweet Potato Fries with Guava Ketchup
Key West Cocktail Sauce

Salt and Cracked Black Pepper Fries with Chive Aioli
Sweet Potato Fries with Balsamic Espresso Ketchup
Firehouse Fries tossed with Hot Sauce and Toasted Dry Chiles
Smoked Eggplant Tahini
Pomegranate Teriyaki Reduction
Cracked Peppercorn Parmesan Ranch
Honey, Brown Mustard and Tarragon Mayo
Spicy Carmel Peanut Satay

Sun Dried Tomato Pesto
Garlicky Gremolata
Hawaiian Black Sea Salt and Caramelized Pineapple Salsa
Red Curry Dip
Rosemary and Wild Mushroom Aioli
Hot Mustard and Horseradish Fondue
Sun Dried Tomato Bordelaise
Orange Honey

Cajun Rémoulade with Chopped Scallions
Crisp Sweet Potato Fries with Chimichurri
Spanish Fries with Chorizo, Pico de Gallo and Oaxaca Cheese
Garlic Herb Fries with a Dark Beer-Whole Grain Mustard Aioli
Black Pepper French Fries with Smoked Red Pepper Aioli
Sweet Potato Fries with Cinnamon Sea Salt

Sweet Potato Fries with Lemon and Habanero Aioli
Greek Fries with Chopped Fresh Herbs, Crumbled Feta and a Lemon-Mint Dipping Sauce
Chesapeake Fries with Old Bay and Marble Cheddar

MASHED POTATO COMBINATIONS

Try topping your mashed potatoes with crispy fried onions or leeks, chopped nuts, fresh herbs or a swirl of any number of flavored oils. Lightly browning in the oven or salamander adds additional texture and is an appealing finishing touch.

Smoked Gouda
Golden Mashed with Truffle Butter
Mojito Mashed with Mint
Roasted Chili
Buttermilk with Tarragon
Wasabi
Crawfish and Chive Mashed Potatoes
Olive Tapenade

Roasted Walnuts
Sun Dried Tomato
Lemon Zest
Caramelized Onion
White Cheddar and Chipotle
Spinach and Roasted Garlic
Cilantro Pesto
Smoked Tomato

Greek Yogurt and Mint
Roasted Banana
Coconut Milk and Toasted Coconut
Bourbon Pecan
Roasted Garlic and Mascarpone Cheese
Mexican Chocolate Mole
Goat Cheese
Horseradish and Smoked Cheddar

Butter Poached Lobster
Caramelized Onion and Thyme
Roasted Poblano
Gorgonzola
Manchego Whipped Potatoes
Dijon
Oven Roasted Tomato
Anchovy with Scallion

Fresh Basil
Black Truffle Oil
Watercress

MASHED POTATO COMBINATIONS

Roasted Eggplant
Green Chili and Cilantro
Grilled Scallion Dijon
Roasted Chestnut Puree
Virgin Olive Oil
Saffron
Caramelized Celery Root
Marble Cheddar

Basil Pesto
Whole Grain Mustard
Shaved Fennel
Gruyere
Roasted Artichokes
Blue Cheese and Bacon
Roasted Shallot
Wild Mushrooms

Prosciutto and Caramelized Shallots
Creamy Horseradish
Sautéed Leeks and Mustard
Three Cheese
Caramelized Sweet Corn
Mint Oil
Sour Cream and Chive
Harissa

Old Bay
Stilton and Caramelized Onion
Red Miso
Green Peppercorn
Roasted Butternut Puree
Foie Gras
Peanut Butter and Bacon
Guinness Fondue

Sofrito
Pancetta Parmigianino
Ranch
Brie
Lemon Oil
Parsley Pesto
Lobster Mashed Potatoes with Merlot Sauce

RICE

There are more and more different and interesting varieties of rice that come onto the market all of the time. Interchange them with all of your recipes and develop new combinations. Basic rice preparations can be enhanced with any variety of flavored oil or compound butter that compliments the dish.

Sunburst Rice with Shallots, Orange and Lemon Zest
Ginger-Coconut Rice with Papaya Salsa
Thai Red Rice Pilaf with Stir-Fried Fresh Basil and Diced Chilies
Jasmine Rice with Crystallized Ginger and Seasoned Rice Wine Vinegar
White Beans and Pumpkinseed Rice
Saffron Basmati Rice with Sautéed Broccoli Rabe
Basmati Rice with Lemon Zest and Lavender
Hazelnut and Wild Rice Pilaf
Orzo Pilaf with Lemon Zest
Ginger Rice with Crispy Shallots

Jasmine Rice with Tangerines and Mint Vinaigrette
Confetti Rice with Tricolor Peppers
Spicy Red Rice with Jalapeños and Fresh Mint
Peking Fried Rice
Apricot Mustard Wild Rice
Jasmine Rice with Spiced Peanuts
Rice Pilaf with Fresh Chives and Mustard Seeds
Arborio Rice with Cucumber and Mint
Red Curry Rice
Basmati Rice with Black Cardamom, Fried Shallots and Toasted Coconut
Brown Rice with Cremini Mushrooms and Pinot Grigio

Bamboo Rice with Grilled Scallions, Toasted Sesame Oil and Rice Wine Vinegar
Mint and Fresh Pea
Brown Rice with Sun Dried Tomato Pesto
Rice with Horseradish and Chives
Basmati Rice with Roasted Garlic
Three Cheese Rice
Jasmine Rice with Lobster Broth and Lemon Zest
Orange and Scallion Basmati Rice
Jasmine Rice with Wasabi and Ginger
Bamboo Rice with Charred Chilies

Brown Rice with Tequila, Lime and Cilantro
Wild Rice with Bacon and Smoked Cheddar
Caramelized Corn and Grilled Scallion Rice
Mushroom Rice topped with Crisp Prosciutto
Three Peppercorn Rice
Rosemary Rice with Orange Zest
Old Bay Rice with Red Pepper Butter

RISOTTO

Can you say "Great Food Cost" ?!!!

Red Wine Risotto with Slow Roasted Lamb
Crab and Truffle Risotto with Fresh Tarragon and Chives
Spring Pea Risotto with Pea Tendrils, Shaved Smoked Ham and Goat Cheese
Sharp Provolone Risotto with Spicy Marinara
Pasilla Chili and Manchego Cheese
Lobster with Mascarpone and Thai Basil
Risotto with Fresh Basil and Lemon
Scallop, Caramelized Onion and Applewood Smoked Cheddar

Black Truffle Risotto with Shaved Logatelli
Sweet Corn and Dried Cherry with Wild Mushroom Pistou
Crab Gorgonzola Risotto
Caramelized Corn, Grilled Scallion and Roasted Fennel
Winter Root Vegetable with Shaved Dry Monterey Jack and Chive Oil
Smoked Salmon and Fontina
Pancetta and Spiced Mascarpone
Lobster with Saffron and Pasilla Peppers

English Pea, Smoked Pork and Stilton
Lemon, Pistachio and Havarti
Pumpkin and Edam with Pecans
Gruyere and Country Ham Risotto with Fresh Peas
Black Truffle, Roasted Red Beets and Gorgonzola
Grilled Portabella and Charred Beef with Chianti Au Jus
Wild Boar Sausage with Mushrooms, Parmesan and Lemon Zest
Sweet Corn and Cherry Risotto with Morels and a Basil Pistou

Risotto of Braised Oxtails with Roasted Acorn Squash, Wilted Kale and Golden Chanterelles
Spinach and Feta with Blistered Grape Tomatoes and Poached Egg
Wild Mushroom with Braised Spring Ramps and White Asparagus
Saffron Risotto with Duck Confit, Butternut Squash, Roasted Shallots and Crispy Prosciutto
Braised Pork and Sweet Corn Risotto with Jalapeño Bacon
Morel Mushroom with Peas, Wild Rocket, Goat Cheese and Brown Butter
Spanish Chorizo, Fire-Roasted Peppers, Oaxaca Cheese and Charred Onions

Shredded Roast Duck with Dried Blueberries and Black Truffles
Acorn Squash with Parmigianino and Crispy Sage
Wilted Swiss Chard with Pea Shoots and Ricotta Salata
Risotto with Grilled Baby Artichokes, Sun Dried Tomato Pesto and Asiago
Toasted Pistachio Duck Prosciutto, Grilled Asparagus and Brown Butter
Smoked Oyster Risotto with Meyer Lemon Confit and Fresh Sage

RISOTTO

Lump Crab and Sweet Corn with Fresh Asparagus Tips and Sherry Wine Butter
Grilled Lobster with Wild Mushrooms, Melted Leeks and Black Truffle Oil
Red Rice Risotto with Smoked Gouda and Golden Raisons
Meyer Lemon with Grilled Asparagus and Crab
Oxtail Risotto with Three Onions and White Truffle Oil
Chardonnay Risotto with Roasted Pumpkin, Baby Spinach and Toasted Pine Nuts
Beet Risotto with Smoked Ham, Roasted Shallots and Dill-Lemon Cream
Scallop and Lobster with a Champagne Truffle Sauce

Seared Scallop with Truffles and Lemon Olive Oil
Sweet Potato, Smoked Pork and Lime Risotto
Crab with Japanese Parsley and Meyer Lemon
Black Rice Risotto with Bacon Confit and Roasted Carrots
Smoked Chicken with Mascarpone and Chive Oil
Pasilla Chili and Chorizo
Asiago Risotto in Smoked Tomato Broth
Lobster with Mascarpone and Lemon Verbena

Roasted Poblano and Chorizo
Shrimp and Scallop Risotto with Orange Zest and Thai Basil
English Peas with Mascarpone and Kalamata Olive Oil
Pastina Risotto with Roasted Tomato and Pepper Sauce
Butternut Squash and Chanterelle Mushrooms
Sweet Potato Lime
Wild Mushroom with Parmesan and Porcini Oil
Lobster with Lemon and Fines Herbs

Smoked Bacon and Red Potato
Roasted Pumpkin with Fresh Sage and Mushroom Jus
Caramelized Corn and Black Bean Risotto
Roasted Red and Yellow Beets with Dill
Walnut Risotto with Asparagus
Pumpkin with Apples and Cider Oil
Leek and Gorgonzola
Cardamom Scented Risotto with Lemon Zest
English Pea Risotto with Grilled Shrimp and Lemon Zest

Smoked Shrimp and Granny Smith Apples
Bay Scallop with Grilled Andouille, Roasted Corn, Scallions and Black Bean Puree

MAC AND CHEESE

Over the last couple of years we have seen the old side dish stand-by macaroni and cheese elevated to a feature item both as a much improved side dish and as an entrée. For side dishes use ingredients that correspond with the entrée that they are being served with like a wild mushroom macaroni and cheese with a beef entree. A slightly more complex combination can be the star with simpler entrees. A spinach and gorgonzola macaroni and cheese will go well with a basic baked chicken. It can be the traditional spoonful serving or you can bake the Mac and Cheese into a firm preparation and cut it in any number of shapes and sizes. It can also be breaded and fried or set in a base of sauce or purée. Don't forget that you can change the pasta you are using in a particular dish. Not only the shape and size of the pasta but you can try whole wheat or other whole grains or try Saba or rice noodles. Flavored pastas could be used like spinach, sun dried tomato or cracked black pepper.

Spanish Mac and Cheese with Orecchiette Pasta, Spanish Chorizo and Enchilado Cheese
Crispy Chicken Mac and Cheese with Honey Hot Sauce
Gruyere Mac and Cheese with Pancetta and Charred Balsamic Onions
Mac and Cheese Fritters with Horseradish Cheddar and Roasted Red Pepper Coulis
Smoked Edam Mac and Cheese with Duck Confit and Sun Dried Tomatoes
Mac and Cheese Muffins with Maple Butter and Chipotle Dipping Sauce
Deep Fried Smoked Gouda Mac and Cheese Bars with Honey BBQ Sauce for Dipping
Beer Battered Macaroni and Cheese Fritters with a Smokey Chipotle Ranch Dip

Brie with Roasted Apples and Pears
Mac and Cheese Fritters with Banana Pepper Rémoulade
Crab and Fontina
Roasted Butternut Squash with Colby-Jack
Lobster Macaroni and Cheese with Melted Leeks
Braised Swiss Chard with Caramelized Onions and Hazelnuts
Mac and Cheese Fritters with Smoked Tomato Compote
Short Rib Mac and Cheese with Marble Cheddar

Roasted Pumpkin with Soubise Onion Cream Sauce
Crab and Old Bay with Smoked Gouda
Chèvre and Goat Cheese with Buttered Rosemary Bread Crumb Crust
Bacon, Caramelized Apple and Smoked Gouda
Wild Mushroom, Smoked Ham and Gorgonzola
Fontina with White Truffle Oil
Angry Mac - Pepper Jack, Chorizo, Roasted Poblano
Bel Paese and Mozzarella with Fresh Tarragon and a Crunchy Asiago Crust

Crispy Macaroni and Cheese with Bourbon Barbecue Sauce
Colby Cheese with Chorizo and Cornbread Crumble
White Cheddar and Sliced Grilled Hot Dogs
Tasso Ham with Roasted Okra
Cotija Cheese and Jalapeno Bacon

MAC AND CHEESE

Asadero with Spicy Chili Crust
Shrimp and Shiitake Mushrooms with Raclette Cheese
Andouille, Charred Onion and Sweet Pepper
Smoked Cheddar and Grilled Apple
Gruyère with Truffles
Spicy Sausage and Queso Blanco with Tortilla Chip Crust
Manchego Cheese and Tasso Ham with Roasted Peppers
Butter Poached Lobster with White Truffle Oil

Mac and Cheese with Crumbled Italian Sausage, Smoked Ricotta and Provolone
Baked Macaroni and Cheese with Crisp Pancetta and Sun Dried Tomatoes
Grilled Apples, Brie and Pecans
Pears, Fresh Sage and Hickory Smoked Pork
King Crab and Havarti with Lemon and Parsley
Shrimp and Caramelized Leek with Manchego Cheese and Cracker Crust
Country Sausage and Maple Cheddar
Smoked Gouda with Herb Crumb Topping

Feta, Olives and Tomato
Chorizo, Grilled Onion and Manchego
Buffalo Mac and Cheese with Crisp Fried Popcorn Chicken, Blue Cheese Chunks and Hot Sauce
Red Jalapeno Mac and Cheese
Colby with Crisp Bacon and Chopped Peanuts
Caramelized Onion, Roasted Corn and Chopped Grilled Scallions
Havarti, Spinach and Wild Mushrooms
BBQ Pork and Horseradish Cheddar with dollop of Cilantro Sour Cream

Mac and Cheese Carbonara - Fontina, Asiago, Crisp Prosciutto and Baby Peas
Roasted Butternut Squash, Cremini Mushrooms and Smoked Gouda
Smoked Shrimp and Bel Paese
Basil Gnocchi Mac and Cheese with Oven Dried Tomatoes and Fontina
Lorraine Mac and Cheese with Caramelized Onions, Bacon and Gruyere
Pepperoni and Smoked Mozzarella
Pancetta and Sharp Provolone
Roasted Poblano stuffed with Queso Blanco and Oaxaca Mac and Cheese

Charred Red Peppers and Maytag Blue
Goat Cheese and Sun Dried Tomato Pesto
Smoked Ham, White Cheddar and Fried Sage

Caramelized Cauliflower, Smoked Sausage and Cheddar
Shredded Beef, Gorgonzola and Porcini

STARCHES

Montrachet Cheese and Orzo Croquettes with a Tomato and Saffron Sauce
Golden Raisin and Roasted Pistachio Couscous
Creamy Grits with Smoked Chicken and Wild Mushrooms
Caramelized Corn and Cannelloni Bean Cassoulet
Dried Fruit Spoon Bread
Mint Dumplings with Chopped Fresh Thai Basil and Diced Red Chilies
Roasted Onion Spaetzle
Crispy Polenta Logs with Sherry-Parmesan Cream Dipping Sauce

Red Potatoes and Asparagus with Porcini Mushroom Butter
Cold Peanut Noodles with Chilies, Bitter Greens and Grilled Scallions
Sage and Roasted Chestnut Bread Pudding
Smokey Mesquite Onion Rings
Garlic Polenta with Crisp Pancetta
Creamy Herb and Prosciutto Polenta
Wild Mushrooms Polenta with Rosemary Oil
Smoked Cheddar and Caramelized Onion Grits

Quinoa with Toasted Walnuts and Golden Raisons
Farro with Blistered Cherry Tomatoes and Chives
Horseradish Cheddar Bread Pudding
Sweet Potato Dumplings with Chicken Jus
Roasted Wild Mushroom Cornbread Pudding
Buckwheat Groats with Grilled Apples and Toasted Pine Nuts
Lemon Mascarpone Polenta

Grilled Artichoke and Red Potato Sauté
Roasted Potatoes with Caramelized Cauliflower and Chives
Parmesan Polenta with Toasted Pistachio Butter
Creamy Blue Corn Grits
Farro with Eggplant and Fresh Oregano
Pistachio Spaetzle
Polenta Cake with Grilled Fresh Fennel
Quinoa with Wild Mushrooms

Lemon Poppy Seed Spaetzle
Brown Butter and Sage Polenta
Stir-fried Rice Noodles with Chili and Thai Basil
Organic Farro with Mascarpone and Chives
Yellow Lentil Pilaf Cakes on Smoked Tomato Curry
Crispy Macaroni Croquette with Sharp Cheddar Fondue
Chili Black Bean Cake with Cilantro Sour Cream
Roasted Tomato Smashed Sweet Potatoes
Smoked Cheddar Grits with Cilantro
Dried Fruit Couscous

STARCHES

Farro with Cranberries and Almonds
Baked Penne and Creamed Spinach Gratin
Parmigianino Polenta with Balsamic-Butter Sauce
Red Quinoa with Caramelized Onion and Roasted Chilies
Bleu Cheese, Honey Roasted Apple and Sweet Potato Gratin
Israeli Couscous with Wild Mushrooms and Shaved Asiago
Crispy Grits Cake with Cheddar and Jalapeños
Wild Mushroom Croquettes with a Reduced Balsamic Cream Sauce

Baked Quinoa and Cheese Casserole
Buckwheat Groats with Yogurt and Fresh Dill
Mascarpone and Caramelized Onion Polenta
Sesame Noodles with Fresh Mint and a Chili-Garlic Sauce
Saffron and Currant Couscous
Rye Bread Pudding with Toasted Caraway
Quinoa with Black Beans, Caramelized Corn and Cilantro
Creamy Herbed Soft Polenta with Madeira Sauce

Roasted Corn Johnnycakes with Fermented Black Bean Puree and Cilantro Crema
Curried Lentils with Maitake Mushrooms, Pan Roasted Chickpeas and Mint Sour Cream
Caramelized Sweet Potatoes with Spice Roasted Pecans

Polenta scented with Rosemary and Layered with
Sun-Dried Tomatoes, Spinach and Roasted Shallots

Truffle Grits with Wild Mushrooms
Chili-Rubbed Onion Strings with Blue Cheese Chunks and Chipotle BBQ Sauce
Corn and Pea Croquettes with Mint Butter
Quinoa and Braised Bok Choy Compote

Smashed Red Potatoes with Roasted Garlic and Chicken Jus
Whole Wheat Dumplings with Sage Butter
Quinoa with Spinach and Pine Nuts
Chive Dumplings with a Sweet Corn Puree
Golden Cornbread with Charred Scallions and Goat Cheese Butter
Chickpeas Fritters with Roasted Garlic Aioli
Heirloom Potato Cassoulet with Andouille, and Fried Cabbage
Grilled Polenta with Porcini Mushrooms and Burnt Brandy Cream Sauce

Red Quinoa with Fresh Thyme and Lemon Zest
Farro with Swiss Chard and Dried Apricots
Smoked Tomato and Caramelized Onion Whole Wheat Bread Pudding
Roasted Red Pepper and Grilled Scallion Croquettes
Semolina Dumplings in a Smoked Tomato Cream
Whole Wheat Egg Noodle Bake with Corn Flake Crust
Colby-Jack and Cilantro Rice Cakes

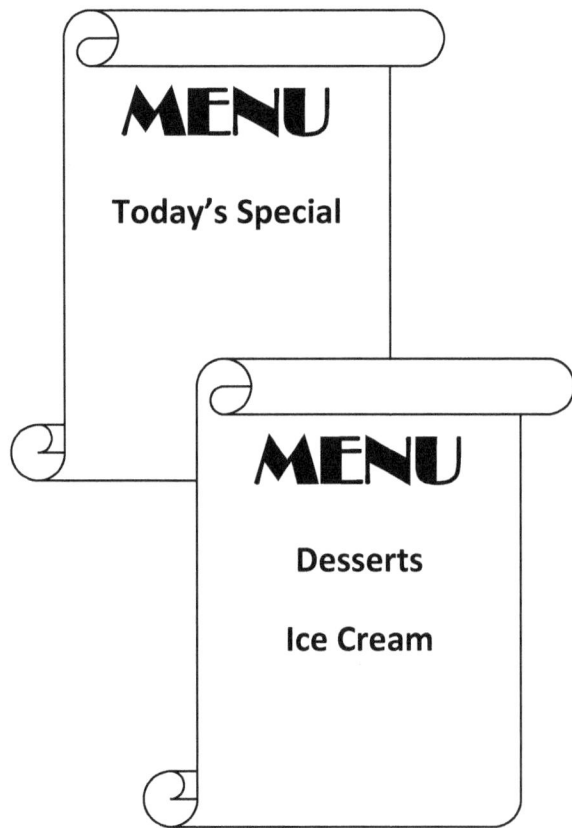

DESSERTS

Various Desserts
Cheesecakes
Ice Cream
Sorbet

Chapter Notes, Ideas and Conversions

Main Ingredient	Element 1	Element 2	Element 3	Sauce	Texture

DESSERTS

Roasted Pear Tart with Gorgonzola Mascarpone and Chianti Reduction
Warm Plum Empanada with Spicy Cabernet Ice Cream and Caramel Sauce
Lady Kisses -Miniature Macaroons topped with Chocolate Mousse and dipped in Chocolate
Strawberry Crumb Cake with Basil Ice Cream
Pretzel Stick Skewer with Strawberry, Marshmallow and Pineapple dipped in Chocolate or Caramel
Toffee and Bourbon Bread Pudding with Brown Sugar Cream
Irish Whiskey Chocolate Tiramisu with Mocha Cream
Dark Chocolate and Orange Crème Brûleè

Crisp Cannoli with Lemon Zest-Blackberry Ricotta
Raspberry Mint Buttermilk Cake
Bittersweet Chocolate and Dark Cherry Crème Brûleè
Warm Pear and Cranberry Crisp
Butterscotch Pots de Crème with Espresso Syrup and Crushed Walnuts
Bay Leaf Panna Cotta with Black Raspberries
Fresh Orange Tart with a Vanilla and Brown Butter Custard
Pink Grapefruit Sorbet with Orange Blossom Honey Drizzle

White Chocolate Boston Cream Pie
Tres Leche Cake with Mango and Raspberry Syrup
Kahlua Infused Espresso Panna Cotta
Chocolate Ganache Cake with Coconut Jam and Macadamias
Smoked Almond Tart with Kaffir Lime Syrup
Banana Croissant Bread Pudding with Dark Cherry Reduction
Peanut Butter – Roasted Banana Crème Brûleè
Vanilla Profiteroles with a Dark Chocolate Caramel Sauce

Chocolate Cheesecake Lollipops with Caramel Cashews
Lemon Blueberry Curd with Hazelnut Beignets
Caramelized Orange Pound Cake with Merlot Syrup
Roasted Pear and Butterscotch Bread Pudding
Mojito and Toasted Coconut Panna Cotta
Kaffir Lime Crème Brûleè with Loganberries
Dark Chocolate Cake with Espresso Milk Chocolate Sabayon
Port Wine Poached Pears

Warm Bread Pudding with Brandy Apples and Cranberry Flambé Topping
Caramel Profiteroles with Espresso Ice Cream and Candied Walnuts
Baked Apple with Warm Rum Raisins and Vanilla Ice Cream
Chocolate Fudge Layer Cake with Malted Crème Anglaise
Raspberry Pecan Shortcake with White Chocolate Mousse
Warm Almond Cake with Caramelized Apples and Cider Hard Sauce
Caramelized Orange Shortbread

DESSERTS

Triple Chocolate Cake with Orange Cream and Raspberry Reduction
Cherry Panna Cotta with Walnut Carmel Syrup
Spiced Chocolate Fondue with Petite Cookies and Fresh Fruits
Blood Orange Crème Brûleè with Blackberry Puree
Key Lime Baked Alaska
Brandied Fig Bread Pudding with Crème Anglaise
Warm Chocolate Tart with Marshmallow Cream
Lemon Crème Brûleè with Shortbread Crust

Pear and Port Sorbet
Chocolate Bread Pudding with Brown Butter Raisins and Caramelized Milk
Sticky Toffee Bread Pudding
Raspberry Rhubarb Crisp with Vanilla Mascarpone Ice Cream
Roasted Banana Cake with Pecan Raison Ice Cream and Dark Rum Syrup
Orange Panna Cotta with Toasted Hazelnuts
Chocolate Crunch Cake with Hazelnut Praline
Galliano and Candied Citron Crème Brûleè

Milk Chocolate and Bourbon Panna Cotta
Grilled Sugar Peach Tart
Deep Fried Candy Bar of the Day with Burnt Sugar Whipped Cream
Warm Walnut Bread with Melted Brie and Aged Fig Sauce
Roasted Pumpkin Mousse with Dark Chocolate Sauce
Poppy Seed Pound Cake with Meyer Lemon Curd and Mint Syrup
Bittersweet Chocolate Ganache with Cranberry Marmalade and Dark Cocoa Whipped Cream
Roasted Cinnamon Sugar Plantains with Pecans and Maple Crème Fraîche

Black Walnut Cake with Dried Fruit Compote and Vanilla Bean Ice Cream
Blackberry Ice Cream with Warm Burgundy Sauce and Cream
Date Pudding with Sticky Toffee Sauce
White Chocolate and Lemongrass Parfait with Chopped Macadamias
Warm Plum Amoretti Crumble with Orange Blossom Honey Whipped Cream
Vanilla Bean Crème Brûleè with Candied Lemon
Roasted Pear Tart with Crunchy Pecan Brittle and Lemony Cream
Maple-Walnut Bread Pudding with Warm Rum Raison Compote

Warm Chocolate Fudge Cake with Peanut Butter Sauce
Meyer Lemon Tart with Chocolate Almond Shortbread Crust
Chestnut Pot De Crème with Macaroons and Chestnut Honey
Ginger Snap Sandwiches with Apple Cinnamon Ice Cream
Blackberry Panna Cotta with a Pecan Shortbread Crust
Coconut Cake with Mango Compote and Burnt Sugar
Warm Banana Tapioca with Macadamias and Toasted Coconut

DESSERTS

Warm Raison Bread Pudding with Apple-Pear Compote and Molasses Ice Cream
Brown Sugar Soufflé with Bittersweet Chocolate Sauce and Toasted Hazelnuts
Whisky Shortcake with Vanilla Ice Cream and Apple Cider Sauce
Roasted Banana and Hazelnut Bread Pudding with a Warm Caramel-Fig Sauce
Toffee Pudding with Warm Tangerine Compote
Lemon Tiramisu with Blackberries and Crushed Walnuts
Honey Panna Cotta with Stewed Blood Oranges
Coconut Ice Cream Sandwich with Macadamia Nuts and Pineapple Compote

Dark Chocolate Pâté with Brûleè Bananas and Lavender Cream
Kailua Tiramisu
Chocolate Profiteroles with Amaretto Ice Cream and Warm Caramel Sauce
Lemon-Vanilla Bean Panna Cotta with Blackberry Compote
Green Apple, Caramel and Dark Rum Tart with Whipped Mascarpone
Brioche Bread Pudding with Bourbon and Caramel Crème
Key Lime Tart with Blueberry Syrup
Warm Caramelized Ginger Cake with Apricot-Rum Compote

Coconut Ginger Jasmine Rice Pudding with Lemongrass and Kaffir Lime Syrup
Dark Meyer's Rum Soaked Génoise with Vanilla Ice Cream and Caramelized Pineapple Sauce
Honey Roasted Pears with Walnut Cake and Basil-Coconut Sorbet
Grand Marnier Tiramisu with Warm Honey Poached Oranges
Butterscotch Flan with Pecan Wafers
Caramelized Pineapple Cake with a Cilantro Buttermilk and Mint Sorbet
Strawberry Sabayon with Lemon Zest and Mint

Flourless Hazelnut and Dark Chocolate Torte
Toasted Coconut Rice Pudding with Rum Raisins
Granny Smith Apple and Dried Cranberry Crisp with Brown Butter Ice Cream
Grilled Peach Panna Cotta with Warm Ginger Syrup
Roasted Bananas on Cashew Shortbread with Toffee Ice Cream
Plum Nectarine Strudel with Crystallized Pecans
Chocolate Peanut Butter Mousse with Dark Chocolate Whipped Cream
Warm Peach Beignets with Toasted Almond Ice Cream

Meyer Lemon Bread Pudding with Fresh Blueberries
Grilled Pear Crisp with Huckleberry Sauce
Double Dark Chocolate and Bourbon Panna Cotta
Galliano and Candied Orange Crème Brûleè
Strawberry Napoleons with Roasted Mango Coulis
White Chocolate and Raspberry Bread Pudding
Fig-Cherry Compote with Black Pepper Ice Cream
Rose Infused Crème Brule

DESSERTS

Cappuccino Parfait with Espresso Custard and Dark Chocolate Ice Cream
Key Lime Brûleè
Grilled Peach Melba with Red Currants
Fig and Raspberry Tart with Toasted Almond Ice Cream
Blood Orange and Pomegranate Tartlet
Lavender Honey Ice Cream with Fresh Raspberries
Tawny Port Soaked Raspberries with Mascarpone Chantilly
Cappuccino Profiteroles with Carmel and Mocha Whipped Cream

Summer Peach and Strawberry Crisp with Butter Pecan Ice Cream
Banana and Macadamia Bread Pudding with Coconut Rum Cream and Drizzled Chocolate
Steamed Fresh Orange Pudding with Ginger Chantilly
Cinnamon Crème Brûleè
Grilled Peach and Raspberry Crisp
Crème Fraîche Panna Cotta with Blackberries
Caramelized Apple Tartlet with Mulberry Ice Cream

Plum and Cardamom Sorbet
Roasted Banana and Toasted Almond Strudel
Peanut Butter and Mocha Cream Martini with Dark Chocolate Ganache
Three Berry Parfait with Pomegranate Whipped Cream
Pear Tart with Tangerine Custard
Baked Bananas with Macadamia Nuts and Caramel Sauce
Strawberry Topped Lime Mousse Tart
Dried Cherry Bread Pudding with Vanilla Bean Ice Cream and Merlot Syrup

Crystallized Ginger and Black Currant Rice Pudding
Oven Roasted Plums and Peaches with Beaujolais Glaze and Toasted Walnuts
Stem Strawberries with Chocolate and Butterscotch Dipping Sauces
Marsala Sponge Cake with Citrus Cream Cheese Icing
Mile High Banana Meringue Pie
Caramelized Pineapple Cake with Ginger Cream
Dark Rum and Pineapple Brûleè
Cinnamon Poppy Seed Cake

Lemon Custard Phyllo Cups with Black Raspberries
Caramelized Apple Cake with Warm Butterscotch Sauce
Pecan, Macaroon and Fresh Fig Tart
Banana Bread Pudding with Foster Sauce
Peach and Raspberry Crisp
Hazelnut Napoleons with Mascarpone and Oranges
Caramel Apple Tart
Chocolate Raspberry Bread Pudding

DESSERTS

Rum Soaked Chocolate Cake topped with Chocolate and Banana Cream
Fresh Pear Cake with Brown Sugar Syrup
Chocolate Zabaglione with Toffee Crisps
Raspberry and White Chocolate Tart
Brownie Sundae with Peanut Butter Ice Cream and Hot Fudge
Orange Poppy Seed Cake with Berries and Crème Fraîche
Chocolate and Peppermint Stick Pie
Exotic Fruit Salad with Rum Cream

Triple Chocolate Mousse Tort
Golden Pineapple and Caramel Cake
Cappuccino and Espresso Sorbet with Petite Macaroons
Chocolate Crepes with Caramel Butterscotch Cream Filling
Crispy Chocolate Cups with Cabernet Mousse
Sour Cherry Brown Butter Tart
Grilled Peaches with Black Raspberries and Merlot Reduction
Chocolate Cream Puffs with Cappuccino Cream

Raspberry Pistachio Cake
Banana Upside Down Cake
Peanut Butter Cake with Butterfinger Icing
Strawberry Napoleons with Lemon Cream
Dark Chocolate and Hazelnut Pie
Lemon Pound Cake with Warm Blueberries
Tia Maria Cream Fondue with Assorted Fruit
Chocolate Crepes with Caramelized Pineapple and Macadamia Cream

Pineapple Pecan Bread Pudding
Chilled Chocolate Cake Soaked in Hazelnut Syrup
Peach and Raspberry Parfait
Chocolate Rum and Banana Cream Torte
Fresh Strawberry Cream Éclairs
Caramelized Apple and Pear Stack with Cinnamon-Cider Ice Cream
Toasted Almond Lemon Cake
Chocolate Croissant Bread Pudding with Warm Butter Caramel

Lavender Scented Meyer Lemon Shortcake
White Wine Poached Peaches with Lemon Verbena Anglaise
Golden Raison and Cranberry Tart
Chocolate Macadamia Flan in Crispy Layers
Chocolate Hazelnut Tarts with Frangelico Crème Anglaise
Pear Cranberry Crisp with Ginger Ice Cream
Chocolate Crepes with Cappuccino Mousse

DESSERTS

Chocolate Ricotta Sponge Cake Soaked in Espresso and Dark Rum
Cherry Champagne Ice
Blackberry Hazelnut Gelato
Orange Walnut Crème with Chocolate Lace
Lemon Mint Sorbet in Crisp Crepe Shells
Almond Meringue Napoleons with Dark Chocolate Mousse
Rum Pistachio Custard in Glazed Phyllo Cups
Brandied Peach Ice Cream Napoleon

Pineapple Macadamia Baked Alaska
Cappuccino Ice Cream in Praline Baskets
Raspberry and Sour Cream Layer Cake
Coconut Caramel Flan
Warm Apple Bread Pudding with Fresh Cider Cream
Dried Apricot Pecan Pie with Butter Rum Sauce
Red Plum Sorbet with Grilled Fruits
Triple Chocolate Terrine

Espresso Mousse in White Chocolate Cups
Plum Strudel with Kirsch
Chocolate and Banana Cream Pie
Orange Chocolate Chunk Brownies
Peach and Blueberry Cobbler
Banana Cream Pie with Banana Caramel Crust
Vanilla Rice Pudding with Dried Cherries
Chocolate Crepes Layered with Raspberry Compote and Peanut Butter Mousse

Caramelized Banana Purses with White Chocolate Sauce
Black Bottom Butterscotch Pie
Chocolate Tiramisu with Orange Sauce
Orange Pecan Pie
Chocolate Bread Pudding with Warm Caramel Sauce and Cinnamon Ice Cream
Cherry Chocolate Soufflé
Chocolate Cannoli filled with Toasted Almond Cream
Walnut Spiced Layer Cake with Kahlua Cream Cheese Frosting

Macadamia, Macaroon and Fig Tart
Chocolate Butterscotch Bread Pudding
Pumpkin Crème Brûleè
Apple Crumb Tart with Caramel Sauce
Chocolate Pistachio Crème Brûleè
Chocolate Mint Cake with Raspberry Compote
Chocolate Caramel Flan

CHEESE CAKES

Ricotta Cheesecake with a Port Wine and Dried Cherry Compote
Chocolate Espresso Ganache
Pistachio Cheesecake with Blackberry-Tequila Jam
White Chocolate Orange
Lemon Ricotta Mint
Caramelized Spiced Apple and Butterscotch
Pumpkin Bourbon
Sweet Potato with Candied Pecans
Caramel Apple with Streusel Topping
Limoncello
Kona Coffee
Honey Ricotta
Key Lime
Caramelized Pineapple with Guava Coulis and Candied Ginger
Caramel Apple

Mango Basil Lemon
Mascarpone and Orange with Toasted Almond Crust
Espresso-Hazelnut with Orange Caramel Sauce
Ricotta Raisin
Blueberry Pecan
Caramel Flan
Roasted Pumpkin and Mascarpone with Amaretto
Habanero Lime and Pear
Mint Chocolate
Margarita Ice
Mojito Mint
Pecan-Pumpkin Spice with Ginger Snap Crust
Brown Sugar with Sherry Poached Pears
Passion Fruit
Honey Tangerine

Ginger with Sour Cherry
Caramel Peach
Lemon with Blueberries
Chocolate Chambord
Peanut Butter and Jelly
Apricot Amaretto
White Chocolate Cheesecake with Toffee Crust
Maple Walnut
Heath Bar Crunch
Frangelico and Chocolate Chip with Hazelnuts
Orange Cranberry
Ginger Pear
Raspberry Chocolate Chunk
Pineapple Raisin

ICE CREAM

Malted Milk Chocolate
Lemon Buttermilk
Salted Caramel
Banana Daiquiri
Angry Mango
Brown Butter
Crème Fraîche Gorgonzola

Caramel Green Apple
Almond Milk
Brown Sugar Vanilla
Chestnut Puree Cinnamon
Guinness
Fior di Latte

Candied Cashew Cream Cheese
Lemon Custard
Banana Caramel
White Chocolate Sour Cream
Espresso Brown Sugar
Orange Blossom Honey
Dark Molasses
Cinnamon Cider
Caramel Brittle

Honeyed Pineapple
Cherry Yogurt
Strawberry Basil
Roasted Vanilla
Mojito
Red Jalapeno Tangerine
Toasted Coconut

Lavender Yogurt
Watermelon Cucumber Mint
Raspberry Crème Fraîche
Rosemary Honey
Sour Cream
Sundried Sour Cherry Kirsch

Roasted Ginger
Blueberry Banana
Grilled Peaches and Cream
Chocolate Butterscotch
Grand Marnier
Fig and Basil
Cilantro, Buttermilk and Mint
Blackberry Hazelnut
Basil Coconut

Vanilla Toasted Pine Nut
Roasted Banana
Buttered Popcorn
White Russian
Sour Cherry
Peach Bourbon
Strawberry Soy Ginger

Tupelo Honey
White Pepper
Fig and Honey
Coconut Mint
Coffee Amaretto
Cardamom

Caramel Thyme
Nutty Roasted Orange
Pecan Brittle
Smoked Earl Grey
Caramelized Banana
Apple Cinnamon
Mulberry
Chestnut Allspice
Lemon Meringue Pie

SORBET

Huckleberry Swirl
Lemon Balm
Green Apple
Chocolate Brandy
Meyer Lemon
Pomegranate Grapefruit
Intense Berry
Crème Fraîche
Spiced Strawberry
Blood Orange
Pink Peppercorn
Plum and Cardamom

Pomegranate Rhubarb
Buttermilk Cantaloupe
Thai Basil
Drunken Peach
Orange Yuzu
Satsuma Mandarin
Plum Wine
Spiced Cider
Apricot Passion Fruit
Chai Tea
Rhubarb
Yuzu

Concord Grape
Poached Pear
Orange Blossom Mango
Pink Grapefruit
Mango Habanero
Cranberry Orange
Hibiscus Tea
Dark Rum Mojito
Piña Colada
Lemon Praliné
Spiced Pear
Whipped Cream Vodka

ON HAND ITEMS

Muffin and Sweet Breads
Compound Butters
Salsas, Chutneys, Pickles and Relishes
BBQ Grilling Sauces

Chapter Notes, Ideas and Conversions

Main Ingredient	Element 1	Element 2	Element 3	Sauce	Texture

MUFFIN AND SWEETBREAD COMBINATIONS

Many of these combinations can work well when incorporated into a cake/loaf bread preparation like a zucchini or banana bread, cornbread or in biscuit dough.

Caramelized Corn with Monterey Jack and Jalapeno
Lavender and Sweet Butter
Grilled Apples, Raisin, Carrot and Bran
Roasted Banana and Mascarpone
Strawberry Buttermilk
Zucchini and Fresh Basil
Cream Cheese and Chive
Orange Cranberry
Roasted Corn with Chipotle
Banana Walnut
Pineapple Macadamia Nut
Lemon Pomegranate
Spiced Pumpkin and Molasses
Raspberry Sour Cream
Peach Cinnamon

Zucchini, Toasted Sunflower Seeds and Orange
Honey Granola
Vanilla Poppy Seed
Apple and Caramelized Onion
Pumpkin Chipotle
Lemon Blueberry
Sage and Prosciutto
Bacon and Scallion
Peach Pecan
Orange Zest with Ricotta
Citrus Zucchini
Peanut Butter Muffin with Jelly Filling
Brown Sugar Praline
Apple, Peanut Butter and Bacon
Raspberry White Chocolate

Carmel Muffins with Streusel Topping
Orange Pecan
Maple, Walnut and Cream Cheese
Apple, Sour Cream and Chive
Honey and Bran
Candied Spiced Yam and Pecan
Peanut Oatmeal
Rosemary and Cracked Pepper
Spicy Almond
Saffron and Golden Raisin

COMPOUND BUTTERS

Combine and wrap the prepared butter in parchment paper or plastic wrap. The "roll" can be round, triangular or square shape. Additionally, the butters can be frozen in individual molds that might correspond to the dish that they are going to be served with. Store in the freezer and slice off the rounds as needed for service. Use for flavoring fish, steaks, vegetables, potatoes or rice dishes. Traditionally, compound butters are sliced and placed on top of the item just as it is to be served, slightly melting from a few seconds under the heat lamp and from the heat of the food. You may also use many of these selections as a whipped butter to accompany the bread service. Be sure to reduce thin liquids and cook out alcohol before combining.

Smoked Tomato-Lobster
Roquefort Burgundy
Horseradish and Grilled Scallion
Apricot Brandy
Roasted Chestnut
Smoked Crawfish
Toasted Macadamia Nut

Red Miso and Wasabi
Honey and Green Peppercorn
Roasted Red Pepper and Jalapeño
Toasted Sesame Ginger
Molasses
Whiskey Lemon
Cabernet and Roasted Shallot

Miso Rosemary
Toasted Pine Nut and Sun Dried Tomato
Smokey Ancho
Foie Gras
Lemon Fennel
Blue Cheese and Fresh Chives
Orange, Lime, Chipotle
Fresh Ginger and Apple

Pumpkin Honey
Caramelized Pear and Chopped Walnut
Mint and Allspice
Port Wine and Bacon
Red Curry
Roasted Tomato and Caramelized Onion
Smoked Salmon and Dill
Caraway and Bacon

Roasted Red Pepper
Green Onion and Dijon
Chianti and Roasted Garlic
Date Walnut
Confetti Sweet Pepper
Kalamata Olive
Pistachio Parsley

Dried Cherry and Toasted Coconut
Creole Mustard and Cilantro
Harissa
Chocolate Mole
Goat Cheese and Peppercorn
Tequila Lime
Chili Pepper Mint

Roasted Pear and Cinnamon
Pommery Mustard and Guinness
Cherry Pepper Relish
Preserved Lemon
Caramelized Ginger Chutney

Raspberry Balsamic
Old Bay
Stilton and Black Currant
Cranberry Pomegranate
Pinot Noir

SALSAS, CHUTNEYS, PICKLES AND RELISHES

Blackberry and Mint Compote
Poblano-Avocado Relish
Caramelized Onion and Dried Cherry Chutney
Grilled Pineapple and Dark Rum Salsa
Pickled Pears with Cinnamon, Cloves and Oranges
Spicy Tomato and Red Chili Chutney with Mint

Cranberry, Caramelized Ginger and Lemon Chutney
Green Apple and Kumquat Relish
Smoked Tomatillo Salsa
Candied Onions
Kiwi, Serrano and Cilantro Salsa
Spicy Lime Relish
Green Tomato and Apple Chutney
Lemon Okra Pickles

Mint and Cumin Pickled Carrots
Tangerine-Pomegranate Relish
Pistachio and Parsley Pesto
Roasted Banana-Tamarind Salsa
Cranberry and Apricot Chutney
Mango Black Bean Relish
House-Made Lime Pickles
Caramelized Apple Marmalade

Fresh Pear and Toasted Walnut Relish
Ginger Red Onion Chutney
Curried Peaches
Tangerine-Pomegranate Relish
Spicy Pickled Carrots
Cranberry Pineapple Salsa
Almond and Apricot Compote
White Currant and Tomato Chutney
Red and Green Pepper Relish
Orange and Cucumber Salsa

Avocado and Black Bean Salsa
Peach Chutney
Ginger Apple Relish
Spiced Cranberries
Tomato Cranberry Chutney
Cranberry, Kumquat and White Raison Relish

BBQ GRILLING SAUCES AND GLAZES

Dried Cherry Chipotle
Chocolate Espresso
Spicy Root Beer
Bourbon Molasses
Mango Habanero
Ancho and Roasted Tomatillo
Caribbean Jerk with Mango
Three Citrus and Dark Rum

Roasted Shallot and Balsamic
Prickly Pear and Tequila
Roasted Peanut and Red Chili
Peach Dijon
Caramelized Onion and Poblano
Cola and Spice
Tamarind and Pineapple
Tangerine Teriyaki

Roasted Poblano, Molasses and Dark Rum
Chipotle BBQ
Pineapple Honey with Juniper Berries
Fig and Habanero
Tarragon and Apple Cider
Apricot Ginger
Chinese Five Spice with Rice Wine Vinegar
Maple Syrup and Caramelized Onion

Mango Pomegranate
Dried Cranberry and Apple Cider
Tandoori with Mint
Brown Sugar Dijon
Ginger Peanut
Orange Plum
Herb and Honey
Caramelized Ginger

Orange Honey and Chipotle
Smoked Red Chili
Jalapeno Mint
Spicy Peach
Plum Ginger
Dried Cherry Orange

EVENTS

Italian Antipasti
Holiday Picnic and Barbecue
Summer Brunch
Boxed Lunches
Father's Day
New England Clambake
Children's Halloween Party
Thanksgiving
Meeting Breaks
The Cheese Cart
Eggrolls

AN ITALIAN ANTIPASTO

Delighted with the ease of service but long weary of the typical "salad bar" selections, I often use this Antipasto Table. Sometimes there are many items and sometimes as few as five or six. It can be used as a quick lunch buffet or a late afternoon meal and you can add entrées and it becomes a full dinner. Select menu items according to inventory, price and prep time. I keep a list of items that can be prepared from the existing inventory and then chose a limited number to be served depending on the meal time or event. Most selections hold well for service and have a good shelf life. As a matter of fact, most get better after flavors have time to blend so don't be afraid to begin prep a day or two ahead. When serving a large number of selections, hold back a few dishes to replace depleted items. When a bowl or plate is about half empty, I remove it replacing it with one of the items that had been held back. I then re-plate it in the kitchen in a smaller vessel and return it to the buffet. If there are items leftover at the end of the meal, they can be used to make a great single serving antipasto plate for lunch or side dish specials.

Grilled Fresh Anchovies with Lemon, Oregano, Parsley and Dill
Crisp Crostini with Gorgonzola and Walnuts
Eggplant and Hot Peppers in Mint and Olive Oil
Roasted Peppers with Goat Cheese and Grilled Scallions
Fontina filled Rice Croquets with a Smoked Pepper Coulis
Greens with Pasta, Parmesan and Toasted Pine Nuts
Red Pearl Onions Braised in White Wine, Bay Leaves and Garlic
Gorgonzola and Roasted Garlic Custard
Calamari with Gaeta Olives, Capers and Golden Raisons
Fennel and Sausage Strudel
Deviled Eggs Stuffed with Sun Dried Tomatoes and Chives
Roasted Eggplant Rounds with Fresh Mozzarella and Purple Basil Leaves
Grilled Vegetables with Aged Balsamic Drizzle
Fried Ravioli with Spicy Fra Diablo Aioli
Red Lentils with Crisp Pancetta and Caramelized Shallot Oil
Roasted Peppers with Garlic and Anchovies

Beef Capriccio with Shaved Logatelli and Black Truffle Oil
Fried Olives Stuffed with Sausage and Fontina
Grilled Onions with Balsamic Vinegar
Eggs Stuffed with Roasted Peppers, Capers and Anchovies
Artichoke and Bel Paese Fondue
Chick Peas and Red Beans with Prosciutto and Roasted Shallots
Arborio Rice and Muscat Raisin Salad
Spinach and Vegetable Crepes with Fontinella
Roasted Eggplant with Sun Dried Tomatoes, Gaeta Olives and Goat Cheese
Crispy Calamari tossed with Pickled Cherry Peppers, Arugula and Lemon Aioli
Dried Salt Cod Salad with Onions and Tomatoes
Snails with Fennel Seed, Garlic, White Wine, Parsley and Shallots
Fried Cabbage with Pancetta and Roasted Garlic
Cold Pasta with Smoked Duck and Sage
Saffron Rice with Peas, Green Onion, Flat Leaf Parsley and Crisp Bacon
Fresh Tuna with White Beans and Oven Dried Tomatoes

AN ITALIAN ANTIPASTO

**No antipasto table would be complete without the expected assortment
of olives, peppers, cured meats and cheeses.**

Spiced Olives   Cured Olives   Marinated Olive Mix
Fried Hot Peppers   Roasted Sweet Peppers

Abruzesse	Mortadella	Sopressata	Bresaola
Cappicola	Genoa Salami	Prosciutto	Calabrese
Cubed Fontina	Shaved Asiago	Pecorino	Wedges of Gorgonzola

- For balance, I will add one or more of the soup selections. If offering more than one soup, I would make one seafood and one non-seafood. If only offering one soup try the <u>Little Neck Clam and Italian Sausage Soup</u>. It resembles a red Manhattan clam chowder in taste and texture and I leave the clams in the shell. It makes a great presentation!

Little Neck Clam and Italian Sausage Chowder
Italian Wedding Soup
Pasta and Bean Soup
Charred Golden Tomato and Grilled Fennel Chowder
Country Minestrone with Prosciutto
Meatball and Roasted Fall Vegetable
Sausage and Lentil
Cream of Roasted Garlic
Roasted Tomato Bisque with Gorgonzola Croutons

- In addition to a good quality sliced Italian bread and rolls, you can offer one or more of the following bread ideas;
Gorgonzola Biscuits
Parmigianino Sage Ciabatta
Rosemary and White Raisin Rolls
Char Grilled Lemon Olive Oil Bruschetta
Garlic and Sesame Seed Breadsticks
Oven Roasted Tomato Focaccia

- To finish off this area, make butter available and a few choices of good olive oil. You can flavor a few of the olive oils with herbs or roasted garlic and butters can be enhanced by whipping them with gorgonzola, chopped Kalamata olives or orange and lemon zest. Take it one step further with these accompaniments;

Walnut, Ricotta, Garlic and Parsley Spread
Sun Dried Tomato Pesto
Prosciutto, Roasted Garlic and Whipped Mascarpone

- To make this a truly grand event, entrees might be added in the form of a pasta station or any number of hot buffet entrees or traditional Italian dishes that can be found in the entrée and pasta sections of this guide.

HOLIDAY PICNIC AND BARBECUE

Boneless Loin of Pork with Rosemary and Garlic Butter
Skewered Shrimp with Thai Ginger Sauce
Grilled Chicken -- Legs, Wings and Boneless Breasts
Make your own Taco and Nacho Table
Homemade Bourbon Beans, Husk Grilled Corn on the Cob with Cajun Butter
Caesar Salad, Tri-color Pepper Slaw, Fresh Green Bean Salad, Marinated Mushrooms
Sliced Onion and Hot Pepper Salad, Chilled Roasted Vegetable Gazpacho with Crab
Fresh Fruits and Ice Cream Novelties
Lemonade, Iced Tea, Flavored Iced Teas and Iced Coffees

Condiment Table

The star here is the condiment table. Add as much variety as possible. Lettuce, tomatoes, red and white onions, sliced black olives. Assorted mustards and flavored mayonnaise combinations, salsa, shredded and sliced cheeses, sour cream, hot sauce and blue cheese dressing. Warm sautéed mushrooms, crisp bacon and barbecued onions for burgers, hot dogs and tacos. Taco seasoned beef and chicken; assorted taco and tortilla shells, nacho chips and cheese sauce.

Dessert

For dessert, use whole fresh fruits like peaches, plums and clusters of grapes, sliced melons and assorted berries. Chill the fruit and check for ripeness (an often skipped step). Offer ice cream novelties for variety and quick service. You can scoop ice cream cones to order for smaller groups. Don't forget bowls and spoons if you are dipping ice cream. You can add sundae toppings to take it another step.

The benefits of this menu are the controllability of the entree items and the ability to add a lot of variety at the condiment table.

- Add the skewers of shrimp, raw boneless chicken breasts and other par cooked chicken parts to the grill as guests arrive.
- Hold the pork loins whole on the grill and carve to order. Keep additional pork loins in a low oven in the kitchen.
- For larger groups, all items can go into chaffers.
- For service, the entree items can be eaten with a knife and fork or they can be suggested as a sandwich, taco filling or on top of Caesar salad. Have the carver help by cutting to suitable size at the carving board.
- Suggest that chicken wings be turned "Buffalo" style with hot sauce and blue cheese at the condiment table.
- Have hamburgers and hot dogs available. Keep the burger size small for quick cooking and don't be afraid to offer "doubles" to adults. I'd rather they fill up on burger than shrimp.
- You may want a little BBQ sauce on some of the chicken, but just grilling it is the idea here.
- Skewer 21/25 shrimp with two skewers for ease in handling. Don't forget to presoak the skewers and trim some of the excess to prevent charring on the grill.
- Offer both chopped onion for tacos and sliced onion for burgers and sandwiches. Use the same idea for tomatoes, lettuce and several types of cheeses. Control the amount placed on the table by the container size. As the picnic slows, reduce the size of the containers. Keep this area neat and have things well labeled.

SUMMER BRUNCH

Imported Cheeses and Country Pate' served with Flatbreads and Crackers
Fresh Melon and Prosciutto
Sectioned Grapefruit Halves Broiled with Honey and Almonds
Pineapple wedges studded with Strawberries
Fruit Salad with Maple Yogurt Dressing
Fresh Spinach, Romaine and Baby Greens
Salad accompaniments including items for Spinach and Caesar Salads
Chicken Salad with Red Grapes and Walnuts
Cold Crepes with Smoked Salmon and Dill Cream Cheese

Omelet and Pasta Bar	Waffle, French Toast or Pancake Station
Scalloped Apples with Sausage	Mushrooms Au Gratin with Puff Pastry Shells
Scrambled Eggs	Crisp Bacon
Vegetable Stir Fry	Home Fried Potatoes

Glazed Canadian Bacon and Roast Sirloin of Beef Carved to Order
Assorted Breads, Muffins Danish and Pastries
Flavored Butters, Jellies and Fruit Toppings

Assorted Juices, Coffees and Teas	Bloody Mary Bar and Assorted Mimosas

- Start with the usual hot items and build around them. A couple nice hot dishes, the omelet and pasta station and either the french toast, pancake or waffle set-up should about do it for hot foods. Guests get their fill of these things quickly.
- I think you get much more "splash" for your buck concentrating on two areas. First is the appetizer and salad area. This is usually the first part of the buffet that the guests see. It's a good place to splash color and variety. The second is the bread and pastry area. Breads and rolls are very important. You can make them from scratch, easy to use mixes, frozen or bakery items. Have a lot of variety and keep the item size small. Use flavored butters and cheese spreads.
- Offering separate scrambled eggs on the buffet will take some of the pressure away from the omelet cook. Keep egg whites on hand for a lower cholesterol selection.
- Add Pastas to the Omelet station. You can use the same toppings for both. You can also use the same cook depending on the amount of customers. Keep the sauces simple for the pasta. A basic red sauce, an Alfredo and offer Aurora sauce (half Marinara, half Alfredo) to folks that can't decide. Have clarified butter and good olive oil for sautéing and a few herbs and roasted garlic on the pasta side. Pre-cook some items like mushrooms, sweet peppers, onions and such. This greatly reduces cooking time out front.
- A waffle station can really add to the brunch but don't try this if you do not have the equipment. Quality commercial waffle irons are required for bigger groups. Good waffle irons re-heat quickly and have staying power. If you do not have the capacity for waffles, substitute a pan of thick-cut french toast or pancakes as an alternative. You can locate various toppings, whipped cream and assorted syrups nearby. It's OK to duplicate the flavored butters here, too.
- A carving station offering a whole glazed Canadian bacon and very thin slices of a well trimmed roasted sirloin might be included depending on the particular event.

BOXED LUNCHES

There are several occasions when you may want to offer boxed lunches. Golf outings, bus trips, sports events or a conference lunch break on a spring day. When boxed lunches are made up ahead of time, they are a great way to feed larger groups that may be arriving all at once or at unknown intervals. Offered in addition to the regular menu, a good boxed lunch following can take some of the pressure off a busy kitchen. You know you are doing well when repeat customers buy the daily boxed special sight unseen, trusting your creativity to come up with great surprise combinations. Sometimes you may want to keep boxed lunches more traditional. For example, there might be an all male golf outing. In this case, a great Ham and Swiss on Rye with a few Hard Pretzels with brown mustard for dipping and a ripe banana for an afternoon potassium lift will about do it. Here are just a few menus don't be afraid to experiment. Surprise can be part of the fun!

- When looking for suitable containers, don't overlook things like small oriental food cartons. They are great for salads, cheese cubes, olives and marinated vegetables.

- Lidded soufflé cups hold dipping sauces and condiments.

- Make sure that items are packed so that they don't shift when moved.

- Be aware that the completed boxed lunch may sit for an extended amount of time and liquids such as marinades may make items soggy.

- Don't forget a wet nap and good plastic ware wrapped in a napkin with salt and pepper packs. Extra napkins are usually a good idea, too.

- If appropriate include Splits of Wine or Champagne.

BOXED LUNCHES

Miniature Croissants with Sliced Chicken Breast and Fresh Herb Aioli
Chilled Asparagus Spears
Miniature Cheese Cake

Grilled Shrimp Cocktail
Bruschetta with Sun Dried Tomato Pesto
Three Pepper Slaw
Fresh Dark Cherries

Cracked Stone Crab Claws with Mustard Sauce
Marinated Mushrooms
Cubed Cheeses with Sourdough Bread Rounds
Gourmet Jelly Beans

BOXED LUNCHES

Prosciutto and Provolone on a Hard Roll
Assorted Olives
Tangerines
Chocolate Chunk Cookies

Country Pâté on Peasant Biscuits spread with Pepper Jelly
Roasted Baby Beets with White Balsamic Vinaigrette
Casino Stuffed Mushrooms
Angel Food Cake

Chilled Blackened Tuna on Snowflake Roll
Fresh Melon Balls
Pepperoni and Cheese Flags
Cupcakes

Mini Hard Shell Tacos of Cajun Roasted Vegetables and Queso Fresco
Slices of Spanish Chorizo Sausage
Saffron Rice and Golden Raison Salad
Cinnamon Sugar Plantains

Smoked Salmon and Scallion Cream Cheese Purses
Chilled Grape Leaves stuffed with Lamb and Fresh Oregano
Orange and Cucumber Slices
Dark Chocolate Drops

Asian Breaded Chicken Tenders with Dipping Sauces
Sesame Peanut Noodles
Watercress and Fresh Mint Salad
Fortune Cookies with event appropriate fortunes inserted

Marinated Fresh Mozzarella and Cherry Tomato Skewers
Grilled Pear Slices wrapped in Parma Ham
Spiced Cashews
Macaroons

FATHER'S DAY

Father's Day has never been the busiest restaurant day of the year. A lot of guys are out playing golf or fishing or just relaxing in the yard. I could never tell what volume of business we were going to have. Back to the old rule: use what is already in the inventory and items that are quick to prep. So along with your regular menu try this:

FATHER'S DAY STEAK OUT

Wheel out a cart or set up a cutting station with whole New York Strips, Tenderloins and Rib Eyes. Trim them but leave them whole. Ask Dad (or anyone else), what kind of steak he wants and what size to cut it. Have a scale available and charge by the ounce. Keep the rest of the meal simple but "Dad Sized". Try a big basket of onion rings and a good sized baked potato. Offer sour cream, shredded cheddar, real bacon bits and chopped scallions at the table. Throw in a Caesar Salad if you think it needs it. Have good warm bread. For dessert try Banana Splits or Huge Banana Boats for the whole family to share.

NEW ENGLAND CLAM BAKE

The story of the New England Clam Bake or the story I was told and love to relate goes something like this; it is held on the beach and is a daylong event. Early in the morning you dig a large pit. Next, collect smooth faced rocks from along the beach or surrounding area. Line the entire pit, sides and the bottom with the rocks. Gather a lot of wood and start a fire in the pit and keep adding wood all day. You get those rocks very hot. After the rocks are ready, you layer seaweed and the food into the pit. Lobsters, clams, mussels, shrimp, crabs, oysters, crawfish or whatever local seafood is available. Even small whole firm-fleshed fish fare well here. Potatoes, husk-on corn, sausages and chicken help round it out. Add a good seafood seasoning and you get a great blending of flavors. Layer it according to how long it takes to cook. Use a wet layer of seaweed between each food. Add a couple buckets of sea water for salt and steam and cover with a canvas tarp till done.

Don't forget plenty of drawn butter and I always include some kind of bread. Unfortunately we all don't have a beach, smooth rocks and seaweed to work with. If you want to offer the *Clam Bake* in-house you just have to adapt with what you have. Offer the feast on a hot platter. I've seen it served in small tins or small aluminum trash cans with lids. I press into service those buckets from the bar that say "A Bucket of Rolling Rocks". Heck, include a bucket of Rolling Rocks! I do think it works best if you offer the *Clam Bake* for two or more family-style. If you have a large group, offer the *Clam Bake* buffet style and add a few items to stretch out the group. Try clams and oysters on the half shell, clam chowder or seafood gumbo. Cole slaw, macaroni salad or a platter of sliced fresh tomatoes also goes well. If you want a dessert try fresh peach cobbler with a sweetened biscuit crust. Have fun and HAPPY CLAM BAKING!

THE CHILDREN'S HALLOWEEN PARTY

Few times are more special to kids than Halloween. Having a children's party is a great way to involve the whole family and generate sales. A few tips;

- Prepare a hand-out for the parents when they arrive telling them the schedule of events and approximate times.

- I suggest feeding the little darlings as soon as they get there: Buffet-style pizza, pasta and salad bar. Keep it as simple as that. Don't go crazy. Include some fruits as salad selections. Don't forget the ginger snaps and apple cider. Have the buffet food ready as soon as they arrive. The young ones will be excited and will find it hard to sit at the table while an order is taken and food prepared.

- Try to plan the activities so they are simple and safe. Instead of just handing out the candy, try easy games where everyone gets a prize. Things like a cut-out of a witch's face for a bean bag toss or rings around the soda bottle painted as ghosts would fit the bill. Ask your kids' they probably have a few ideas.

- For prizes, you can give out a little bit of candy and small prize trinkets. Trinkets can be ordered in bulk from catalogs or on-line. Consider ages and safety factors in selecting trinkets. Same applies when selecting candy. Choking hazards for less than three years is a particular safety threshold.

- A haunted walk or haunted trail is an activity kids like. Make it spooky. Unless they are toddlers, kids are not easy to scare. You get a lot of "that's so fake" but they still like it and have fun. They really like the gross stuff, Slimy "ca-ca" stuff! Put your hand in the mystery box is also a popular event.

- A fun parent/child activity to do is letting the kids make their own caramel apples. Don't forget to wash the wax off of the apples if they are not fresh-picked. Dip them in caramel or chocolate. Make sure the caramel and chocolate are just warm and not too hot to prevent any safety issues and parental supervision is a must. Have available for rolling on top; coconut, chocolate chips, chopped peanuts, almonds, macadamia nuts, Oreo cookie crumbs, chocolate and rainbow jimmies, gummy worms or whatever is available. To help manage any potential mess, keep the work areas clear and within easy reach of both the parents and children. You will need wax covered paper plates at the ready for finished apples and there should be boxes or wrap available so the apples can be taken home. A large bowl of wet-naps should see a lot of use also.

- The other thing they will enjoy is "Painting your own pumpkin" (washable paints or markers). Let them chose their own pumpkin from the pile and do as they like. Have a table to display the finished art work.

- Finish the evening and signal that the staff has had enough and it is time for festivities to end with a costume parade. Parents like the kids costume parade the best. I try to stay away from prizes for best of this or that. The fewer hurt feelings the better.

THANKSGIVING

The Thanksgiving meal is a time for variety. The original event must have been similar to a pot luck dinner where everyone brings a dish. A lot of fall vegetables and staples were the most likely fare. Side dishes were made with recently harvested or dried for the winter ingredients. Pickles and relishes that were "put up" were also brought. The holiday has evolved into a celebration around the meal. Obviously the turkey is the centerpiece of the meal. A turkey slowly roasted, basted in butter and evenly browned will always be a winner. Injecting the turkey or spreading a flavored butter or liquor just under the skin will enhance the taste and help keep them moist. If nothing else, I use a well-seasoned stock or broth to baste the bird during the roasting process. I love to go outside the box when flavoring the turkey and in addition to adding flavor to the skin the baste can add color and crispness.

Here are just a few suggestions for Glazing or Basting, don't be afraid to be **Bold** !

Apple Cider and Cranberry Juice
Orange Juice and Grand Mariner
Herb Butters
Brown Sugar and Amaretto
Roasted Garlic and Walnut Butter
Honey, Tequila, Lime and Ancho Powder
Pomegranate Glaze
Smoky Bacon and Sweet Onion Butter
Kona Coffee and Kahlua
Spicy Root Beer

SIDE DISHES

Side dishes add the real flavor to the Thanksgiving meal. This is where the meal becomes personalized for each guest. We all remember the green bean casserole and the candied sweet potatoes with marshmallows we had every year. Whether we liked them or hated them they were part of the meal. Try a few of the following selections:

Husk on Corn - Amish Limas - Red Cabbage with Bacon and Apples
Mashed Potatoes with Roasted Onions - Brussels Sprouts with Chestnuts
Roasted Butternut Squash with Apples - Caramelized Corn Pudding

Caraway Sauerkraut - Creamed Mushrooms
Cider Mashed Yams - Roasted Parsnips with Rosemary
Braised Celery with Mushrooms - Sweet Potatoes with Praline Topping

Maple Glazed Carrots with Pecans - Baked Onions with Herb Crumb Topping
Stuffed Acorn Squash with Oranges, Walnuts, Nutmeg and Golden Raisins
Spiced Cranberries - Savory Corn Relish - Pickled Beets with Red Onions

Cranberry Raison Relish - Green Tomato and Apple Chutney
Red and Green Pepper Relish - Cranberry Waldorf Salad

THANKSGIVING

DRESSINGS

I like to offer a variety of dressings and three is a good number to work with. With the popularity of rice dressings I might add one of these as an additional option. The first choice should be basic bread stuffing for the die-hard traditionalists, then maybe something with oysters or another shellfish. Round it off with a fruit and or nut selection and try to incorporate a smoky bacon, sausage or ham into one of these three. A great way to add flavor is to try different breads such as ryes, sourdough, pumpernickel, cornbread or raisin bread. You can also mix and match various herbs and spices. Just as in the basting process, flavored butters and the like can add body to your dressings. Here are a few combinations and a list of often included ingredients that you can add:

DRESSINGS

Smoked Oyster and Wild Mushroom
Apples, Country Ham, Marble Rye
Wild Rice, Toasted Almond and Dried Cherry
Sun Dried Tomato and Fresh Basil with Olive Bread
Corn Bread, Roasted Poblano and Grilled Scallion
Caramelized Onion, Bacon and Pumpernickel
Roasted Chestnuts, Grilled Pears and Smoked Turkey Sausage
Andouille, Cajon Rice and Crawfish
Cured Olives, Grilled Rustic Saffron Bread and Currents
Crab, Dried Cranberries and Old Bay Crackers

Interchange or add any of the following;

Walnuts - Pistachios - Chestnuts - Pine Nuts - Raisons - Golden Raisons
Mixed Dried Fruits - Fresh Pears - Oranges - Fresh Fennel - Dates - Figs
Apricots - Spinach - Grapes - Leeks - Fresh and Dried Mushrooms
Truffles - Cranberries - Sweet Peppers - Italian Sausage - Chorizo
Andouille - Cubed Pâté - Oysters - Shrimp

GREAT GRAVY !!!

Obviously, great gravy is as important as the turkey! All parts of the meal are going to end up covered in it. The turkey, the stuffing, the potatoes, and most of the side dishes will undoubtedly come in contact with it before it is over. "Gravy as a beverage" I have heard it called.

I very seldom offer actual recipes assuming that as pros we all know the basics, but here is my tried and true method. Remove some of the fat from the roasting pan. Leave enough fat to later make a roux. Remember that some of this fat is water and will evaporate. Put the roasting pan on the stove and cook out the water and caramelize the fat and the fond on the bottom of the pan. Add flour to make a roux and brown the roux while scraping the bottom of the pan and releasing the fond. Stir while cooking out the flour. When browned, turn off the heat and allow it to sit for a few moments to cool a little. Add hot turkey stock and bring to a boil to thicken. Check for thickness and adjust seasoning. You don't have to flavor the gravy, but some people like to add some variety. Try wild mushrooms, giblets, marsala, truffles or truffle oil, dry sherry, herb butters, cracked peppercorns, caramelized shallots or red onions.

MEETING BREAKS

If you have private rooms, think about selling it as a room for business groups who can use it to hold seminars or training sessions. Many places charge a room rental, but offer to waive the room rental for some guaranteed lunch business. If they have 20 people get a guarantee for that many lunches. You can also offer coffee and pastry service for breakfast and great afternoon breaks. After the event kick in a free drink and happy hour prices for all attendees to keep them there after the conferences and you have made profit from that same group all day.

No matter how dynamic the speaker or topic is a late afternoon break is a must. It's a chance to get up and stretch, use the rest room or just get some fresh air. If possible, set up the break in a completely different area from the meeting room. Try outside on a nice fall day, near the fireplace in winter or at the swimming pool in summer. Two tips: don't overfeed the folks, (they will fall asleep the minute they get back to work), and don't make the break too long.

FALL FLING
Caramel and Candy Apples, Pumpkin Cookies, Apple Cider

HEALTH CLUB
Granola Energy Bars, Fresh Fruit, Bottled Waters, Individual Yogurt, Trail Mix, Fruit Juices

CHESAPEAKE BAY
Cocktail Shrimp, Half Shell Clams and Oysters, Lemons, Cocktail Sauce, Virgin Bloody Mary Bar

ESPRESSO BAR
Espresso, Latte, Biscotti and Mini Cannoli

TAKE ME OUT TO THE BALL GAME
Miniature Hot Dogs, Soft Pretzels, Peanuts, Root Beer

ICE CREAM PARLOR
Ice Cream Sodas, Hand Dipped Ice Cream, Penny Candy, Cup Cakes

WINTER WARMER
Hot Chocolate, International Coffees, Warm Apple Cider
with Cinnamon Sticks, Old Fashion Cookies

FANCY TEA
Assorted Tea Sandwiches, Scones, Butter Cookies, Assorted Teas

A TASTE OF ITALY
Antipasto, Miniature Bruschetta, Italian Water Ice, Cappuccino

KING KONA
Pineapple Chunks dipped in Chocolate, Macaroons, Island Smoothies, and Iced Kona Coffee

MEETING BREAKS

MORNING MULLIGAN
Cool Coffee Drinks, Honey Bran Muffins, Mini Danish, Fruit Salad

MEXICAN FIESTA
Nachos, Mini Tacos and Virgin Frozen Margaritas

SUMMER BREEZE
Fresh Vegetable Tray with Spicy Yogurt Dip, Popsicles, Fudgsicles, Lemonade

ASIAN AFFAIR
Sushi, Spring Rolls, Fortune Cookies and Green Tea

GAY NINETIES
Vanilla, Chocolate and Strawberry Ice Cream, Chocolate Syrup, Whipped Cream, Chopped Nuts, Maraschino Cherries, Chocolate covered Strawberries, Macaroons

PARIS CAFÉ
Chocolate Croissants, Red and White Grape Juice served in wine glasses, Brie and Crackers

WORKOUT WAKEUP
Fresh Fruit Smoothies, Protein Shakes and Power Bars

FLORIDA ORANGE
Fresh Squeezed Orange Juice, Creamsicles, Tangerines, Orange Drop Cookies

SOUTH PHILLY
Six Foot Hoagie, Cream Sodas, Warm Homemade Potato Chips, Dill Pickles and Cherry Peppers

A HALLO EVE
Mini Pumpkin Tarts, Gingersnaps, Cherry Cider, Candy Corn

THE IRISH ARE COMING
Non-alcoholic Irish Coffees, Guinness Cheese Fondue with
Soda Bread for Dipping, Shamrock Cupcakes

CHRISTMAS PAST
Mint Hot Chocolate, Candy Canes, Non-alcoholic Eggnog, Fruitcake Bites, Ribbon Candy

GREAT SCOTCH
Smoked Salmon Canapés, Shortbread, Butterscotch Iced Coffee, Marmalade Crisps

JAMAICA ME HAPPY
Island Pork Canapés, Mango Salsa with Chips, Tropical Punch

EGG ROLLS

Egg rolls are not just for breakfast anymore! Be prepared for those strange looks when you tell them this one but by the end of recent tasting with the wait staff we converted every naysayer. Try egg rolls anywhere: breakfast, lunch, dinner, bar snacks and desserts. Egg rolls make a great accompaniment for soups and salads too.

You can add small savory egg rolls to the bread basket. For added texture, savory egg rolls might be coated with melted cheese or a flavorful reduction and sprinkled with herbs. They can also be seasoned with various spice blends. Miniature chocolate or cinnamon egg rolls make great giveaways with the coffee service. With sweet or dessert rolls, try finishing by dipping in chocolate, caramel or raspberry glaze. They can also be dusted with cocoa or flavored sugars and are very receptive to an ice cream accompaniment. You may want to add a dipping sauce for some selections, but many combinations can stand alone.

The larger wrappers are easier to work with but vary the individual size for the appropriate course and presentation. To make crisper egg rolls, blanch them first in the deep fryer and allow them to cool before re-frying. Try some of these fillings.

The Miami - Grilled Shrimp, Orange Salsa, Spicy Cuban Rice
Crab with a Tie - Dungeness Crab, Asian Spiced Peanuts, Thai Jicama Slaw and Sweet Chili Sauce
French Class - Sweetbread and Morel Mushroom Spring Rolls with Pea Tendrils and Mint Aioli
Thai Juan On - Shrimp and Diced Chilies with Thai Basil and a Soy and Scallion Dipping Sauce
Wild Goat - Charred Chicken, Goat Cheese and Wild Mushroom

On Fire Jerk! - Fiery Jerked Pork and Caramelized Plantains with a Sugarcane and Garlic Sauce
Crab Cali - Crab and Shrimp, Daikon, Avocado, Mint and Pea Greens
Just Ducky - Duck Confit, Caramelized Onions, Carrot Matchsticks, Bok Choy and Hoisin Sauce
Anna Cubana - Roast Pork, Smoked Ham, Swiss, Pickles and an Ancho Mustard Sauce
Chilly Mexican - Chili Spiced Chicken, Avocado, Pico de Gallo and Habanero Sour Cream Dip

Rose's Rib - Short Rib, Apple and Onion Slaw with a Rosemary BBQ Sauce
Relish the Minute - Lobster, Cucumber-Mint Relish, Diced Red and Yellow Peppers
A Sinful Duck - Thai Spiced Duck and Daikon Slaw with Chili-Apricot Sauce
Lob Me Far East - Lobster and Asian Vegetables with Spicy Teriyaki Sauce
Fall of the Pig - Pulled Pork with Caramelized Onions and Fall Vegetables

Sicily Silly - Pepperoni, Roasted Eggplant and Fried Long Hots with Smoked Tomato Coulis
Wake Me for Shrimp - Soy Marinated Smoked Shrimp, Wakame, Pickled Ginger, Wasabi Aioli
Corny Crab - Crab, Roasted Sweet Corn, Napa Cabbage Slaw with a Spicy Garlic Sauce
Baton Rouge - Andouille, Crawfish, Dirty Rice

EGG ROLLS

Far South of the Border - Chili, Jack Cheese, Refried Beans, Jalapenos and Red Onions
Hot Italian - Spicy Sausage, Mozzarella, Diced Tomatoes and Peppers
Gobbler - Turkey, Bread Stuffing and Dried Cranberries served over Homemade Gravy
Gyro - Shredded Lamb, Feta, Diced Tomatoes and Scallions with Cucumber Yogurt Dip
The Carolina -Smoked Brisket, Onion Jam and Chive Sour Cream
The Diner - Meatloaf, Green Peas and Garlic Mashed Potatoes served with Onion Gravy

And I'm Past Ya - Cappicola, Diced Salami, Sharp Provolone, Chopped Olives and Pesto
Carbonara - Cooked Fettuccine, Gorgonzola, Petite Peas and Prosciutto
Filet Fling - Grilled Steak, Wild Mushrooms and Bleu Cheese
Cornel Klink- Corned Beef, Mustard Seed Sauerkraut and Swiss Cheese
Pair of Duck Feet - Duck Confit, Roasted Pears, Spicy Black Bean Oyster Sauce

Smokey Past - Grilled Pastrami, Colby Cheese, Broccoli Slaw and Smoked Tomato Aioli
Full of Philly - Shaved Steak, Grilled Onions and Mushrooms, Provolone and Roasted Garlic Aioli
Porky Pete - Roast Pork, Broccoli Rabe, Extra Sharp Provolone and Cherry Pepper Relish
Dusty Duck - Roasted Duck with Orange-Blackberry Compote and a Porcini Dusting
Fourth of July - Diced Deli Meats with Summer Slaw and Green Goddess Dipping Sauce
Hot in Buffalo - Popcorn Chicken, Blue Cheese and Diced Celery with a Texas Pete-Ranch Dip

Sunrise Egg Rolls

Eyes Wide Open - Bacon, Scrambled Eggs, Smoked Gouda and Hash Brown Potatoes
S O S - Chipped Beef, Scallion Cream Cheese and Grilled Onions
Benedict - Asparagus, Canadian Bacon and Scrambled Eggs Topped With Hollandaise
Pepper and Egg - Scrambled Eggs, Roasted Peppers and Provolone Cheese
Toast to the Pig - Diced French Toast, Maple Bacon, Sage Sausage and a Ginger Yogurt Dip

Dessert Egg Rolls

Banana Slam - Roasted Banana, Heath Bar, Macadamia Nuts
Smoors - Marshmallows, Graham Crackers, Chocolate Chips
Nutty Reese - Peanut Butter, Chocolate Chunks and Peanuts
Pina Colada - Candied Pineapple, Toasted Coconut and Rum Cream
Caramel Apple - Cooked Apples, Caramels and Chopped Peanuts
Brown Eyed Girl - Brownie Chunks, Dried Cherries and Butterscotch Bits

THE CHEESE CART

You don't see the Cheese Cart or Cheese Table offered as much anymore. Although it can be a great finishing touch to a meal, there are things you must take into consideration when deciding the viability of a cheese cart or table. The first is that you are using expensive products with the potential for a lot of waste. The second is that the wait staff must be well trained. It's also important that your server have the time to do the service. They should not have to be rushed and they need to be able to make it fun for the guest. The cart service is not just dessert but a show. The wait staff also has to be comfortable and confidant at tableside. Servers must be knowledgeable about the products and the proper service of the cheeses and they must be able to handle a knife for peeling and portioning fruit. You can have as many cheeses as you wish. As few as three selections will do. Certainly ten or more offerings make it much more interesting.

- Use only quality cheeses. First, decide the number of selections you will be offering. Then determine the breakdown of texture or types that you want. How many semi-firm cheeses, how many soft-ripened and so on. It's nice to offer a few of the same types for comparison like offering Roquefort, Stilton and Gorgonzola. Point out the differences and the characteristics of all of them. If artisan or local cheeses are available, try to work them into the selections.

- Serve the cheeses at the proper temperature for best flavor and texture.

- Compliment the cheeses with some fruit and a selection of crackers, crostini and flat breads.

- If you want to start out small, go to a cheese shop and start with small quantities. Even if the price is higher, buying retail may still be less expensive than purchasing large quantities of a product that you do not have an outlet for. A good cheese shop can also be a great source of information about the products.

- Make the table or cart self-contained. Stock it with serving plates, silverware, folded napkins and bowls for peelings and cutting waste. Be sure the server has everything they need. Nothing kills the show faster than having to wait while the busboy runs to get forgotten silverware. A small pair of kitchen shears makes it easy for snipping grapes into small clusters at the table. Look around for a pair of antique scissors or other vintage tools that can be used. Really impressive tools are antique apple peelers and corers.

- Remember the product loss potential here. Try to keep in mind possible uses for remaining product. To further minimize waste, set exacting after service breakdown and storage procedures.

- Make it nice and be sure to price it accordingly. It works best if it can be sold to several or all of the customers at the same table.

Don't forget that this is a great opportunity for additional wine sales.

GLOSSARY

THIS WORKING CHEF'S GLOSSARY OF TERMS

Adobo Sauce - Made from ground chilies and vinegar, this Mexican paste is often used to marinate Chipotle peppers.

Aglio E Olio - A basic sauce of garlic and olive oil. The garlic can be chopped, pounded or sliced very thin. This basic sauce is heated gently, slightly toasting the garlic and is often served on pastas but can be used for vegetables as well.

Agneau - French term for "lamb".

Agnolotti - Stuffed pasta in a crescent shape. The shape is formed by filling a small round of pasta and folding it over.

Ahi - Hawaiian term for high grade tuna. Most often a reference to Yellow Fin tuna but sometimes can be associated with Blue Fin or Big Eye.

Aioli- A garlic, egg yolk and oil sauce in the style of a mayonnaise and served as a condiment for seafood, meats and vegetables. May also be infused with flavors other than garlic.

Al Forno - Italian term for something cooked in the oven.

Amaretti - Italian almond flavored cookies often made with almond paste. These are similar to macaroons.

Amaretto - A sweet almond flavored liqueur.

Amoroso - A light to medium sweet sherry.

Amuse Bouche - French term for "amuse mouth" this very small portion appetizer is served as a first course to stimulate the palate for things to come.

Anaheim Chili - A mild green elongated chili. This pepper is commonly available fresh although it can also be found canned. The canned chilies are usually roasted or fire charred.

Ancho Chili - This dried Poblano chili ranges from dark red to almost brown. This drying condenses the flavor. Ancho can be mild to hot and have a deep pepper flavoring.

Andouille Sausage - A spicy smoked sausage with a rich flavor. This sausage is used in Cajun cooking and has the ability to impart its distinct flavor throughout the dish the longer it cooks.

Aquavit - A clear caraway flavored liquor from Scandinavia.

Arborio Rice - A thick, round grained rice most often used to make to make Risotto. It has a high starch content which gives the dish a creamy texture.

Arroz - Spanish word for rice.

Arugula - A small leaved member of the cabbage family. It has a peppery flavor that has a slightly bitter aftertaste.

Au Jus - A term used to describe a meat served in its own juice. A very basic sauce made from roasting juices and pan drippings.

Au Lait - French term for with milk.

Baccala - Italian term for dried and salted cod.

Baklava - From the Mediterranean area around Greece, this is a pastry made with phyllo dough, chopped nuts and an orange-lemon and spiced flavored honey syrup.

Ballottine - A dish of meat, poultry or fish that has been stuffed rolled and tied with corresponding forcemeat. It is either baked or gently braised.

Bard -To cover lean meats or poultry with a layer of fat to keep them from drying out. Layers of pork fatback or bacon are commonly used. Caul fat is also an excellent item for barding. The fat is usually tied to the meat. The fat flavors the meat while it roasts. Often, the barding fat is removed before the roast is done, allowing the meat to brown before serving.

Basmati Rice - A fine texture, long grain rice. It has a sweet nutty flavor that is very fragrant. It is commonly used in Indian or Middle Eastern dishes.

Béarnaise - A sauce made by combining a hollandaise with a reduction of tarragon vinegar, tarragon, shallots and white wine.

Béchamel - This is a basic white sauce of cream or milk thickened with a roux. This is one of the five "Mother" sauces.

Beignet - A deep fried fritter made of yeast dough. One popular variety is from New Orleans where is served hot with plenty of confectionary sugar.

Bel Paese - A very rich Italian semi-soft cheese.

Beurre - The French word for butter.

Beurre Blanc – A basic sauce made from wine, vinegar and a flavoring reduction. This reduction could be peppercorns, shallots, mushrooms or any aromatic blends. The sauce is thickened by whisking in cold butter until it thickens.

Beurre Noisette – Brown butter. Cook raw butter over low heat until it is a medium brown color. Once it begins to brown you must be ready to remove it from the fire and the pan as it will continue to cook. Typically served with fish or shellfish.

Biscotti - A very crisp Italian cookie. It is given its shape and hardened texture by first baking a slightly flattened loaf of dough then slicing the dough and re-baking it.

Bisque – A thick soup usually made from shellfish. The soup is pureed and finished with cream.

Blintz - A thin pancake filled with sweet or savory filling and then rolled. It can then be sautéed or baked.

Blue Point Oyster - These excellent half shell oysters are originally from the area of Blue Point Long Island.

Bockwurst – A lightly seasoned veal sausage. This German sausage is almost white in appearance and is usually sold fresh and uncooked.

Boeuf – The French term for Beef.

Bocconcini - Small balls of fresh mozzarella cheese.

Bok Choy – A type of Chinese cabbage. It has dark green leaves with white stalks. It has a very mild flavor and holds its crisp texture very well.

Bolognese – An Italian term for a rich sauce flavored with meat and pungent vegetables usually including mushrooms and may include red wine. Normally a slow cooked sauce; it may be finished with heavy cream.

Bombe – A frozen dessert that has layers of ice cream, sherbet or flavored ices. Alternating colors and flavor the "Bombe" may have a fruit or cream center.

Bonne Femme – A sauce or garnish of a white wine and lemon cream sauce. This sauce characteristically contains mushrooms and shallots and is most often served with seafood especially lightly flavored poached fish.

Bouillabaisse – A thick soup or stew made with regionally available shellfish and meaty fish. This tomato based dish also contains olive oil, saffron, tomatoes, garlic, onions and a full bodied white wine. This dish in customarily served over crusty bread.

Bouillon – The liquid that remains after cooking meat, fish or poultry with vegetables and seasonings.

Boule – A rounded loaf of bread made in the shape of a bowl.

Bouquet Garni – Herbs tied together in cheesecloth for easy removal from stocks or stews. It may be any combination of herbs but if specific herbs are not noted you would normally find bay leaves, whole peppercorns, thyme and parsley.

Bourguignonne – A sauce or garnish made from a rich demi-glace, red wine, mushrooms and shallots. This sauce is commonly used with hardy meats such as beef or game.

Boursin - A rich French cheese with a soft almost crumbly texture.

Braciola – An Italian dish made of beef or pork and herbs. The meat is pounded flat with a thick coating of herbs then rolled and tied. The meat is then slowly braised in a rich tomato sauce until tender with the meat and herbs flavoring the sauce.

Braise – To cook in a small amount of liquid over low heat for a long period of time. The amount of liquid should not cover more than one third of the item. The item is browned in fat or oil prior to the braising. This method is used to slowly tenderize tougher cuts of meat. Braising can be done on top of the stove over low heat or in the oven and should be covered. The remaining liquid develops a deep flavor and is served as part of the dish.

Bratwurst – A hearty German sausage flavored with caraway, coriander, parsley and nutmeg. It contains pork and veal is available both fresh and smoked.

Bresaola – Air dried beef that has been salt cured and aged. It is customarily sliced very thin and drizzled with olive oil, fresh herbs and a squeeze of lemon.

Brine – A term for the liquid or a process of using a heavily salted solution of water and seasonings for pickling foods. The solution may or may not be sweetened.

Brioche – Airy bread made with yeast and extra butter and eggs. It may be made into large or small rounds or have a circular base and a top knot.

Brisket – A cut of beef that is slow cooked, either by braising in liquid or slow cooked in a smoker. The available cuts are "First Cut" which is leaner or the "Point Cut" which contains more layers of fat, thus being more flavorful and better for the drier smoked method.

Broccolini - A combination of broccoli and kale this vegetable has a mild flavor.

Broccoli Rabe - A green leafy vegetable with very small broccoli like ends. This vegetable may be very bitter and sometimes requires blanching. Closer to the turnip family it can be prepared in many ways similar to kale or spinach.

Brochette – A food cooked on a skewer.

Bruise – To crush an ingredient to help release its flavor. Frequently done with garlic, shallots or herbs.

Brule - A molded custard of starch, eggs and cream or milk.

Bruschetta - A thick toast made using hearty bread. The bread is drizzled with olive oil before being grilled, preferably over an open flame or charcoal grill then rubbed with fresh garlic.

Bulgur Wheat - Dried wheat that is a staple in Middle East cooking. It has a nutty flavor and a chewy texture. It is available in coarse and fine grinds.

Cacciatore - Prepared in the style of the "Hunter" this Italian sauce, garnish or preparation contains mushrooms, onions, tomatoes and peppers.

Calamari - Squid

Cambozola - A cheese that is a combination of Camembert and Gorgonzola.

Canard - French for duck.

Cannelloni - A large hollow pasta that is stuffed.

Cannoli - An Italian dessert specialty that is a crunchy pastry tube filled with a flavored ricotta filling.

Caper - A small flower bud that most often has been pickled in a vinegar solution.

Capon - A young castrated chicken that is considered more flavorful and tender.

Caponata - An Italian condiment or side dish made with eggplant, anchovies and capers. It may contain other ingredients all simmered in olive oil.

Cappuccino - A coffee drink made from strong coffee and steamed or frothed milk.

Cappellini - A very thin spaghetti shaped paste slightly thicker than "Angel Hair".

Cappelletti- Small pieces of pasta that are stuffed.

Caramelize - The process of browning the sugars of a product. It can relate to sugar itself or the sugars found in meats, fruits and vegetables.

Carbonara - A sauce or garnish commonly associated with pasta. The sauce is made with cream, eggs and Parmigianino cheese. Bacon, prosciutto or baby peas are also sometimes added.

Carnitas - This Mexican pork is a slow cooked item made from the pork shoulder or other less tender cuts. After braising until the meat falls apart, the meat is then quickly browned in hot fat. It can be used as a topping for enchiladas or nacho chips or as a filling for other Mexican dishes.

Carpaccio - This very thin cut of beef filet is frequently served as an appetizer. It is drizzled with olive oil and sometimes fresh lemon juice. It is commonly topped with shaved Parmigianino cheese and fresh cracked pepper. It may also be served with capers and thinly sliced red onion.

Carpetbag Steak - This thick steak has a pocket cut into it and is stuffed, most often with oysters, before grilling. Breadcrumbs and fresh herb butter may be added to the oysters to make the stuffing. If necessary the pocket may be tied before cooking.

Cassoulet - This classic dish from France contains white beans, pork, duck and sausage. It is covered and cooked at low heat until the meats are tender and the flavors blend.

Caul - A very fatty membrane from the abdominal cavity of a pig or sheep. It is used to wrap item such as roasts, pates or forcemeats. As the fatty "lace" melts, it bastes and flavors the item.

Celeriac - A celery-turnip combination also known as celery root or celery knob. Only the bulb is edible. It can be eaten cooked or raw.

Cepe - A brown wild mushroom variety.

Ceviche - Also spelled Seviche, this dish from Latin America consists of raw seafood marinated in lime or other citrus juice. The dish also commonly includes tomatoes, onion, peppers and fresh cilantro. The seafood is cooked by the acid from the citrus juice. You must only use very fresh fish or seafood for this preparation. To check to see if the fish is done, look for a firming of the fish and an opaque color.

Chalupa - This crisp fried corn tortilla that usually has a savory filling and is shaped into a scoop shape. It makes a great appetizer platform.

Champignon - French term for mushroom.

Chanterelle - A mushroom that ranges in color from light yellow to a mild orange. This mushroom has a dense flavor and is typically found in the dried form but may be found fresh during late summer through the fall.

Chantilly Cream - A sweetened whipped cream that may be lightly flavored.

Chasseur - A garnish or sauce that contains mushrooms, tomatoes, shallots and wine and combined with flavorful demi-glace.

Chaurice Sausage - Spicy pork sausage usually found in Cajun cooking.

Chiffonade - Thin cuts of vegetables, usually leafy types of greens or herbs used as a garnish. They may be cooked quickly or used raw.

Chili Bean Paste - Made of fermented soy bean or black beans, garlic and aromatic spices. This item is found in many oriental dishes.

Chiles Rellenos - This is a Mexican dish of stuffed peppers most often the Poblano variety. The peppers are typically roasted first then stuffed with a blend of cheeses and may contain some seasoned rice or potatoes. The peppers are then coated with eggs or egg whites and fried crisp.

Chili Paste - This red colored paste is made of fermented beans with the addition of spicy chili peppers. Much spicier than Chili Bean Paste, it is used in oriental cooking. It can also be found in a milder form sold as Sweet Chili Paste.

Chimichanga - A crisp fried folded burrito. Traditional fillings are beef, pork or chicken. Fillings may contain rice, beans or diced potatoes. Non-traditional fillings may also be used.

Chimichurri - A mildly spicy mixture of chopped parsley, oregano, onions, garlic and olive oil.

Chinese Five Spice - This is most often a combination of star anise, fennel, cloves, cinnamon and Szechuan peppercorns.

Chipotle - A smoked Jalapeno pepper. This pepper has a very pungent smoky sweet flavor.

Chorizo Sausage - A spicy pork sausage. It may be fresh as in the Mexican variety or smoked as in the Spanish or Portuguese variety.

Churro - A Mexican deep fried dough stick commonly finished with cinnamon and sugar.

Cioppino - A fish stew made with local fish and shellfish in a very flavorful seasoned tomato broth.

Clotted Cream - The thickened layer of cream obtained from reducing unpasteurized milk.

Compote - Made with fresh or dried fruit that has been slowly cooked in simple syrup with flavoring and spices. Some compote is prepared using savory ingredients.

Confit - Meat that has been salted and slowly cooked covered in its own fat. The meat is then put into a crock and covered with the fat to preserve it.

Consommé - A broth or bouillon that has been clarified and strengthened by simmering using a "raft" of the corresponding protein, egg whites and vegetables.

Coq Au Vin - A slowly cooked French dish of poultry, mushrooms, shallots, red wine and spices. It may contain smoked ham and pearl onions.

Coulis - A sauce typically made from a fruit or vegetable puree such as roasted peppers or mangos.

Couscous - A grain type pasta made from semolina. It is produced by being pushed over a medium sieve. It can be made fresh but is commonly found in the dried form. Unlike customary forms of pasta the preparation method for couscous is similar to the preparation of rice whether it be simmered or steamed in a perforated pan.

Crème - French for "cream"

Crème Fraîche - A thickened cream with a slightly pungent flavor. Its non-curdling properties make it ideal as an addition to soups or sauces. It may also be used as a topping for fruit or desserts.

Crevette - French term for tiny Shrimp.

Crostini - Small slices of hardy bread that have been toasted or grilled. May be used plain as a garnish for soups or may be topped as a canapé.

Croustade - An edible bowl or container. It may be made of bread, pasta or pastry and can hold a variety of fillings from thick soups and stews to dessert fillings.

Deglaze - To remove the "fond" or the remaining food particles left on the bottom of a pan by heating a small amount of liquid in the pan. This is a very flavorful liquid that is used as a base for sauces and stocks.

Demi-Glace - A rich brown sauce made by combining one part espagnole or brown sauce with one part rich beef or veal stock and reducing by one half

Devein - To remove the vein from the back of a shrimp.

Dim Sum - Assortment of small dumplings and other bite size dishes found in Asian cuisine. They are most often steamed, poached or fried.

Duxelles - Finely chopped mushrooms that have been cooked in butter with shallots and herbs. The mixture is cooked until almost all of the moisture has been evaporated. Heavy cream may be added for flavor and texture.

Empanada - Mexican half moon shaped pastry that may have a sweet or savory filling.

Emulsify - To merge together two ingredients that would normally not stay together. An emulsion of oil and wine might be one example. Egg yolk would be added to the wine and oil would be added by slowly whisking it into the yolk and wine.

Enchilada - Mexican dish of a filling wrapped with a tortilla, most often a corn tortilla. These are usually baked in a sauce.

En Croute - To wrap a product in a pastry or similar wrapper.

En Papillote - Food baked and thus steamed inside parchment paper.

Espagnole Sauce - One of the mother sauces. A rich brown sauce made from beef stock, a browned "meripoix", herbs and tomato. This sauce is thickened with a browned roux and simmered for a long time to allow the flavors to develop.

Espresso - A strong dark Italian coffee.

Essence - Concentrated liquids that are used to enhance dishes.

Etouffée - A Cajun dish or procedure that gets its thickness, flavor and dark color from a deeply browned roux. Usually made with seafood and aromatic vegetables such as peppers, onions and celery. As a dish it is typically served over rice.

Fagioli - Italian for "bean".

Fajita - Mexican dish of meats or seafood cooked quickly with onions and assorted peppers and served with tortillas.

Falafel - Made from chickpeas, this Middle Eastern item is generally eaten with pita and accompanied with a light yogurt based sauce.

Farina - Made from high protein grain this meal is often cooked in water and eaten as a breakfast cereal.

Fish Sauce - A very strong and pungent sauce made from fermenting fish. It has a salty flavor and is found in Asian recipes. It may be used as a table condiment and is also known as Nuoc Nam.

Flan - An egg based custard that may be sweet or savory.

Flauta - A corn tortilla that is filled, most often with a savory filling then deep fried.

Focaccia - Italian flat bread that is used both as table bread and as a platform for sandwiches and appetizers.

Foie Gras - The enlarged liver of a duck or goose that has been force fed therefore producing a very flavorful and high fat content liver.

Fond - The browned particles that remain at the bottom of a pan after sautéing or roasting. These flavorful bits can be released by heating the pan with a small amount of liquid. The liquid can then be strained into a sauce or stock.

Fondant - A mixture of sugar, water and sometimes cream of tartar. When heated and cooled it becomes very pliable.

Fontina - An Italian soft semi-firm cheese.

Forcemeat - A ground mixture of meat and other savory ingredients that may be used as a stuffing or cooked as it is.

Frijoles - Mexican word for "bean".

Frittata - An Italian unfolded omelet that is prepared by combining the savory ingredients with the eggs. The surface of the frittata is slightly browned imparting a distinct flavor to the dish.

Fritter - Sweet or savory foods mixed with batter and fried.

Frito Misto - An Italian dish of mixed foods often fish, shellfish or vegetables that have been fried.

Fromage - French for "cheese".

Fumet - A stock commonly made from fish or shellfish. This stock will often be made with the head and bones of the fish or the shells of lobster and shrimp and will include a variety of aromatics such as a meripoix or herbs.

Gaeta Olive - A small dark Italian olive.

Galantine - Flavorful forcemeat that has been wrapped in cheesecloth or the skin of its corresponding ingredient and poached in a stock.

Ganache - A mixture of chocolate and heavy cream that is combined by heating. It can be used as an icing as is or whipped to the consistency of a heavy whipped cream.

Garam Masala - An Indian spice mixture that contains any combination of several spices such as cinnamon, allspice, cumin, cardamom and chilies. It may be added directly to a dish or used as a table condiment.

Gazpacho - A tomato based vegetable soup that is served cold.

Gelato - A very dense Italian ice cream.

Glace De Viande - A beef stock that has been reduced down to a thick consistency. This is used to flavor soups and sauces.

Gnocchi - A small Italian dumpling made from flour, potatoes and eggs.

Gremolata - Condiment made with garlic, fresh parsley and lemon zest.

Grits - Most often made from corn, grits are cooked in a boiling liquid such as milk or water. They can be eaten at any meal but until recently were most often a breakfast accompaniment to eggs. They can be flavored with many savory additions such as herbs or cheeses.

Hallah, or Challah - A traditional Jewish bread made with yeast and plenty of eggs. Evenly browned and usually braided this bread is great for French toast or grilled sandwiches.

Haricot Vert - French for Green Beans.

Harissa - From the Northern Africa region, this is a spicy sauce made from chilies, garlic and spices. It is used to flavor many dishes and can also be used as a table condiment.

Hoisin Sauce - This sauce used in oriental cooking is made from soybeans and assorted spices. It has a spicy sweet flavor. It is sometimes added at the end of the recipe or offered at the table.

Huevo - The Spanish word for egg.

Hummus - This puree is made by combining chickpeas, garlic, olive oil and lemon juice. It may have other savory flavors added such as roasted peppers or olives.

Infused Oil - An oil that is flavored by combining with other ingredients.

Insalata - Italian for "salad".

Jamaica Jerk Seasoning - A spice blend that may contain cinnamon, ginger, cloves, assorted chilies and thyme as well as garlic. It may or may not be spicy hot as determined by the individual combination.

Jasmine Rice - An aromatic rice from Thailand.

Jicama - A Mexican root vegetable with a nutty flavor. Can be eaten raw or added to the cooking process.

Jus - The natural juices from meat.

Kaffir Lime Leaves - From Asia, kaffir lime leaves are very aromatic and flavorful. They are simmered or steeped and used to flavor a variety of dishes.

Kalamata Olive - A dark skinned elongated Greek olive.

Key Lime - A small yellow skinned lime from Florida.

Kobe Beef - A type of beef raised in Japan that has an extremely high fat content that leads to a very tender and flavorful product.

Lait - French for "milk".

Langoustine - French for "prawn".

Macerate - To allow foods to absorb flavoring liquids by letting them soak in the liquid. Normally associated with fruits.

Macedoine - A mixture of cut fruits or vegetables. The mixture is often found sweetened with sugars or honey.

Mache - A type of lamb's lettuce.

Marzipan - A pliable paste of ground almonds, sugar and egg whites.

Mascarpone - An Italian cheese with the consistency of cream cheese. It has double cream content and can be used in sweet or savory preparations.

Medallion - A small round cut of meat.

Mesclun - A mixture of young lettuces and salad greens.

Mesquite - Hardwood from the American Southwest and Mexico used for grilling and smoking.

Mexican Chocolate - A vanilla and cinnamon flavored chocolate which is heaver grained than typical chocolate. It is the ingredient used in the preparations of Mole as well as other regional drinks and dishes.

Mignonette - Originally this term referred to an aromatic sachet but for our purposes it is a combination of course cracked pepper, onion and vinegar that are used as a dressing or condiment. Additional elements may be added to correspond with the end use such as raw oysters on the half shell.

Meripoix - A mixture consisting of two parts onion, one part carrots and one part celery.

Mirin - A sweet rice wine used in Japanese cuisine.

Mise en place - French term for having all tools, items and ingredients ready for preparation.

Miso - A fermented paste made from soy beans. It comes in a variety of colors, textures and flavors.

Mole - A rich sauce made from chilies, aromatics and Mexican chocolate. It is not necessarily a sweet concoction but has deep savory flavors.

Morel - An elongated honeycomb shaped mushroom. It has a smoky, woodsy flavor.

Mousse - A puree that has added volume from egg whites or whipped heavy cream. They can be sweet or savory and served hot or cold.

Naan - A flat lightly browned yeast bread found in Indian cuisine.

Noisette – 1)-The French term for brown as in beurre noisette, browned butter. 2)-A small round cut of meat, slightly smaller than a medallion.

Nori - Very thin sheets of dried algae or seaweed commonly used for sushi or as garnish in Japanese dishes.

Oeuf - French for "egg".

Okra - An oblong thick skinned vegetable pod used in southern cooking.

Orecchiette - Small "ear-shaped" pasta.

Ouzo - A sweet Greek liqueur.

Pad Thai - A Thai dish that combines rice noodles with various vegetables, spices, aromatics and proteins.

Paella - A Spanish dish of rice, shellfish, sausage and meats with aromatics, saffron and tomatoes added.

Paillard - A very thin cut of meat that may be pounded out then grilled quickly.

Pancetta - A cured but un-smoked bacon from Italy.

Panko Crumbs - A white course breadcrumb found in Japanese cooking, this crumb is great for breading anything from chicken and seafood to vegetables.

Panna Cotta - An Italian egg custard. Most often served sweetened as a dessert but more and more it is being flavored with savory ingredients.

Pappardelle - A wide flat noodle with curved edges.

Parma Ham - A very high quality prosciutto ham from the Parma region of Italy.

Peperonata - An Italian mixture of grilled eggplant, peppers, garlic, onions, olive oil and tomatoes. Served as a dip or table condiment.

Pesto - A raw sauce made from basil, pine nuts, parmesan cheese, olive oil and garlic. Other fresh herbs or nuts may be substituted for the basil and pine nuts.

Phyllo Leaves - Very thin layers of pastry dough. Used in all types of Greek and Mediterranean preparations.

Pico de Gallo - A salsa type preparation often consisting of tomato, onion, peppers and garlic. It may contain an assortment of other ingredients and is used as a table condiment to Spanish or Mexican dishes.

Pignoli - Pine nuts.

Pilaf - Rice preparation that always begins with toasting the rice in butter or another fat. Stock and aromatics are then added to complete the coking process.

Piquante Sauce - A brown sauce that contains vinegar, white wine, shallots and chopped pickles.

Pistou - A condiment of un-cooked chopped basil, garlic and olive oil.

Po' Boy - A hoagie type sandwich from the Deep South. Common ingredients are breaded oysters, shrimp or crawfish with shredded lettuce and sliced tomato and an accompanying sauce.

Poivre - French term for pepper.

Polenta - An Italian cornmeal mixture that can be baked poached or grilled. It can be flavored with any number of ingredients including but not limited to herbs and cheeses.

Pommes - French for "potato".

Ponzu Sauce - Japanese sauce made with rice wine vinegar, soy sauce, dried bonito flakes and Mirin.

Porc - French for "pork".

Portobello Mushroom - A very large cap dark mushroom that is the mature variety of the Cremini. The stems and gills are often discarded before preparation.

Pot Stickers - Oriental style dumpling made with various fillings. They can be steamed, poached or fried. They can also be prepared by a combination of frying then steaming in the same pan.

Poussin - A small young tender chicken.

Prosciutto - An air dried salted ham from Italy and Spain.

Provencal - A sauce or garnish that contains garlic, tomatoes and olive oil.

Puttanesca - A spicy cooked sauce containing black olives, anchovies, capers, tomatoes, garlic and various fresh herbs with olive oil.

Quahog - A large hard shell clam.

Quenelle - A poached dumpling made with ground meats or vegetables. They have an elongated shaped and are held together with eggs.

Quesadilla - A meat, cheese or vegetable filled flour tortilla folded into a half moon and baked or fried.

Queso - Spanish word for cheese.

Queso Fresco - A fresh Mexican cheese with a slightly salty taste and a crumbly texture. It is also referred to as Queso Blanco.

Quinoa - A South American grain that has an off white color and a very mild taste.

Ragout - A thick, rich slow cooked preparation of assorted ingredients that allow flavors to blend and develop.

Ramp - A wild leek that has a garlic onion flavor.

Risotto - An Italian rice dish made by first toasting the rice in butter or another fat then adding hot stock in increments allowing the stock to be absorbed before adding the next amount of stock. The risotto can be flavored by adding an assortment of additions from meats and cheeses to vegetables and herbs.

Romesco - Spanish sauce made with tomato, onion, peppers, garlic, olive oil and nuts, typically almonds.

Roulade - A thin cut of meat that has been filled with any number of ingredients.

Roux - Combination of one part flour to equal part fat, usually butter. Roux is used to thicken stocks, soups or sauces. By cooking the roux you change the color and flavor as required by the individual recipe.

Saffron - This spice is the yellow- red stigmas from a crocus flower and has a slightly anise flavor and aroma.

Salsa - Mexican term for "sauce". It can be any variety of ingredients either cooked or raw. Most commonly a salsa might contain tomato, cilantro, onions, garlic and peppers.

Sambal - A Indonesian condiment that may contain any number of regional ingredients including coconut milk, chilies, onions and tamarind as well as assorted spices and aromatics.

Sashimi - Sliced raw fish. It may be accompanied by wasabi, pickled ginger and a soy-rice wine mixture.

Satay - Skewered pieces of meat that are grilled. The most common accompaniment is a spicy peanut sauce.

Shallot - This garlic-onion flavored "bulb" has a delicate flavor. Peel and use as you would for garlic or onion.

Shirred Eggs - Eggs baked in a small dish or ramekin. They may be topped with any assortment of accompaniments such as bacon or sliced onions and may also be topped with cream. The eggs are baked until the whites are firm but the yolks are still liquid.

Soba Noodles - A buckwheat noodle found in oriental preparations.

Sofrito - A sauce made from Annatto seeds, oil and aromatics.

Soft Shell Crab - A crab that has shed its hard shell and has not yet grown a new one. After removing the eyes and gills, the entire remaining crab even the legs and soft shell can be eaten.

Soubise - A white sauce that has been additionally thickened with cooked onion puree.

Spaetzle - German dish of small dumplings that have been forced through a colander or Spaetzle press and cooked in boiling water or stock. The Spaetzle may be flavored with a variety of ingredients such as roasted garlic or fresh herbs.

Star Anise - A star shaped seed pod used in oriental cooking. It can be used whole and then removed before serving or ground. This is a key ingredient in Chinese five spice powder.

Stracciatella - An Italian soup made by straining beaten eggs into rich chicken broth and flavored with Parmesan cheese.

Sunchoke - A Jerusalem artichoke.

Tabouleh - Middle Eastern salad made with bulgur wheat, chopped tomatoes, onion and parsley and mixed with olive oil and lemon juice.

Tahini - A paste made from pureed sesame seeds.

Tagliatelle - A pasta made into long thin strips.

Tamale - A Mexican dish made by placing a masa cornmeal mixture that has been filled with any number of savory fillings in a corn husk wrapping before steaming or roasting.

Tapenade - A coarse paste made with capers, black olives, anchovies, olive oil and spices.

Timbale - A tall cone shaped mold or dish. It could be made with rice, custard, vegetables or forcemeats.

Tiramisu - An Italian dessert made with espresso soaked cake or lady fingers and a mascarpone filling.

Tomatillo - A small tomato shaped fruit that has a papery skin and a firm green to yellow flesh. Used in Southwest and Mexican cooking, it has a citrus, apple to pear flavor. It can be used raw but cooking mellows the flavor and softens the texture.

Truffle - A fungus prized for its earthy, pungent flavor. Its color may be from an intense black to off white.

Tzatziki - A cold Greek sauce made with yogurt, cucumber and garlic.

Vegetable Protein - Sometimes referred to as TVP, textured vegetable protein. An extraction of soybeans, this is often used as an extender to ground meats, usually in institutional operations.

Veloute - One of the Mother sauces made from light colored stocks thickened with a roux. Usually made from chicken it can also be made with veal, fish or shellfish.

Vermicelli - Very thin long shaped pasta. It falls between "angel hair" and regular spaghetti in thickness.

Veronique - A garnish of seedless peeled white grapes.

Vert - French term for "green".

Wakame - Edible seaweed found in Asian cooking. It can be fresh, dried or frozen in brine.

Wasabi - An oriental type horseradish. Green in color it is usually sold in its powdered form. The dry powder is mixed with water to form a paste. Allowing this paste to set for a few minutes will develop its very spicy pungent flavor.

Weisswurst - A white veal sausage with a very light flavor.

Wild Rice - Not really rice, wild rice comes from a tall wetland grass. This product usually takes longer to cook than white rice varieties and develops a sweet nutty flavor.

Wood Ears - A mushroom type fungus used in oriental cooking. Found often in the dried form. After reconstituting, the liquid is normally poured off before using.

Yorkshire Pudding - A mixture of flour, eggs and milk that is poured into very hot beef drippings and baked. Most often served with Prime Ribs of Beef, it should be served immediately as it collapses when removed from the oven.

Zabaglione - Sauce or dessert made with egg yolks, sugar and Marsala. The mixture is whisked over a double boiler until thickened.

Zest - The outer non-white layer of citrus fruit. This oily aromatic skin has an intense flavor.

Ziti - Hollow tubes of pasta usually about an inch and a half long.

Zuppa - The Italian word for soup.

www.ingramcontent.com/pod-product-compliance
Lightning Source LLC
LaVergne TN
LVHW081315060426
835509LV00015B/1526